PRAISE FOR *THE BRAIN*  FOR

21st-Century man

"This book will encourage many educators to teach 21st-century students via 21st-century policies and practices that are grounded in the dramatic advances occurring in the cognitive neurosciences."

—**Robert Sylwester**
Author of *A Child's Brain: The Need for Nurture*
Emeritus Professor of Education
University of Oregon, Eugene, OR

"Teachers will find the content valuable and can implement the Brain-Targeting Teaching concept very easily."

—**Steve Hutton**
School Improvement Specialist
Villa Hills, KY

"Mariale Hardiman offers a unique model that teachers can use to assess the extent to which they are considering brain-friendly concepts when they plan their lessons."

—**David Sousa**
Consultant in Educational Neuroscience
Author of *How the Brain Learns*
Palm Beach, FL

"The emphasis on integrating the arts with content areas is timely and welcome. An additional strength are the examples from 'expert teachers' which show how the model can be implemented while addressing curriculum standards."

—**Jacqueline LaRose**
Assistant Professor of Education
Eastern Michigan University, Ypsilanti, MI

"This book provides a teacher-friendly model that teachers can use to establish student-friendly classroom environments and effective teaching strategies and activities."

—**Darla Mallein**
Director of Secondary Social Sciences Education
Emporia State University, KS

"The Brain-Targeted Teaching Model for 21st-Century Schools has much to offer all educators. The book contains a wealth of knowledge from cognitive and neuroscience and presents it in a way that is accurate and accessible. Hardiman's work creates a vision of education in which scientific discoveries about thinking and learning are taken full advantage of."

—**Jay N. Giedd**
Chief of Brain Imaging Unit
Child Psychiatry Branch, NIMH
Bethesda, MD

"Few educators bring Dr. Hardiman's ability, experience, and scholarliness to the increasingly rich exchange between educators and neuroscientists. She has succinctly synthesized a large body of information into a must-read for educators, researchers, and anyone else interested in how neuroscience and cognitive science can make a difference in the classroom."

—**Kenneth S. Kosik, MD**
Harriman Professor of Neuroscience
University of California
Santa Barbara, CA

"Hardiman's book provides a practical way for educators to operationalize theoretical principles, and teach in a way that can effectively engage students on different and meaningful levels. The research and strategies presented in this book emphasize the very important notion of supporting students' personal, social, and academic development and achievement."

—**Fay E. Brown**
Director of Child and Adolescent Development
Yale School Development Program
Yale University

"One of the central components of Hardiman's remarkable book is creativity—the ability to generate something new. Promoting the development of this unique attribute is critically important for the success of our students, and I applaud Dr. Hardiman for showing that neuroscience can and should inform the process of education."

—Charles J. Limb, MD
Associate Professor
Johns Hopkins University Schools of Medicine and Education
Baltimore, MD

"This book is a tour de force, providing not only a comprehensive understanding of cognitive and neuroscience research, but also a well-constructed model providing teachers with the practical tools they need to integrate it into their classrooms. Dr. Hardiman has become a leading authority in the emerging field of neuroeducation."

—Paula Tallal
Board of Governors Professor of Neuroscience
Rutgers University
Cream Ridge, NJ

"Dr. Hardiman provides clear explanations of what is currently known about the functions of the human brain, along with practical examples of ways to apply these understandings in the classroom. With this book she offers a significant contribution to the field of education."

—Dee Dickinson
Founder
New Horizons for Learning
Seattle, WA

"Dr. Hardiman's Brain-Targeted Teaching Model is one of the most powerful and research-based methods of achieving greater learning retention—its focus on the arts and creative problem-solving moves teaching from traditional 'drill and kill' methods to one that engages students for the demands of 21st-century teaching and learning."

—Linda Casto
Advisory Board
Johns Hopkins University Neuro-Education Initiative
Malibu, CA

"The Brain-Targeted Teaching Model has informed my teaching in so many ways. I love the model's infusion of the arts as the arts lend themselves to creative expression for all children. There is no question that the Brain-Targeted Teaching Model enhanced the quality of my teaching."

—Andrea Jackson
5th Grade Teacher
Baltimore, MD

"The Brain-Targeted Teaching Model provides a framework for teaching that makes sense not only in K–12 but also in higher education settings. I hope to continue spreading the word that higher education coursework can be significantly enhanced by using the tenets of Brain-Targeted Teaching."

—Vicky M. Krug
Assistant Professor
Pittsburgh, PA

"As a leader of a new school, I looked for an approach to teaching that would help teachers to be intentionally thoughtful about every aspect of their day. Brain-Targeted Teaching by Dr. Hardiman provides teachers with the structure to plan thoughtful, intentional, arts integrated units. The clear explanation of neuro and cognitive research, along with examples, allows teachers to develop a connection between the research and best practice. Roots and Branches School is very excited about using Brain-Targeted Teaching as our means of instructional practice."

—Jenifer Shaud
Founder
Roots and Branches Charter School
Baltimore, MD

The
BRAIN-
TARGETED
Teaching Model
for 21st-Century Schools

Mariale Hardiman
Foreword by Martha Bridge Denckla

CORWIN
A SAGE Company

CORWIN
A SAGE Company

FOR INFORMATION

Corwin
A SAGE Company
2455 Teller Road
Thousand Oaks, California 91320
(800) 233-9936
Fax: (800) 417-2466
www.corwin.com

SAGE Ltd.
1 Oliver's Yard
55 City Road
London EC1Y 1SP
United Kingdom

SAGE India Pvt. Ltd.
B 1/I 1 Mohan Cooperative Industrial Area
Mathura Road, New Delhi 110 044
India

SAGE Asia-Pacific Pte. Ltd.
33 Pekin Street #02-01
Far East Square
Singapore 048763

Acquisitions Editor: Arnis Burvikovs
Associate Editor: Desirée A. Bartlett
Editorial Assistant: Kimberly Greenberg
Production Editor: Amy Joy Schroller
Copy Editor: Amy Rosenstein
Typesetter: Hurix Systems Pvt. Ltd
Proofreader: Dennis W. Webb
Indexer: Sheila Bodell
Cover Designer: Karine Hovsepian
Permissions Editor: Karen Ehrmann

Printed in the United States of America

Library of Congress Cataloging-in-Publication Data

Hardiman, Mariale M. (Mariale Melanson), 1951-
  The brain-targeted teaching model for
21st-century schools / Mariale Hardiman ;
foreword by Martha Bridge Denckla.
    p. cm.
  Includes bibliographical references and index.
  ISBN 978-1-4129-9198-8 (pbk.)
  1. Educational psychology. 2. Learning—
Physiological aspects. 3. Brain. 4. Teaching—
Psychological aspects. I. Title.

  LB1057.H26 2012
  370.15—dc23

                                2011049854

This book is printed on acid-free paper.

14 15 16 10 9 8 7 6 5 4 3 2

Contents

Online Resources Included

Access a Reading Companion and Study Guide for
The Brain-Targeted Teaching Model for 21st-Century Schools
at **www.braintargetedteaching.org.**

List of Expert Teachers by Chapter

Chapter 4: Brain-Target One

Sharon Delgado—*To Make a Friend, Be a Friend*

Dev Sharma—*Calamity Jane and Positive Emotions*

Scott Williamson—*Visual Symbols and Emotional Connection*

Chapter 5: Brain-Target Two

Alexandra Fleming—*Novelty in the Classroom*

Amanda Kowalik—*Let the Light Shine*

Michelle Hartye—*Montessori and the Silence Game*

Angela (David Hallam's student)—*Vanilla Makes Me Happy*

Elizabeth Levy—*A Taste of Spain*

Chapter 6: Brain-Target Three

Amanda Kowalik—*How to Start a Learning Unit: Concept Mapping*

Susan Rome—*Mapping the Journey of Learning*

Meredith Adelfio, Victoria Douglas, Vicky Krug, Kelly Murillo, Jeremy Mettler—*Classification of Two-Dimensional Shapes*

Carol Lautenbach, Harriett Saviello, Misty Swanger—*How to Grow a Democracy: The Three Branches of Government*

Amy Cotugno, Marian Derlet, Emmalie Dropkin, Dev Sharma, Juliet Stevens—*Fables: Learning to Make Wise Choices*

Sharon Delgado—*Native Americans in Pre-Colonial Maryland*

Chapter 7: Brain-Target Four

Vanessa Lopez-Sparaco—*Eye of the Beholder*

Stephanie Rafferty—*Physics and the Arts—A Natural Fit*

Joseph Izen—*Shakespeare and Hip-Hop*

Kathy Rivetti—*A Picture Is Worth a Thousand Words*

Foreword

*T*he Brain-Targeted Teaching Model for 21st-Century Schools is a welcome update to the 2003 book that introduced educators to Dr. Hardiman's "Brain-Targeted Teaching Model." Both that book and the new edition share the ambitious goal of providing teachers with valuable knowledge from the neuro- and cognitive sciences in a form that can be readily understood and applied in practice. The strength of Dr. Hardiman's approach is that in addition to carefully describing research findings, she frames those findings in terms of an accompanying pedagogical model that educators can use to interpret, organize, and apply the information they are receiving. From the viewpoint of a researcher and clinician, this is exactly what teachers need—a way to connect the information we provide with the kind of practical expertise that can only be gained in real-life school settings.

Too often, efforts to translate scientific research for use by educators run into serious difficulties. One way to go wrong is to water down the science and describe important ideas only colloquially or metaphorically, with little or no documentation of sources. Broad-brush "research-based" recommendations for practice may be offered, but these usually represent little more than common sense, and the support they garner from scientific research tends to be trivial. Allusions to brain science serve to make existing ideas seem "cutting edge"—as though they hold some great new promise for "fixing" education in one fell swoop.

Despite widespread enthusiasm for the idea of joining together the work of scientists and educators, other frameworks like the Brain-Targeted Teaching Model have not emerged. Instead, there has unfortunately been only a proliferation of pseudoscientific "brain-based" educational products and workshops, many promoted in the media. Though research scientists are wise to steer well clear of these enterprises, this leaves no one to counter the "neuromyths" or misconceptions teachers are left with. In contrast, Dr. Hardiman is unique in her vigilance to avoid overreaching beyond what can be reasonably concluded from scientific research. This is one of the main reasons why scientific researchers are willing to work with her. Though her background is that of an educator—foremost as a long-time, nationally honored urban school principal—she has forged professional relationships with research scientists at her own institution, Johns Hopkins University, as well as others around the country.

She is determined to make sure that her claims are grounded in rigorous scientific research and are well-referenced. This does not mean, however, that research findings relevant to education must be presented as they would be in a scientific journal, without thorough explanations of vocabulary, basic concepts, or logical implications for practice. When educators have to try on their own to understand research conclusions and "translate" them into educational frames of reference, they become vulnerable to the possibility that much is lost in translation; they may misunderstand or overgeneralize. Teachers (like anyone) may go astray when the work of helping them understand and apply scientific ideas is left undone. Teachers do not work in a vacuum, and their success often depends on collaboration with others whose belief in rigorous, evidence-based practices provides the format for practice. A global commitment to the training of all who provide educational services to students at all levels must include a commitment to this scientific approach to understanding learning, the cognitive processes associated with learning from the earliest grades through higher education, and the use of research to promote innovative, creative, and effective teaching.

Whereas many educational researchers exhibit a strong ideological bent and often try to recruit scientific research to support a predetermined agenda, Dr. Hardiman starts with rigorous research and works in a highly pragmatic way to build a pedagogical framework on the foundations of scientific knowledge. She is able to lean on her experience as a longtime practitioner to consider the needs of teachers and schools. Because Dr. Hardiman understands so well how teachers think, she is able to seek out the scientific information that teachers want to know and deliver that information in a way that makes it accessible and useful.

With all of the advances that have come in the neuro- and cognitive sciences since Dr. Hardiman's 2003 book, it is great to have an updated version of the Brain-Targeted Teaching Model. Many educators are already familiar and comfortable with her framework; they will finish this book and return to the classroom with great new ideas that are based in up-to-date and sound research. For those who may only now be learning about Dr. Hardiman's work, this book will reveal a pedagogical model that resonates with educators' goals and strategies as well as a plethora of useful information from the brain sciences. The collective hope is that this book serves as a road map toward creating ever-better outcomes for your students and better collaborative professional practices in your school.

Martha Bridge Denckla, MD
Batza Family Endowed Chair
Director, Developmental Cognitive Neurology
Kennedy Krieger Institute
Professor, Neurology, Pediatrics, Psychiatry
Johns Hopkins University
School of Medicine

Preface

The Emotional
Climate

Evaluation and
Assessment

The Physical
Environment

Application of
Knowledge

Mastery of Content,
Skills, and Concepts

Big Picture
Learning Design

The Brain-Targeted Teaching Model

Since the publication of my first book, *Connecting Brain Research With Effective Teaching: The Brain-Targeted Teaching Model* (Hardiman, 2003) much has changed in the landscape of educational neuroscience or *neuroeducation,* an emerging field at the intersection of the brain sciences and education. Research in the neuro- and cognitive sciences has produced numerous findings that educators have increasingly viewed as important to expanding their understanding of how children learn. Like professionals in other emerging "neuro" fields—neurolaw, neuroeconomics, neuroaesthethics, neuroethics—many educators seek to not only become familiar with the advancing knowledge of human cognition and learning, but also to understand how this knowledge can inform their work.

Currently, research from the scientific community that is *specifically intended* for teaching audiences is scant. Still, promising findings from neuro- and cognitive science research in areas such as attention, memory, emotions, creativity, executive function, sleep, and exercise continue to expand our understanding of cognition and learning and can directly inform how teachers and educational policymakers craft the educational experiences of students at all ages. This growing knowledge, however, creates the need for translation of relevant research findings to determine appropriate connections to educational practice.

WHO SHOULD READ THIS BOOK

This book is intended to serve as a bridge between research and practice by providing any educator with a cohesive, usable model of effective instruction informed by educational research as well as findings from the neuro- and cognitive sciences. The research and instructional strategies presented are designed to be relevant to a wide range of educators, from early childhood practitioners to higher education faculty. Examples of practical applications of research span various subject areas and extend from early elementary grades to college classrooms.

For educators at any level, it is critical that relevant research on cognition and learning be approached systematically and realistically, rendering a better understanding of the developing child and adult learner, greater precision in instructional techniques, and enhanced educational outcomes for students. It is also important that the growing attention on *brain-based learning*—a term often used to refer to learning that uses strategies that are based in research in the brain sciences—does not generate just another short-lived initiative.

In my own work as a school principal in an urban school district and now at the university level, I have found that too often teachers are handed an ever-changing array of initiatives and programs that rapidly come and go. Well-meaning educational leaders may not understand how this serves only to dilute teacher effectiveness rather than support it. Teachers may "wait out" one initiative in hopes that a better one will come along or feel confused as they try to meld a new program with the previous one. Accordingly, without a cohesive classroom-based model, teachers may easily be confused by the plethora of instructional strategies that claim (some appropriately, some not) to be based on research from the brain sciences. Usable knowledge may be confounded with myths that divert teachers' time and waste valuable resources.

THE CENTRAL PURPOSE OF THIS BOOK

A PEDAGOGICAL FRAMEWORK—THE BRAIN-TARGETED TEACHING MODEL

The basis of this book is to bring relevant research from the brain sciences to educators through a pedagogical framework, the Brain-Targeted Teaching (BTT) Model (Hardiman, 2003). The model provides teachers with a cohesive structure for interpreting research findings from the neuro- and cognitive sciences and applying them to their own practice. Teachers who have adopted the model as a guide for planning and delivering instruction have recounted how it has enhanced teaching practices (www.braintargetedteaching.org), and preliminary research has demonstrated its efficacy (Bertucci, 2006).

The BTT Model is neither a curriculum nor a marketed product. Rather, it is a way to plan effective instruction informed by research from the neuro- and cognitive sciences and research-based effective instruction (see Marzano, Pickering, & Pollock, 2001). It was designed, in part, from the thinking skills frameworks of Dimensions of Learning (Marzano, 1992), Multiple Intelligences (Gardner, 1983, 1993), and Bloom's Taxonomy (Bloom & Krathwohl, 1956). Important, however, to the development and expansion of the model is the emphasis of translating and applying findings from recent and ongoing scientific research.

The model presents six important domains, or "brain targets," of the teaching and learning process. These include the following:

- Brain-Target One—Establishing the emotional climate for learning

- Brain-Target Two—Creating the physical learning environment

- Brain-Target Three—Designing the learning experience

- Brain-Target Four—Teaching for the mastery of content, skills, and concepts

- Brain-Target Five—Teaching for the extension and application of knowledge

- Brain-Target Six—Evaluating learning

The BTT Model, which originated as a grass-roots school-based program in Baltimore, Maryland, is now informing educators across all grade levels from California to Greece. The model took root and expanded during my tenure as a principal of a large school serving children in Grades K–8. As our faculty looked to expand the school's approach to instruction, we sought ways to meet the demands of high-stakes testing while also providing an educational program informed by the latest research on how children best acquire, retain, and apply knowledge. At the same time, as part of my doctoral studies at the Johns Hopkins University, my inquiries led me to examine and make sense of findings from the explosion of research from the brain sciences during the 1990s, the "Decade of the Brain." Although the number of studies conducted in school settings was (and still is) quite small, I applied usable knowledge from the neruo- and cognitive science to develop a model of effective teaching.

From its original inception at Roland Park Elementary/Middle School, the model continues to evolve thanks to the dedicated work and experiences of teachers regionally and nationally who received training at workshops and conferences or through study in graduate work in the Mind, Brain, and Teaching Certificate at Johns Hopkins University School of Education. Based on their experiences, teachers (from K–12 to higher education) have shared how the model helps them to conceptualize activities that tap into students' creative thinking and imagination by focusing on problem-solving and application of content to real-world contexts. Teachers also have recounted how meaningful integration of the arts into learning activities leads to heightened student engagement and greater retention of content. From our first experiences in 2004 to now, the framework of the BTT Model has assisted teachers in using relevant knowledge and research from the neuro- and cognitive sciences to inform the design of instruction to promote students' connection to learning, creative thinking, and deeper learning—all important outcomes for 21st-century learning.

SPECIAL FEATURES OF THIS BOOK

This book reviews research from the neuro- and cognitive sciences, discusses how the findings can inform educational practice, and shares classroom activities from many teachers who have used the model in their classrooms. It begins with a consideration of current educational practices and how the emerging field of neuroeducation can promote educational reform toward the goals of "21st-century skills," which explicitly call for teaching all students to become innovative and creative problem-solvers. It then examines themes from neuro- and cognitive science that educators should know, including discerning the differences between meaningful uses of research and common misapplications of findings, known as *neuromyths*. Next, in order to help with understanding of research in subsequent chapters, the book provides fundamental information of how the brain works, including its structure and function. Chapter 3 provides an overview of the BTT Model, and the chapters that follow focus on each of the six brain targets, including research supporting the target as well as concrete examples of applications from practicing teachers—referred to as "expert teachers" throughout the book. We end by considering how the model can be used as a unifying framework in a school, how it aligns with standards and programs in place in many schools, and the various ways it can be implemented within any curriculum or school-based initiative.

Finally, it is important that I explain why I find the concept of "Brain-Targeted Teaching" (a description I coined in the last book) to be more useful than the term *brain-based learning*. A number of people have justly criticized the use of the term *brain-based* as an adjective describing learning. The silliness of the term is exemplified by the question, "Doesn't all learning occur in the brain? . . . After all, we don't think with our feet!" I concur that labeling learning as "brain-based" seems uninformative as all learning indeed occurs in the brain. In contrast, all ***teaching does not result in learning;*** so, while all learning is "brain-based," all teaching is not. Accordingly, I wanted to focus on how *pedagogy* can be informed by knowledge of how the brain learns—how people perceive, process, and remember information. Therefore, the term *Brain-Targeted Teaching* seemed particularly apt.

Research from the brain sciences has demonstrated that the essence of learning is about biological changes. In view of that, focusing on the *science of learning* should be as central to discussions about education as the focus on accountability for the *product of learning*. It is time that policy and practices for schools of the 21st century reflect a focus on the way students think and learn. The emerging field of neuroeducation and the BTT Model can be the linchpin in this work.

Acknowledgments

It is with great pleasure that I acknowledge those whose contributions have been critical in conceptualizing and writing this book. I begin by recognizing the dedicated work of my postdoctoral fellows at the Johns Hopkins University School of Education—Emma Gregory, Luke Rinne, and Julia Yarmolinskaya. As cognitive scientists, they were stellar partners in parsing research findings and considering their relevance to classroom application.

Next, the voices of practicing teachers turn research and theory into rich images of real classrooms with students engaged in meaningful learning. Much gratitude goes to Clare O'Malley Grizzard and Suzanne McNamara, who provide the Brain-Targeted Teaching learning units that thread through this book. Their contributions make each stage of the model come alive with activities that are sure to inspire readers. Special thanks also to Linda Bluth, who embraced the model with zeal early in its development and teamed up with Clare for the creation of one of the units shown in this book.

Within each chapter are excerpts from teachers who have used the BTT Model in their classrooms. I am grateful to these "expert teachers" (as they are called throughout the book) for their enlightened and thoughtful contributions. They teach in public and nonpublic schools as well as universities across multiple states from early elementary grades through higher education graduate courses. I list them in the order they appear in the chapters: Sharon Delgado, Dev Sharma, Scott Williamson, Alexandra Fleming, Amanda Kowalik, Michelle Hartye, Angela (student) from David Hallam's class, Elizabeth Levy, Susan Rome, Meredith Adelfio, Victoria Douglas, Vicky Krug, Kelly Murillo, Jeremy Mettler, Carol Lautenbach, Harriett Saviello, Misty Swanger, Amy Cotugno, Marian Derlet, Emmalie Dropkin, Juliet Stevens, Vanessa Lopez-Sparaco, Stephanie Rafferty, Joseph Izen, Kathy Rivetti, Bob Lessick, Georgia Woerner, Dan Hellerback, Elayne Melanson, Paula Mainolfi, Kristen McGinness, Robin Melanson, Rebecca Singer, and Catherine Gearhart.

I want to thank Gordon Porterfield, my friend and colleague who edited my first book, for once again offering expert advice and sharing the story of his current work as a graduate-level teacher educator that appears at the end of this book. Special thanks to the research assistance of Amy Akers Duggan and Kristen McGinness in the design and field testing of the BTT checklists in Appendix II. I also want to give special acknowledgment to the assistance of Susan McLean, Carolyn Combs, Toni Ungaretti, Sharon Delgado, and Sam Clayton. I would like to acknowledge the graphic designer, Bennett Grizzard, for the creative graphics that depict each brain target in the icons that appear in the book.

Finally, many thanks to Drs. Martha Bridge Denckla, Paula Tallal, and Mary Ellen Lewis who, along with my postdoctoral fellows, offered encouragement and a keen eye toward scientific interpretation and application of research.

Publisher's Acknowledgments

Corwin gratefully acknowledges the following individuals for taking the time to provide their editorial insights:

Steve Hutton
School Improvement Specialist
Villa Hills, Kentucky

Jacqueline LaRose
Assistant Professor of Education
Eastern Michigan University
Ypsilanti, Michigan

David Sousa
Author and Consultant in Educational Neuroscience
Palm Beach, Florida

Robert Sylwester
Emeritus Professor of Education
University of Oregon
Eugene, Oregon

About the Author

 **Mariale M. Hardiman, EdD,** serves as the Assistant Dean of Urban School Partnerships and Chair of the Department of Interdisciplinary Studies at the Johns Hopkins University School of Education. She is the cofounder and director of the Neuro-Education Initiative, which collaborates with various schools and units within Johns Hopkins University.

Dr. Hardiman's publications focus on the intersection of research from the neuro- and cognitive sciences and education, bringing to educators relevant research from the brain sciences to inform teaching and learning. She is a frequent presenter at local, regional, and national conferences.

Dr. Hardiman also served for more than 30 years in the Baltimore City Public School System as a principal, assistant principal, staff developer, and teacher. Under her leadership, Roland Park Elementary/Middle School received numerous awards for continuous student achievement gains as well as its designation as a Blue Ribbon School of Excellence. During her tenure as principal, she devised a teaching framework, the Brain-Targeted Teaching Model, which has generated interest from educators worldwide. Dr. Hardiman earned her undergraduate and graduate degrees from Loyola University Maryland and her doctorate from The Johns Hopkins University.

She may be reached at mmhardiman@jhu.edu; for more information on the Brain-Targeted Teaching Model, visit the website www.braintargetedteaching.org.

To Tara and Krysta and in memory of Bob;
To Our Glorious Gloria and All Her Children.

Introduction

The Emerging Field of Neuroeducation
and 21st-Century Schools

Because of its broad implications for individual and social well-being, there is now a consensus in the scientific community that the biology of mind will be to the twenty-first century what the biology of the gene was to the twentieth century.

—Eric Kandel, *In Search of Memory*, p. xiii

A s lawmakers look to redefine federal legislation that drives national educational policy, efforts to reform American schools should begin by changing the very notion of how to measure educational success, driven by the movement of 21st-century learning and ultimately informed by new knowledge from the science of learning. At present, with no national consensus on what makes an effective school, federal policies have reduced the notion of measuring successful schooling to merely tracking achievement scores in reading and mathematics.

Clearly, educators must not shrink from accountability for student performance. The current practices that measure educational effectiveness, however, are driving school policies and practices and have resulted in a well-documented narrowing of the curriculum, reducing time spent in the social studies and the sciences and—at the same time—diminishing opportunities for many children to participate in the visual and performing arts, physical education, and even recess. This is especially true in urban settings, where budgets are tight and many educators believe that children require more time to work in the tested subject areas. The present focus on narrow educational goals could well be contributing to the fact that nearly half of the students in public school systems in major cities drop out of school (Swanson, 2008)—at a time when a highly educated population is necessary for our country to continue to take part in a global economy. Moreover, narrow accountability measures fail to give

1

the public, from parents to policymakers, the broad measures of school effectiveness they want and deserve.

In a recent study at University of California Riverside, teachers indicated that, while the practice of high-stakes accountability helps identify expectations of student learning, it also cuts down on the time they have to provide students with deeper and more engaging learning experiences (Guggino & Brint, 2010). These teachers represent many across the country who feel continual pressure to improve test scores rather than to help students develop the ability to think critically and apply knowledge creatively. Practices that support narrow, "spoon-fed" thinking are incompatible with our nation's need for workers capable of collaboration, innovation, and creative problem-solving—the hallmark of 21st-century skills.

Educating the citizens of tomorrow will require the redesign of school policies and practices so that students do not merely acquire information, but also are provided with opportunities to apply what they have learned in novel ways. These are the very abilities identified by the Partnership for 21st-Century Skills (www.p21.org) as necessary for the workforce of the future. The framework designed by the Partnership includes four major areas of expertise that students should master in order to be prepared for the demands of work and life in their future. They include the following:

- Core subject knowledge in English, reading, language arts, world languages, art, mathematics, science, history, geography, economics, government, civics as well as the understanding of global awareness literacy in finance, business and health;

- Learning and innovation skills such as creativity, critical thinking, problem-solving, collaboration, and communication;

- Technology, media, and information literacy;

- Career and life skills such as self-direction, leadership, the ability to adapt to new situations, and skills in working in a diverse cultural and social environment.

As we redefine American education to embrace the concept of 21st-century schools, the emerging field of neuroeducation can play an important role by focusing educators on *how students learn* rather than on merely *what they learn* based on narrow achievement goals. As neuro- and cognitive science researchers continue to accrue knowledge about the science of learning, it is important that relevant findings reach educators in a manner that allows them to incorporate this knowledge into policies and practices. As is the norm in medicine, neuroeducation can bring to educators the "bench to bedside" approach through which research informs practice and the needs of practitioners drive research questions.

There is considerable evidence that this approach holds great promise. Neuro- and cognitive scientists have already made important contributions to the work of educators. For example, from her research on executive function and clinical practice with school-aged children, Martha Denckla, M.D., of the Kennedy Krieger Institute encourages educators to examine critical periods in various domains of child development that can inform decisions pertaining to the readiness of preschool-age children for reading instruction or the young adolescent for the conceptual thinking that algebra requires (Hardiman & Denckla, 2010). Paula Tallal, PhD, Co-Director of the Center for Molecular and Behavioral Neuroscience at Rutgers University, has integrated her research on the fundamental role of rapid auditory processing in language development and literacy with basic neuroscience research on neuroplasticity (Tallal, 2004). She has translated this body of research into a series of cognitive skill, language, and reading intervention programs that are used in classrooms around the world to help English language learners, struggling readers, and children with neurocognitive disorders. The work of Ronald Dahl (2004), Jay Giedd (2010), and others encourage educators to examine research on adolescent sleep patterns to inform practices such as school start times. Further, Raizada and Kishiyama (2010) suggest that basic science can demonstrate neural changes underlying the behavioral changes that are observed from specific educational interventions. They suggest that finely tuned neural measures can provide evidence as to whether particular educational interventions are causing anatomical or functional brain changes; this in turn might be predictive of behavioral changes that endure beyond the period immediately following the intervention.

It is clear that a growing number of educators also see the potential of the science of learning to inform the field of education. During the last 10 years, teacher attendance at national, regional, and local conferences related to learning and the brain has grown and teachers report that information from the neuro- and cognitive sciences is highly relevant to their work (Howard-Jones, Pickering, & Diack, 2007). As professional development programs, books, and journal articles have proliferated, however, there has emerged a strong need for some way to separate the wheat from the chaff when it comes to commercial products and textbooks that increasingly tout the use of "brain-based" strategies to improve student achievement (Sylvan & Christodoulou, 2010). Teachers must have ongoing information that helps them become informed consumers of research claims, and a cohesive way to apply relevant research to effective practice.

The BTT Model is presented as a tool for applying neuro- and cognitive science to educational practice that is consistent with the skills associated with 21st-century learning—preparing all students to become the creative and innovative thinkers and learners of tomorrow.

Information From the Neuro- and Cognitive Sciences That Educators Should Know

Separating Neuromyth From Neuroscience

I t is readily acknowledged that the field of neuroeducation is just beginning to bring to educators usable knowledge. Nonetheless, there exists a solid literature base and a growing number of research findings from the neuro- and cognitive sciences that can and indeed should inform the teaching and learning process (e.g., Dubinsky, 2010; Fischer, Goswami, & Geake, 2010; Fischer et al., 2007; Hardiman & Denckla, 2010; Meltzoff, Kuhl, Movellan, & Sejowski, 2009; Tallal, 2004; Varma, McCandliss, & Schwartz, 2008). Unfortunately—and for a variety of reasons—these worthwhile findings are sometimes oversimplified or misinterpreted when attempts are made to apply them to pedagogy. In this chapter, I begin by identifying some of these erroneous constructs of the science, often referred to as neuromyths. Next, this chapter highlights some of the general themes from the neuro- and cognitive sciences that can give educators a broader perspective of child development and learning. Many of these general themes (and associated neuromyths) will be revisited in subsequent chapters as we explore the Brain-Targeted Teaching Model.

◎ There exists a solid literature base and a growing number of research findings from the neuro- and cognitive sciences that can and indeed should inform the teaching and learning process.

NEUROMYTH IN EDUCATION

In considering neuromyths, we must be aware of not only why they are incorrect, but also how they came to be widely believed among educators. In particular, although the media and manufacturers and marketers of commercial educational products improperly sensationalize findings, teachers are the ones who are blamed for incorrectly applying those findings (Goswami, 2006). After interviewing educators on the use of neuroscience in education, Howard-Jones, Pickering, and Diack (2007) reported that teachers felt a sense of embarrassment and even betrayal when they discovered that programs they thought were grounded in neuroscience research actually lacked scientific support. Teachers have been encouraged, for example, to teach to the left or right side of the brain, or to inventory their students' learning styles (see section below for explanation)—activities that, while perhaps alluring, lack scientific support. Teachers' time and school resources are wasted when they are duped by false advertising or forced by policymakers to use products or methods that are not supported by research. To illustrate, I will highlight some popular neuromyths so that we can see why it is important for teachers to become more savvy consumers of neuro- and cognitive science research.

◎ Teachers felt a sense of embarrassment and even betrayal when they discovered that programs they thought were grounded in neuroscience research actually lacked scientific support.

Some of Us Are Left-Brained; Some of Us Are Right-Brained

Fueled by popular media and commercial products, the notion that we can label ourselves and our students as left- or right-brained thinkers has essentially become common knowledge in many educational circles. The idea arose from research on hemispheric specialization in studies of "split-brain" patients, as researchers were able to isolate processing primarily happening in one hemisphere or the other. Scientists demonstrated that the left brain is associated with language processing, logical or "linear" thinking, and memory for facts, while the right side deals with spatial information, forms, and patterns in a more "holistic" fashion (Goswami, 2006). Gazzaniga, Ivry, and Mangun (2009) point out that, while each hemisphere *does have specializations*—for example, Broca's area in the left hemisphere controls much of speech production— (see also the description of Bowden and Jung-Beeman's study in Chapter 8), the two hemispheres are more similar in function than they are different. This explains why those with lesions on one side of the brain still have remarkable capacity for functioning despite damage to critical brain structures (see Immordino-Yang & Damasio, 2007). In reality, unless one has actually had his or her corpus callosum (i.e., the bundle of fibers that connect the two hemispheres) severed, both sides of the brain are critically involved in most tasks. The idea that one hemisphere can "dominate" the other—that people who are better at some kinds of tasks than others must have better functioning in one hemisphere—has no basis in fact. There is simply no scientific evidence that would justify identifying learners as either "left-brained" or "right-brained" and gearing instruction toward one side of the brain or the other.

> ◎ Unless one has actually had his or her corpus callosum (i.e., the bundle of fibers that connect the two hemispheres) severed, both sides of the brain are critically involved in most tasks.

Listening to Mozart Will Make Your Baby Smarter

The idea that listening to Mozart will increase IQ scores and help babies become smarter was endorsed by articles in such reputable sources as the *New York Times* and the *Boston Globe* as well as by books and commercial products that touted increases in mental development when infants listened to Mozart piano concertos (Campbell, 1997). This misconception was derived from a study by Rauscher, Shaw, and Ky (1993) who investigated the effects of listening to Mozart's concertos on spatial reasoning. The researchers found that listening to Mozart produced only short-term (i.e., 15-minute) enhancement of spatial reasoning on a subtest of the Stanford-Binet IQ test, compared with subjects who listened to relaxation music or experienced silence. In other words, Rauscher and colleagues (1993) did indeed find an effect of listening to Mozart on one's score on an IQ test, but that effect was fleeting and was only seen for a very specific subtest associated with a particular cognitive capacity and not intelligence in general. Although the researchers claim that their work was misrepresented, the impact of the study went beyond mere commercialization. In 1998, the governor of Georgia approved funding in the state budget to provide every child born in the state with a recording of classical music.

Mozart lovers need not despair. Jenkins (2001) reported impressive results in reducing epileptic attacks after patients listened to Mozart for 10-minute intervals each hour. Thompson, Schellenberg, and Husain (2001) suggest that temporary changes resulting from listening to Mozart or any music may be attributed to differences in mood and arousal. Moreover, any effects from listening to Mozart are again quite narrow as the authors claim that only music perceived by the listener as enjoyable produces any effect.

After Critical Periods of Development, Learning Shuts Down

Often used interchangeably, the terms "critical period" and "sensitive period" (a deliberate softening of the former) refer to a time during development when children best acquire knowledge or skills in some domain. The notion is that if appropriate stimulation during this period does not occur, the "window of opportunity" for learning closes and the particular skill will never be developed. Although there is certainly evidence of critical and sensitive periods for certain aspects of development, it is important not to overgeneralize this idea to domains for which there is no evidence. And further, for domains in which a critical or sensitive period can be demonstrated, it appears that in most cases the window may narrow somewhat, but only rarely does it completely close. We could certainly learn to play a musical instrument at 60, but we might want to think twice about booking Carnegie Hall.

Language acquisition is a particularly important area in which researchers have proposed the existence of a critical period. Much of this work is based on studies of feral children who, due to abandonment or abuse, were not exposed to language and failed to ever fully develop language skills. Jean Itard's work with Victor of Aveyron in the early 1800s and the case of Genie, who was discovered in 1970, led to the theory that language exposure must occur early in life or language fails to develop. Additional evidence of a critical period for language is based on studies of individuals with brain damage; ensuing language impairments tend to be more severe when the incident occurs in adulthood compared with in childhood. Perhaps the most compelling evidence for a critical period for language acquisition (where the lack of linguistic input is not confounded with extreme social deprivation) comes from deaf children of hearing parents. Some of these children are often deprived of good sign language input until elementary school or later. Unlike children exposed to sign language early in life, children exposed later will not learn sign language in a native-like way (Grimshaw, Adelstein, Bryden, & MacKinnon, 1998; Mayberry & Eichen, 1991).

◎ Language acquisition is a particularly important area in which researchers have proposed the existence of a critical period.

Second language learning is another, much more controversial area in the study of critical periods. According to Singleton and Lengyel (1995), younger children seem to be advantaged in ultimate attainment of a second language. Even though native-like pronunciation is almost never observed in late learners, adolescents and adults can master a second language, especially with respect to vocabulary and syntax (Robertson,

2002). So, although some kind of specialized "critical period" for second language acquisition could exist especially in phonology, there is evidence for high ultimate achievement even among late second language learners.

Although the window of opportunity for language learning seems only to narrow, the same cannot be said of the development of vision. Based on the work of Nobel Prize winners David Hubel and Torsten Wiesel (1970), a kitten temporarily blinded in one eye at an early developmental stage would never recover sight in that eye after the blindfold was removed, thus demonstrating that there is a critical period for the development of the visual cortex.

Research in the area of sensitive periods continues to advance, particularly in the area of adolescent development. Recent studies reveal changes in brain structure and function at the onset of puberty and into early adulthood (Dahl, 2004; Giedd, 2010). Although this, along with the examples described previously, may provide evidence in favor of the existence of critical or sensive periods in certain domains, the idea that this is characteristic of all or even most areas of learning is not supported by scientific research. Similarly unfounded is the idea that it is pointless to try to learn new information after a demonstrable critical or sensitive period has ended. This appears to be true only in rare or extreme cases. So for anyone so inclined, do sign up for those tuba lessons!

> ◎ Recent studies reveal changes in brain structure and function at the onset of puberty and into early adulthood.

We Only Use 10% of Our Brain

With all of the attention in popular media about the workings of the human brain, it is amazing that this myth still perpetuates. Indeed, many believe that 90% of the brain is inactive (Higbee & Clay, 1998). University of Washington neuroscientist Eric Chudler (2010) offers several sources for this myth, including the work of Karl Lashley in the 1930s. Lashley found that rats were still able to perform certain tasks even after having large areas of the cerebral cortex removed. This may be one of several studies where results were misrepresented or exaggerated in a way that contributed to the false conclusion that large areas of the brain were inactive.

In fact, we use all of our brain. Findings from neuroimaging studies demonstrate activity throughout the brain during many different tasks. Chudler (2010) points out that studies involving functional neuroimaging generally only highlight *differences* in brain activity that arise due to the performance of specific tasks. The areas of the brain that appear dark on the scan are likely still active; they simply don't change in response to the task being studied. Thus, when a graphical representation shows only a tiny island of activation, this is in no way indicative of the amount of activity taking place in the brain as a whole.

◎ We use all of our brain.

Teachers Should Assess and Teach to Each Child's Learning Style

A very recently debunked neuromyth in educational literature concerns the concept of "learning styles." Learning style theory assumes that some children learn best through visual, auditory, or kinesthetic methods. According to the theory, teachers should inventory each child's preferred style and adjust instructional strategies to meet each child's assessed style of learning.

This neuromyth is certainly widespread: about 90% of people surveyed reported a belief that everyone has a preferred style of learning (Willingham, 2009). Willingham (2009) argues that this misunderstanding likely comes from popular notions of multiple intelligences and left/right brain processing theories. Unfortunately, the learning style theory as applied to classroom instruction has been aggressively perpetrated by vendors of educational products that promote learning style assessments and strategies for tailoring instruction to specific groups of students. Specifically, learning style theory has been promoted as a way for educators to differentiate instruction based on the "needs" of particular learners. Despite the pervasiveness of learning style theory in educational settings, in an extensive review of the literature Pashler, McDaniel, Rohrer, & Bjork (2008) found no evidence that children taught in their preferred learning style performed any better than if they were taught through a nonpreferred style.

◎ Pashler and colleagues (2008) found no evidence that children taught in their preferred learning style performed any better than if they were taught through a nonpreferred style.

Pashler and colleagues (2008) point out, however, that incorporating diverse teaching methods still appears to be a valid way of reaching *any* student. In particular, they suggest that varying presentation methods based on curriculum or content appears to be an efficient teaching strategy. With regard to meeting individual needs, there are potentially more efficient means of differentiation, such as considering prior knowledge, background in the content, level of mastery of skills, interest level, or learning differences and goals identified in individualized educational programs.

We Are Born With All the Brain Cells We Will Ever Have

Many of us believe that the brain is a static organ incapable of any significant changes. This is one of the most important myths to dispel for educators as it may influence teachers' attitudes and perceptions about children's capacity to learn (Hardiman & Denckla, 2010). As we will see from the discussion of plasticity and neurogenesis below, the brain is an amazing organ capable of tremendous change throughout life.

◎ The brain is an amazing organ capable of tremendous change throughout life.

IMPORTANT THEMES FROM THE NEURO- AND COGNITIVE SCIENCES THAT EDUCATORS SHOULD KNOW

Now that we have dispelled a number of the most insidious neuromyths, I turn to areas from the neuro- and cognitive sciences that can and should inform the philosophical beliefs as well as practices of educators at all levels. Each of these topics will also be considered in discussing the related components of the Brain-Targeted Teaching Model in subsequent chapters.

Plasticity

Plasticity is the term used to explain how the brain is modified with experience. Learning involves changes in the strength between neural synapses after a sensory input or motor activity. Neurons branch new dendrites, grow new axons, develop new synapses, and modify or eliminate established neural connections over the lifespan of the human being. Genetic makeup and environmental interactions set the course for the brain to change with experience (Shonkoff & Phillips, 2000). Just as muscles are strengthened with repeated exercise, brain networks are strengthened with repeated use.

◎ Just as muscles are strengthened with repeated exercise, brain networks are strengthened with repeated use.

Neurogenesis

Until recently, most neuroscientists believed that, although connections between cells continue to increase in number throughout life, the brain produces no new cells. The discovery of neurogenesis, the production of new cells in certain brain regions, represented an enormous breakthrough in

understanding the human brain. In animal studies, researchers have demonstrated the genesis of new brain cells in the cerebellum and in other impor-

> ⊚ The discovery of neurogenesis, the production of new cells in certain brain regions, represented an enormous breakthrough in understanding the human brain.

tant regions such as the hippocampus, an area associated with memory (Gould et al., 1999). In addition, it appears that neurogenesis can be enhanced through exercise, nutrition, and stress reduction (Kempermann, Wiskott, & Gage, 2004).

Emotion and Stress

Study of brain structure and function reveals the intricate interplay between cognition and emotion. Perhaps the words of Jill Bolte Taylor, a neuroscientist recovering from a severe stroke, best express this interplay. Taylor explains a major breakthrough in her thinking about brain function as she chronicles her brain's healing process. She states, "Although many of us may think of ourselves as *thinking creatures that feel*, biologically we are *feeling creatures that think*" (Taylor, 2008, p. 19).

Many of us were trained in our teacher preparation programs to believe that rational and emotional processing should not mix. Schools and classrooms, we believed, must focus on developing cognitive processes; emotion must be shut down for learning to take place. Now we know that it is impossible to separate emotions and learning. We will explore this topic in more depth in the chapter on Brain-Target One, Establishing the Emotional Climate for Learning.

(Cannot separate emotion from learning...duh!)

The Role of Attention in Learning

Regulation of attention to relevant tasks (or even elements of tasks) clearly affects every aspect of learning. Posner and Rothbart (2007) identify three neural networks—or systems of interconnected brain regions—involved in attending behaviors: the alerting network, which allows us to maintain an alert state; the orienting network, which helps us attend to sensory events; and the executive network, which sustains attention to an event (p. 59). They point out that effortful control of attention develops from early childhood into adolescence. Their studies have shown changes in patterns of neural activity underlying attentional processes and improvement in behavioral measures of attention after subjects received specific training in tasks requiring effortful control of attention

> ⊚ Effortful control of attention develops from early childhood into adolescence.

(p. 115). The chapter on Brain-Target Two will address how the classroom environment can be shaped to maximize attending behaviors in children.

Executive Function

The term *executive function* is used to describe basic cognitive processes that underlie on-going, goal-directed behaviors and higher-order thinking skills. These basic functions, which are often associated with neural processing in the frontal lobe, include holding information in working memory, initiating as well as inhibiting an action, and shifting perspective or the focus of attention, and together allow us to carry out more complex actions such as planning future events, organizing processes, self-monitoring, and regulating emotional response. Many children diagnosed with Attention Deficit Hyperactivity Disorder (ADHD) display deficits in one or more of the skills associated with executive function. Although executive function is necessary for most, if not all aspects of learning, this topic will be addressed in conjunction with Brain-Target Five, which focuses on the higher-order thinking processes and application of knowledge. This is one area in which executive function is especially critical for effective learning as it requires being able to draw novel associations and flexibly use information in different contexts. — *use information not only for class but life experiences too*

◎ Executive function is especially critical for effective learning as it requires being able to draw novel associations and flexibly use information in different contexts.

The Importance of Movement and Learning

Long recognizing the importance of movement in cognition and learning, Maria Montessori (1967) noted that "one of the greatest mistakes of our day is to think of movement by itself, as something apart from the higher functions . . . Mental development must be connected with movement and be dependent on it" (pp. 141–142).

Consistent with Montessori's idea, in his latest book, *Spark*, John Ratey (2008) explains that movement and exercise do more than just produce chemicals that make us feel good; physical activity actually affects cognitive development by accelerating the production of specific chemicals necessary for memory consolidation and spurring the development of new neurons from the hippocampus (p. 53). Within the Brain-Targeted Teaching Model, we will see the critical role of movement on attention in Brain-Target Two as well as in content acquisition and retention when we consider Brain-Target Four, which emphasizes active learning and arts integration.

Arts and Learning

Although the number of arts programs seems to be shrinking in our nations' schools, a growing body of research maintains that there are important positive effects of arts engagement in educational settings. Besides serving as a creative and enriching experience for children, the arts have been shown to have benefits on learning of various sorts. For instance, heading the Dana Foundation Arts and Cognition Consortium, Michael Gazzaniga (2008) reports a tight correlation between study of the arts and improvement in attention and various cognitive abilities. In addition, James Catterall (2009) reports significant differences in academic achievement and social behaviors between youth highly involved in arts programs compared with those with no arts engagement. What is more, researchers have shown changes in brain structure even with relatively small amounts of music training (Hyde et al., 2009). Hyde and colleagues found that students who were given just 15 months of music training showed significant changes in specific brain regions that were also correlated with improvements in musically relevant motor and auditory skills. Building from these connections between the arts and learning, Brain-Target Four explores how integrating the arts into content instruction may play a role in long-term retention of information and more robust habits of mind that transfer to all tasks.

> ◎ Researchers have shown changes in brain structure even with relatively small amounts of music training.

Adolescents, Sleep, and Learning

Research in the neuro- and cognitive sciences is beginning to shed light on the way brain changes during adolescence as well as on what patterns of neural activity may accompany at least some of those changes. National Institutes of Health researcher Jay Giedd (2009, 2010), for example, points out that the onset in puberty brings dramatic brain changes. Compared with prepubescent children, children entering puberty exhibit greater connectivity among various brain regions during task completion, reduction in grey matter volume, and changing balance between connections in the limbic and frontal executive function systems. A recent study demonstrated significant brain plasticity during the teen years evidenced by both biological and behavioral measures. Ramsden and colleagues (2011) found changes in verbal and non-verbal IQ scores (both higher and lower) during the teen years compared to earlier testing. These scores correlated with changes in associated local brain structures involved with verbal and non-verbal processing.

In addition to changes in neural and cognitive processing, sleep patterns also typically show significant changes. The circadian rhythms of adolescents point to a tendency for later sleep onset in the evening and later arousal in the morning (Dahl, 2004). This finding suggests that a school day that begins later in the morning may be more consistent with the sleep patterns of adolescents.

> ◎ Circadian rhythms of adolescents point to a tendency for later sleep onset in the evening and later arousal in the morning.

Brain changes may also account for the tendency of adolescents to shift from seeking approval from adults to seeking approval from same-age peers as well as for adolescents' having a greater propensity toward thrill-seeking behaviors (Giedd, 2009). Promising new research in this area could be used to assist educators and caregivers in understanding and preventing the increase of morbidity and mortality that comes with this sensitive time in human development. We will examine adolescent emotional development in discussions of Brain-Target One.

Creativity

As a hallmark of "21st-century skills," creativity in teaching and learning has become a topic of conversation and heightened interest in both the academic literature and popular media. In a special *Newsweek* issue dedicated to the topic, Po Bronson and Ashley Merryman (2010) point out that although IQ scores for children over the last 30 years have improved, creativity indices have declined. They cite analyses that examined the declining scores of more than 300,000 children and adults on the Torrance test, a popular measure of creative thinking. Sir Ken Robinson (2001) believes that concentrating on high-stakes testing in relation to an ever-increasing multitude of content standards is squeezing creativity out of our schools and classrooms.

> ◎ Concentrating on high-stakes testing in relation to an ever-increasing multitude of content standards is squeezing creativity out of our schools and classrooms.

While educators grapple with how to build more creative activities into overcrowded curricula, scientists have continued to demonstrate differences in how the brain processes information when people are engaged in creative, spontaneous tasks, as opposed to ordinary activities that depend on rote knowledge (Berkowitz & Ansari, 2010; Chávez-Eakle, Graff-Guerrero, García-Reyna, Vaugier, & Cruz-Fuentes, 2007; Fink, Benedek, Grabner, Staudt, & Neubauer, 2007; Limb & Braun, 2008). In our discussion of Brain-Target Five, we will examine this research on creativity, considering neuroimaging studies as well as behavioral studies. We will explore how teachers might be able to teach content in greater depth in order to move children beyond the mere acquisition of information to creative thinking and problem-solving tasks.

The next chapter provides a basic overview of brain structure and function, information that is important as we discuss research that supports the components of the Brain-Targeted Teaching Model.

Brain Structure and Function

In a similar chapter in my first book, I suggested that knowing basic information about brain anatomy was not necessary to implement teaching methods based on knowledge of the workings of the human mind and brain (Hardiman, 2003). However, after observing and studying how findings from the brain sciences can inform teaching, I believe that educators need at least some knowledge of brain structure and function in order to incorporate these findings into their teaching practice. As emerging research in neuro- and cognitive sciences continues to detail how children learn, fundamental knowledge of how the brain works should be an important component of teacher preparation programs. Though teachers might not need sophisticated scientific knowledge of neuroscience, a fundamental understanding of brain structure and function will allow educators to become better consumers of scientific research. For example, it will allow educators to more readily discern usable information from sensational headlines that serve only to propagate neuromyths. So, let's take a brief journey through the human brain, starting with the basics of its parts and processes and then examining in more detail how the brain is organized.

> ◎ Fundamental understanding of brain structure and function will allow educators to become better consumers of scientific research.

BRAIN FACTS

Looking at a human brain, one would describe it as the size of a grapefruit and the shape of a walnut. It weighs just under 3 pounds, most of which is water (about 78%), fat (about 10%), and protein (about 8%). It makes up about 2.5% of total body weight and consumes about 20% of the body's energy, a rate 10 times that of other body organs.

The brain is part of the human nervous system, a system that receives, processes, and stores information in order to coordinate actions. The nervous system is divided into two major parts: the central nervous system (CNS) and the peripheral nervous system (PNS). The CNS includes the brain and spinal cord, and the PNS consists of sensory and motor neurons that extend to all parts of the body. The CNS acts as the conductor, storing and analyzing the sensory signals it receives from the PNS and directing motor and chemical responses. The PNS sends sensory signals to the CNS and transports motor signals from the CNS to muscles, glands, and organs.

◉ The brain is part of the human nervous system, a system that receives, processes, and stores information in order to coordinate actions.

Brain Cells: Neurons and Glial Cells

The brain consists of several hundred billion cells of two main types: neurons and glial cells.

Neurons

Nerve cells or neurons receive and transmit information to other cells through electrochemical signals. Looking like a bulb with sprouting roots and a long tail, neurons typically consist of a cell body or soma (the bulb), dendrites (the sprouting roots), and an axon (the long tail). Each part of the neuron has a specific function. Like all other cells, the cell body of the neuron serves a metabolic function and contains molecules in cytoplasm within a cell membrane. The axon and dendrites are features unique to neurons, however. Dendrites branch out from the cell body and receive information from other neurons while the axon carries messages from the nerve cell to dendrites of other cells. Furthermore, the cell body of each neuron, in addition to its metabolic functions, processes or "sums up" the signals it receives from other neurons and responds by passing along signals of its own.

This process of cell communication is the essence of brain functioning. Signals are transmitted when neurons "fire," sending information outward from the cell body along the axon in the form of an electrical impulse. Communication between cells occurs when signals cross a tiny gap between the axon of one neuron and the dendrite of another called a synapse. Some synapses channel electrical impulses directly while others are traversed through biochemical processes as electrical impulses produce a release of chemicals called neurotransmitters from sacs at the end of the axon. These neurotransmitters bind to specialized receptors on the receiving (dendrite) side of the synapse, sending signals from one neuron to the next. Each neuron connects with thousands of other neurons, and as a result, the process of cellular communication can involve highly intricate neural pathways.

◎ Each neuron connects with thousands of other neurons, and as a result, the process of cellular communication can involve highly intricate neural pathways.

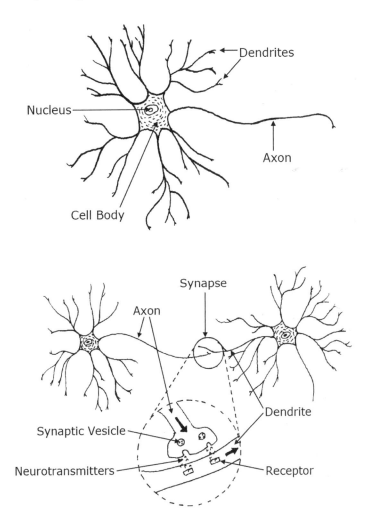

Glial Cells

Accounting for more than half of the brain's volume and far outnumbering neurons are glial or neuroglial cells. One function of these cells, whose name derives from the Greek word for glue, can be to provide structural support to neurons (Gazzaniga, Ivry, & Mangun, 2009).

Another critical function of glial cells is the formation of myelin, a fatty sheath that surrounds the axons. Myelin is essential for protecting and insulating the axon and also allows electrical impulses to travel at greater speeds, making communication between brain cells more efficient. Because myelin is white in color, these cells are referred to as the white matter of the brain.

Cerebral Organization

Before we review three major sections of the brain—the hindbrain, the limbic system, and the cerebrum (see figures on pages 21, 22, and 23 respectively)—we should note that the brain consists of two halves or hemispheres and the majority of brain structures discussed below are paired or occur in corresponding areas of the left and right hemispheres.

The Hindbrain

The hindbrain, consisting of the pons, medulla oblongata, and cerebellum, is considered the oldest part of the evolving human brain.

Pons and Medulla Oblongata. The pons and medulla oblongata control autonomic functions such as respiration, heart rhythms, and states of consciousness such as wakefulness and sleep. They control sensory processes, including auditory and visual sensation and motor control of the face, mouth, throat, respiratory system, and heart. These structures are located along the midline of the brain and thus are not paired.

Cerebellum. Though small in size, the cerebellum, sometimes referred to as the little cerebrum, plays a large role in brain and body functioning. Although it consists of only 10% of the brain, it contains approximately 11 billion cells that control important motor and sensory processes (Pinel, 2000). It is central to the body's balance, posture, walking, and planning motor commands for the coordination of harmonious movements. When you hit that perfect forehand in tennis without giving it a thought, your cerebellum is actively engaged. The ability to perform tasks automatically—like riding a bicycle, driving a car, or writing—relies heavily on the cerebellum; this automatic muscle memory frees up the higher cortical areas to process new information (Ratey, 2008). Recent discoveries have demonstrated that the cerebellum may also perform functions well beyond muscle memory. Patients with damage to the cerebellum have demonstrated difficulties with verbal tasks (Ivry & Fiez, 2000) and difficulty in regulating emotion (Schmahmann, 1997). Brain imaging studies suggest that children with Attention Deficit Hyperactivity Disorder (ADHD) who demonstrate lack of impulse control have a cerebellum that is reduced in size (Castellanos et al., 2002).

> ◎ When you hit that perfect forehand in tennis without giving it a thought, your cerebellum is actively engaged.

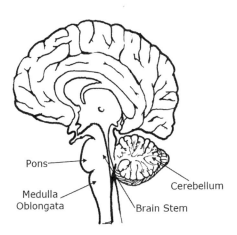

Pons

Medulla Oblongata

Cerebellum

Brain Stem

The Limbic System

Moving up from the hindbrain, we find the limbic system, a collection of structures that play an important role in emotional processing, learning, and memory. The structures we will examine here include the thalamus, hypothalamus, hippocampus, and amygdala.

Thalamus. At the core of the brain rests a walnut-sized structure that serves as the traffic cop, directing information received from the senses (excluding the olfactory) to other parts of the brain for further processing.

Hypothalamus. This structure serves as a relay station as it monitors information coming from the autonomic nervous system. It regulates the body's functions to maintain homeostasis. For example, when the body's temperature rises, the hypothalamus will increase perspiration to lower body temperature. The hypothalamus also regulates the endocrine system and some emotional processes.

Hippocampus. The shape of a seahorse, the hippocampus may be thought of as the workhorse of the memory system. It holds memories of the immediate past and serves to consolidate memories into the long-term memory system.

Amygdala. This almond-shaped structure is mostly associated with emotional states and processes. Although multiple neural systems are involved in processing emotional information, the amygdala is considered to have a key role (Gazzaniga et al., 2009). The amygdala is especially involved in our response to fearful situations. It is interesting to note that sensory information extracted from the external environment arrives in the amygdala for emotional processing before it reaches the cortex, the part of the brain where rational thought takes place (Sapolsky, 2004). More specifically, according to LeDoux (1996), the amygdala receives stimuli 40 milliseconds before the cortex. This finding indicates that fearful responses precede any conscious, thoughtful responses to stimuli.

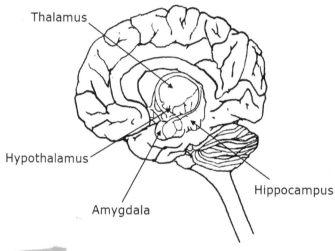

Thalamus

Hypothalamus

Amygdala

Hippocampus

The Cerebrum

The cerebrum is the largest area of the brain, accounting for more than 80% of the brain's weight. It is divided into halves referred to as cerebral hemispheres. The left and right hemispheres are connected by a thick bundle of nerve fibers called the corpus callosum. The corpus callosum contains 200 million or so tightly packed axons that bridge communications between the brain's hemispheres. Within each hemisphere, the cortex is divided into four lobes, each associated with particular brain functions.

◉ The corpus callosum contains 200 million or so tightly packed axons that bridge communications between the brain's hemispheres.

Occipital Lobe. Located at the back of the brain, the occipital lobe perceives and processes visual stimuli and their properties, including color, luminance, visual orientation, spatial orientation, and motion (Gazzaniga et al., 2009).

Temporal Lobe. The temporal lobe is located just above and around the ears. This lobe is where auditory stimuli are initially processed. The left temporal lobe includes Wernicke's area, one of several areas that specialize in processing spoken language.

Parietal Lobe. The parietal lobe is located on the top and side of each hemisphere and is responsible for processing sensory information such as pain, body position, temperature sense, limb position, and touch.

Frontal Lobe. Considered the center of thought, the frontal lobe includes the prefrontal cortex and the motor cortex. The prefrontal cortex is associated with executive functions such as planning, carrying out conscious actions, and inhibiting responses. The motor cortex lies between the prefrontal areas and parietal lobe and contains some of the largest neurons in the cerebral cortex, with axons that extend several feet down the spinal cord (Gazzaniga et al., 2009).

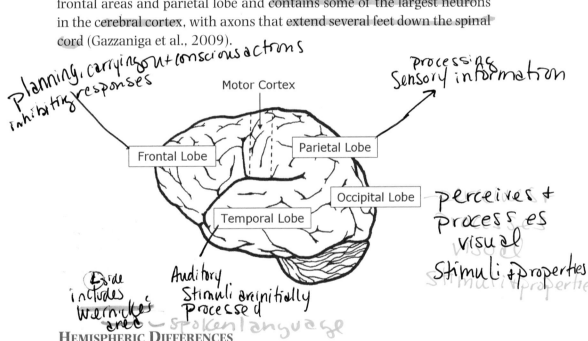

HEMISPHERIC DIFFERENCES

As pointed out in the previous chapter, differences in information processing between the left and right hemispheres of the brain were established and popularized as a result of studies of "split-brain" patients who underwent surgery to disconnect the two hemispheres of the brain in an effort to minimize seizure activity due to severe epilepsy. Specifically, split-brain surgery consists of severing the corpus callosum, the bundle of nerve fibers that serve as an "information superhighway" between the two hemispheres. Early notions of brain asymmetry characterized the left hemisphere as responsible for verbal and "linear" information processing, and the right hemisphere as responsible for spatial and "holistic" processing.

In contrast, more recently developed views of hemispheric specialization suggest that both hemispheres are involved in most tasks, though contributions from each may not be equal (Gazzaniga et al., 2009). Modern neuroimaging techniques such as functional magnetic resonance imaging (fMRI) and positron emission tomography (PET) confirm, for example, that the left side of the brain indeed plays a prominent role in language processing. However, neuroimaging studies also indicate that regions in the right hemisphere are important for some aspects of language as well, in particular for comprehension of abstract thought (Bookheimer, 2002) and prosody, the ability to detect affect or intonation in speech.

> ◎ Both hemispheres are involved in most tasks, though contributions from each may not be equal.

FROM RESEARCH TO PRACTICE

This research in left/right brain specializations demonstrates an important point: as research evolves, popular notions of how the brain works also need to evolve to reflect the latest scientific thinking. As we saw in the last chapter, there is no such thing as being a "left-" or "right-brained" thinker. And although it is harmless for anyone to profess to be left- or right-brained, it is unwise to base instruction on this or any other unscientific pop-culture notion. With a basic understanding of brain structure and function, educators can avoid using mere popular notions of how the brain works and instead translate usable findings on cognition and learning into instructional practices.

> ◎ With a basic understanding of brain structure and function, educators can avoid using mere popular notions of how the brain works and instead translate usable findings on cognition and learning into instructional practices.

Armed now with some basic information of brain anatomy, in the next chapter, we begin our study of the Brain-Targeted Teaching Model, an instructional framework designed to assist teachers in basing instruction on what we know from research from the neuro- and cognitive sciences about how the brain and mind work.

The Brain-Targeted Teaching Model for 21st-Century Schools

The Emotional
Climate

Evaluation and
Assessment

The Physical
Environment

Application of
Knowledge

Mastery of Content,
Skills, and Concepts

Big Picture
Learning Design

The Brain-Targeted Teaching Model

The Brain-Targeted Teaching (BTT) Model is an instructional framework designed to assist teachers in planning, implementing, and assessing a sound program of instruction informed by research from the neuro- and cognitive sciences. The model consists of six stages of the teaching and learning process that I refer to as ***brain targets***— that is, teaching targeted to what we know about how we think and learn.

As we have seen from previous chapters, scientific discoveries in cognition and learning can and should inform the work of educators. However, without a guiding framework, making sense of usable knowledge from this research and integrating it into instructional practices can become challenging. This model synthesizes relevant research into a cohesive pedagogical system for using effective practices in any instructional program from early childhood to adult learning and in any content area. As such, it is not a curriculum nor a stand-alone product, and most sound teaching programs and practices align with one or more of the brain targets, such as the Universal Design for Learning (Rose & Meyer, 2002) or Framework for Teaching (Danielson, 1996). (See Appendix I: Alignment of Brain-Targeted Teaching With Cognitive Taxonomies, Teaching Standards, and Frameworks.)

> ◎ Without a guiding framework, making sense of usable knowledge from this research and integrating it into instructional practices can become challenging.

Although each of the targets is presented as a separate component, all six are interrelated. Thus the model should not be viewed as linear, but as an organic system that guides and informs an approach to instruction both at the level of the classroom and as a unifying school-based system. Fundamental to that approach are teaching practices that lead all students not only to demonstrate mastery of content but also to apply knowledge in creative problem-solving, now referred to as "21st-century skills." Also central to the model is the purposeful focus on the emotional and physical learning environments, designing instruction so that students understand "big picture" concepts, continuous evaluation of learning, and the integration of the arts to foster retention, conceptual development, and higher-order thinking. The section below provides a brief description of each of the brain targets.

> ◎ The model should not be viewed as linear, but as an organic system that guides and informs an approach to instruction both at the level of the classroom and as a unifying school-based system.

Overview of the Brain-Targeted Teaching Model

Brain-Target One: Establishing the Emotional Climate for Learning

Our study of the BTT Model begins with Brain-Target One, an exploration of the interconnection of emotions and learning. As research from the brain sciences continues to shed light on the neural systems underlying emotion, it is important for educators to understand the influence of emotional arousal, both positive and negative, on attention, memory, and higher-order thinking. For example, research is demonstrating the negative effects of stress on learning from prenatal stages to early childhood, adolescent, and adult learning. Conversely, positive emotion has been shown to improve learning outcomes. This research informs instructional strategies designed to promote a positive, joyful, and purposeful climate for learning. We also consider ways to embed into learning units specific activities to provide an emotional connection to the subject matter in order to make learning more meaningful and relevant for students.

> ◎ Positive emotion has been shown to improve learning outcomes.

Brain-Target Two: Creating the Physical Learning Environment

Just as the emotional environment in a classroom can shape learning, elements in the physical environment—the focus of Brain-Target Two—can influence students' attention and engagement in learning tasks. We explore how novelty in the classroom engages students' attention and how it can be achieved by using strategies such as changing seating arrangements and classroom displays. We also look at ways to encourage movement and bring a sense of order and beauty into the classroom environment.

> ◎ Novelty in the classroom engages students' attention.

Brain-Target Three: Designing the Learning Experience

The learning sciences delve into the cognitive processes associated with information processing—how we make meaning and find relationships amidst input from various senses. Brain-Target Three is informed by the notion that we use prior knowledge to categorize stimuli and combine this prior knowledge with new knowledge to create patterns of thinking and learning. Rather than lists of facts, cognitive science tells us that knowledge is organized around global understanding or big ideas. Therefore, we design the learning experience with the use of visual representations to show students "big-picture" concepts and connections between new ideas and prior knowledge. We demonstrate to students how learning goals and objectives connect with daily activities and lead to the attainment of targeted content, skills, and concepts.

> ◎ Knowledge is organized around global understanding or big ideas.

Brain-Target Four: Teaching for Mastery of Content, Skills, and Concepts

Educating students assumes that they acquire knowledge and master skills and concepts so they can lead full and productive lives and become lifetime learners. Learning content, skills, and concepts requires that students retain information and use it meaningfully. Brain-Target Four explores the connection between learning and memory, reviewing how information and experiences are processed, encoded, stored, and retrieved in the brain's memory systems. Research from cognitive science and psychology demonstrates various manipulations that influence long-term memory. We consider these "memory effects" as we explore how retention of knowledge is supported through teaching that integrates the visual and performing arts into content instruction.

> ◎ Research from cognitive science and psychology demonstrates various manipulations that influence long-term memory. Retention of knowledge is supported through teaching that integrates the visual and performing arts into content instruction.

Brain-Target Five: Teaching for the Extension and Application of Knowledge—Creativity and Innovation in Education

Teaching and learning in 21st-century classrooms must not only lead students to mastery of content, skills, and concepts but also must promote the application of knowledge in real-world problem-solving tasks. The hallmark of 21st-century learning is the ability to demonstrate creative and innovative thinking. Brain-Target Five focuses on the growing body of research in creativity and how findings can inform instructional practices so that learning experiences foster divergent thinking and problem-solving.

> ◎ The hallmark of 21st-century learning is the ability to demonstrate creative and innovative thinking.

Brain-Target Six: Evaluating Learning

Evaluation of learning is a critical component of the teaching and learning process. In Brain-Target Six, we explore research that demonstrates how continuous evaluation can enhance learning and memory. We consider how to expand traditional types of assessments to include the use of student portfolios, student-generated products, and performance-based assessments.

◎ How continuous evaluation can enhance learning and memory.

BRAIN-TARGETED TEACHING

RESEARCH TO PRACTICE

In Chapters 4 through 9, we take an in-depth look at each component of the BTT Model. For each brain target, we first review the neuro- and cognitive science as well as educational research that informs the brain target. Then, to demonstrate application of the research into practice, each chapter is followed by strategies that logically stem from the research. These strategies are embedded in the text and also are offered in special sections written by *expert teachers* who have used the model in preK–12 and higher education settings. In addition, below we meet two teachers whose complete Brain-Targeted Teaching units are threaded through the chapters. Clare O'Malley Grizzard describes a language arts unit for elementary grades, and Suzanne McNamara demonstrates a unit implemented in a high school biology classroom. As these units unfold through each chapter, they provide rich examples of how traditional methods of teaching can be enhanced and student learning deepened through the use of strategies associated with the stages of the Brain-Targeted Teaching Model.

WHAT DOES A BRAIN-TARGETED TEACHING UNIT LOOK LIKE IN THE CLASSROOM?

Learning Unit: Surviving Alone in the Wilderness: A study of the novel *Hatchet* by Gary Paulsen

Grade/Content: Fifth-Grade/Language Arts

Author: Clare O'Malley Grizzard

Overarching Goal of Unit: Students will increase language arts skills of reading for understanding through analysis of character, plot, main idea, and symbolic language.

As a visual art teacher and arts-integration specialist, I look for opportunities to bring the arts into traditional classrooms through cross-curricular planning. This unit involved collaboration with Linda Bluth, a veteran fifth-grade language arts teacher, who, in her 29th year of teaching, realized a whole new way of engaging her students through Brain-Targeted Teaching.

Our goals were simple:

- To bring the students back to *a love of reading* which had been lost in an era of high-pressure test preparation and technology;

- *To teach empathy*—enable students to connect emotionally with the character in a novel; and

- To *rekindle the educator's enthusiasm* for sharing a journey with her students through a deep and meaningful exploration of literature.

Hatchet by Gary Paulsen tells the story of a young teenage boy named Brian who is the lone survivor of a plane crash in the Canadian wilderness; he finds that he is left with only a small hatchet in his possession. He experiences an exciting adventure of survival that includes learning to respect the natural environment and his integral place in it and discovering the power of ingenuity in problem-solving and self-reliance. Complete with a tornado, moose attack, food poisoning, skeletons, bears, and desolation, this novel offers a rich opportunity to explore coming-of-age themes, literary objectives, and empathy.

Linda Bluth and I realized the transformative power of the arts as we planned activities to teach this novel to the students. Without shortchanging academic content and reading objectives, students participated in creative work because they were engaged in the adventure of the novel, actively and purposefully. Their writing expressed a deeper involvement with the story with an effortless use of descriptive language and their personal voice. Ms. Bluth and I were transformed, too. Using the BTT Model, we developed strategies and approaches to planning collaboratively that spoke to our individual strengths. I hope you enjoy seeing our unit come to life through the study of each of the brain targets through this book.

◎ Without shortchanging academic content and reading objectives, students participated in creative work because they were engaged in the adventure of the novel, actively and purposefully.

—Clare O'Malley Grizzard

Learning Unit: Genetics and Heredity—Thinking Outside the Punnett Square

Grade/Content: 10th-Grade/Biology

Author: Suzanne P. McNamara

Overarching Goal of Unit: Students will apply their understanding of genetics and heredity in discussions centered on current medical and social issues as well as an appreciation for human diversity.

Having worked in Baltimore City for my entire teaching career, I have constantly struggled to meet the diverse needs of my high school students. I saw the BTT Model as a method to help engage more of my students and motivate them to take ownership of their learning. When I first decided to implement a Brain-Targeted Unit in my classroom, I was especially attracted to Brain-Targets One, Two, and Five. I thought that introducing these elements into my instruction would help me better reach out to my diverse learners. After planning for this unit, however, I realized that this model provided much more than mere student engagement. The BTT Model is an authentic and holistic approach to instruction. It not only forced me to provide opportunities for students to truly engage with the material, but it helped me to focus less on the "facts" and more on how students would engage with the unifying concepts of the unit.

> ◎ The BTT Model is an authentic and holistic approach to instruction. It not only forced me to provide opportunities for students to truly engage with the material, but it helped me to focus less on the "facts" and more on how students would engage with the unifying concepts of the unit.

As a science teacher, I have always been an advocate for a hands-on interdisciplinary approach to learning in my classroom. From my observations, students are more engaged in the learning experience when the lesson is interactive, meaningful, and relevant. Most important, these practices help students to develop versatile skills that enable them to become lifelong learners. Having implemented the BTT Model for the past 2 years, I have seen how its use can have a major impact on student motivation and achievement. At first, I was afraid that this type of holistic teaching may not prepare students for high-stakes testing—but this has proven otherwise in my class. When students immerse themselves in hands-on learning, they develop critical thinking skills that can be applied to various tasks; they have demonstrated that learning on assessments from unit tests to Advanced Placement exams. From my experiences, this model has helped students understand and explore content deeper and promotes better retention of content.

I designed and implemented a high school Brain-Targeted Teaching unit on the topic of genetics for my ninth-grade students titled "Genetics and Heredity—Thinking Outside the Punnett Square." The goal of the unit was for students to apply their understanding of genetics and heredity in discussions centered on current medical and social issues as well as the appreciation of human diversity. Instead of using traditional extension projects to help students better understand the material, I forced myself to find ways to incorporate "21st-century skills" into the unit. My students were constantly required to apply the material to real-world applications in order to solve problems. Without realizing it, I was helping them to make true meaning of the content. Although the Brain-Targeted unit helped me accomplish my initial goal of student engagement, it also made me realize that this non-traditional teaching method is not just an alternative, but a more effective way to meet the developmental needs of my students. It was clear to me that my students had truly mastered genetics.

◎ Although the Brain-Targeted unit helped me accomplish my initial goal of student engagement, it also made me realize that this non-traditional teaching method is not just an alternative, but a more effective way to meet the developmental needs of my students.

Although I was a little wary of integrating the arts into my teaching methodology, I soon realized that it was an extremely powerful way to foster creativity among my students and encourage divergent thinking. Once I found ways to incorporate the arts into genetics topics, I found that these learning opportunities especially helped students to understand the content and apply their learning in meaningful ways. I hope you enjoy learning more about my unit in each of the chapters that follow.

—Suzanne P. McNamara

Brain-Target One

Establishing the Emotional Climate for Learning

A teacher who is attempting to teach without inspiring the pupil with a desire to learn is hammering on cold iron.

—Horace Mann

I ask you to take a few moments to think back into your own school experiences. Think of a time when you may have been publically embarrassed by an insensitive remark by a teacher or classmate. Think about how you felt immediately after the incident. Were you able to concentrate on the learning task after that event? Did it affect how you performed in that teacher's class in the subsequent days or even months? What elements do you remember most about the experience?

These are questions that I've asked thousands of participants in workshops, conferences, and graduate education classes. And the responses are always riveting. At 72, Sarah, for example, described a vivid memory of an event she experienced as a 6-year-old. Sarah shared how her excitement for learning numbers was squelched by her first-grade teacher who criticized her mistakes when she was asked to count by fives. She said that she clearly remembers the teacher saying, "Sit down and be better prepared the next time you try to answer . . . not all of us understand math as well as others." Sarah expressed how, after that remark, she was frightened to respond to any question posed by the teacher, especially in a math lesson. When I asked her how that affected her performance in math that school year, her response was not surprising. She stated, "That incident affected my performance in math for the rest of my school career. I avoided the subject and always struggled with confidence in any math work in the future." Sarah was not the first to share a story that she remembered with such clarity and to view the incident as having a negative impact on her schooling. Jeremy shared a similar situation stemming from an oral report in a seventh-grade social studies class. Negative and embarrassing feedback from the teacher in front of the class prompted him to refuse to speak publically for the rest of his middle school experience.

My rather risky workshop presentation activity may seem strange to the audience; after all, most speakers want the audience to be happy during a presentation, not provoke them into thinking uncomfortable thoughts! Like many others, Sarah and Jeremy openly shared their experiences to help illustrate a critical idea: Each of these shared experiences clearly demonstrates the role of emotions in learning. When placed in situations like those described above, most of us become caught up in negative or stressful feelings and our attention is shifted away from the higher cognitive processes required for learning. Understanding and preventing how attention is shifted under stress is crucial, especially in a school environment, if any learning is to occur.

> ◎ Understanding and preventing how attention is shifted under stress is crucial, especially in a school environment, if any learning is to occur.

The effects of emotions on learning, including how stress impedes learning but also how positive feelings enhance the learning experience, are where we begin our journey through the Brain-Targeted Teaching (BTT) Model. As demonstrated by the activity described above as well as by the present chapter, setting the emotional climate for learning may be the most important task a teacher embarks on each day. In Brain-Target One of the BTT Model, teachers consider the emotional climate through two lenses. First, they design the general climate of the classroom—beginning on the first day of school—to promote a joyful, productive, and safe learning environment. Second, they purposefully plan activities in a learning unit that will provide students with an emotional connection to the content, making the subject matter more personal, relevant, and meaningful. In this chapter, we explore findings from the neuro- and cognitive sciences that shed light on the relationship between emotions and learning as well as what those findings advocate in terms of establishing an emotional climate for learning.

> ◎ Setting the emotional climate for learning may be the most important task a teacher embarks on each day.

Neural Systems Underlying Emotion

In order to consider how teachers might address the emotional climate in the classroom, we should have some understanding of how the brain processes emotions—whether they are negative or positive—and how that functioning influences children's capacity to attend to, perceive, and remember information. Although researchers now recognize that multiple areas of the brain are engaged when we process emotion, studies of the brain's emotional response must begin with the limbic system, which has been most widely recognized as the brain's emotional center (Gazzaniga, Ivry, & Mangun, 2009). The amygdala, located in the brain's medial temporal lobes, is part of the limbic system and is an important structure for processing emotion (e.g., for a review, see Phelps, 2006; Phelps & LeDoux, 2005). The amygdala is engaged not only in implicit emotional reaction, such as an unexpected fearful event, but also in explicit emotional learning, such as learning about a danger and remembering the information.

In addition to the amygdala, explicit emotional learning engages the hippocampus, a key structure involved in memory. We may intuitively know that an emotionally charged event stays in our memory. This relationship between emotion and memory is supported by research demonstrating that the engagement of the amygdala does indeed strengthen memories (Ferry, Roozendaal, & McGaugh, 1999). In other words, the involvement of the amygdala in declarative memories explains why we remember emotionally charged events better than ordinary day-to-day occurrences.

How We Perceive Fear and Threat

One critical aspect of emotional processing and therefore of emotional learning is how our brains respond to fear and threat. In particular, our brain processes threat so that we can both think about it and respond to it. To take a step back, as we receive information from our senses, the sensory signal projects to the thalamus, which then sends information to various brain systems for processing including the cortex, the center for thinking. At the same time, the thalamus sends the signal to the amygdala to assess if the sensory input involves danger or threat. The signal, however, travels from the thalamus to the amygdala through a *quicker* pathway than the signal that is sent to the cortex. Joseph LeDoux (1996) calls this the "low road," a quick and dirty route that allows the brain to prepare for an immediate response to potential threat (p. 163). In contrast, the signal projected to the cortex, the "high road," is slower but more thorough in its analysis. This high road signal, once processed by the cortex, is then routed to the amygdala for a fuller emotional response.

This dual system for sensory perception of threat has its purposes. The quick route to the amygdala, the low road, allows us to take action to a potentially dangerous situation before we fully know the extent of the threat or even if a danger actually exists. In evolutionary terms, the quick but incomplete response system is necessary for survival, as it allows an organism to protect itself from environmental dangers. Yet, although fast and efficient, this system is not designed to be precise in its assessment. Consistent with this imprecision, LeDoux (1996) explains that when we react to fear, our brain systems are in fact designed to respond to sensory information that has not been fully analyzed in the cortex. In this way, the emotional processing system, mostly in the amygdala, "has a greater influence on the cortex than the cortex has on the amygdala, allowing emotional arousal to dominate and control thinking" (p. 303).

◉ When we react to fear, our brain systems are in fact designed to respond to sensory information that has not been fully analyzed in the cortex.

Our emotions and thinking are not the only functions affected when we perceive threat and fear. Once the amygdala senses threat, a cascade of *physical* responses follows. The information processed by the amygdala triggers the hypothalamus, which activates stress hormones to prepare the body for the fight-or-flight response and promotes bodily changes, including elevating blood pressure, increasing heart rate, and contracting muscles.

This biological system—emotional processing of threat that in turn generates a physical response—evolved as a result of stressful events that lasted for a short time. We either were able to run from the saber tooth tiger or we were its lunch. In our lives today, however, stress is often an ongoing event and the effects of constant stress hormones may not be beneficial (e.g., Joëls, Pu, Wiegert, Oitzl, and Krugers, 2004). Chronic stress is known to impair body systems such as the cardiovascular, digestive, and immune systems. In addition, research has shown that constant stress may cause damage in the hippocampus and frontal cortex, affecting memory and information processing (McEwen & Sapolsky, 1995). In the following section, we consider in more detail how these neural and physiological consequences of stress impact cognitive function and learning.

◎ Chronic stress is known to impair body systems such as the cardiovascular, digestive, and immune systems.

EFFECTS OF STRESS ON LEARNING

An area of great concern to the research communities across multiple disciplines is the effects of stress on the developing child. In particular, a growing body of research is examining the relationship between poverty and stress as well as the effects of such stress on cognition and learning. Bradley, Corwyn, Pipes McAdoo, and Garcia Coll (2001) demonstrated a high correlation of childhood stress associated with poverty. They found, for example, that children in lower socioeconomic status (SES) groups had fewer opportunities for learning and less supportive caregiving than those living in homes with higher SES. Children living in poverty tend to have less engaged parental and extended caregiver support systems and fewer opportunities to engage in informal learning experiences. What is more, poverty-driven family stress appears to have an effect on the cognitive development of children. For example, research demonstrates differences in a child's neural processing of selective attention, including the ability to ignore irrelevant information, based on the mother's education and economic level (Stevens, Lauinger, & Neville, 2009). Furthermore, in a recent study of middle-school aged children from low SES households, Farah and colleagues (2008) found relationships between parental nurturing and memory development and between environmental stimulation and language development. In addition to memory, parental nurturance has been to shown to predict brain morphology in the hippocampus, an area associated with memory (Rao et al., 2010). In other words, parental nurturance seems to have an important role not only in the development of cognitive function but also in maturation of the physical brain.

◎ Parental nurturance seems to have an important role not only in the development of cognitive function but also in maturation of the physical brain.

These findings are similar to studies conducted within the general population. Such lab-based studies not only support an effect of stress on learning but also demonstrate the extent to which performance on a simple task is affected when a study participant is under stress. For example, Schwabe and Wolf (2010) found that, when placed in a stressful situation while

> ◎ Although mild stress in specific contexts may enhance performance and recall, prolonged stress appears to reduce the ability to acquire, retain, and recall information.

learning new words, participants' performance declined by at least 30%. Although mild stress in specific contexts may enhance performance and recall, prolonged stress appears to reduce the ability to acquire, retain, and recall information (Joëls et al., 2006).

Stress and School Environments

Given that stress has been shown to affect one's ability to learn, it is imperative that we understand the stress levels of students in schools. Educators and caregivers expect that every child would view school as a joyful and inviting learning experience and not a stress-inducing environment. Unfortunately, rates of drop-outs and suspensions across school districts as well as stories of bullying suggest otherwise. More important, students themselves report a different story. Studies on school environments are beginning to shed light on the emotional world of students in school. Pekrun, Goetz, Titz, and Perry (2002), for example, conducted a series of studies to determine the emotions that students say they experience during the school day. Although a broad range of emotions were cited, including positive emotions associated with learning, the most frequent emotion identified was anxiety, accounting for up to 25% of all emotions reported. In addition, the researchers tested the physiological reaction to stress-related episodes by testing levels of cortisol, a hormone associated with stress. Not surprisingly, they found that students with high anxiety had high cortisol levels. In contrast, students who were able to employ stress-reducing coping strategies did not produce high cortisol levels, suggesting the importance of including purposeful activities to reduce stress in the learning environment. Behavioral problems associated with anxiety have also been linked to cortisol levels (Ruttle et al., 2011). The research demonstrates that when anxiety-driven behavioral problems begin, individuals have increased stress and cortisol levels that become abnormally elevated. If the behavioral problems and thus the stress continue over an extended period of time, stress and cortisol levels become abnormally low, as the body is trying to protect itself from negative effects associated with high levels of cortisol. Unfortunately, this reaction to continual stress may cause the individuals not to worry or care about their performance in school, which in turn leads to poor academic performance. This work suggests that interventions should be put in place as soon as behavioral problems are observed.

> ◎ Studies on school environments are beginning to shed light on the emotional world of students in school.

As research continues to demonstrate behavioral and biological effects of stress on learning, it would seem that high priority must be given to producing a school climate that promotes a positive learning environment. As a first step, teachers might do well to take an "emotional inventory" to determine what might be stressful triggers for children. Such an inventory should also involve assessing students' perceptions about causes of stress as these perceptions may affect actual stress levels. In a recent study involving children and adults, even young children appeared to be aware of the kinds of stressful situations that would impede academic performance. The participants were presented with stories in which the main character experienced either a positive or negative event, and then the character had to perform a difficult cognitive task. The participants were asked to predict the character's performance on the cognitive task. Even young children understood the detrimental effects that negative events such as an argument with a peer, a noisy environment, or even messy hair might have on performance (Amsterlaw, Lagattuta, & Meltzoff, 2009).

> ◎ As research continues to demonstrate behavioral and biological effects of stress on learning, it would seem that high priority must be given to producing a school climate that promotes a positive learning environment.

THE IMPACT OF POSITIVE EMOTIONS

We have seen how emotion, especially the negative effects of stress, impacts attention, learning, and memory. As there are detrimental effects of negative emotion on learning, there are also beneficial effects of positive emotion on learning. For example, Frederickson (1998) points out positive emotions influence broad cognitive associations and results in better performance on creative thinking measures. She argues that positive affect also leads to a greater repertoire of skills to create, explore, and integrate content knowledge. In addition, a recent study by Fredrickson and Branigan (2005) found that after viewing films that elicit positive, negative, or neutral emotions, positive emotions increased subjects' scope of attention, global thinking, and increased thought-action responses (i.e., describing an action that the subject would perform given the emotion).

> ◎ As there are detrimental effects of negative emotion on learning, there are also beneficial effects of positive emotion on learning.

In setting up an emotional climate for learning, another important factor to consider is motivation to learn, which can vary from one student to the next. In fact, recent research by Hart and Albarracin (2009) has demonstrated that individuals who are typically motivated by achievement goals perform better when a task is presented as achievement-oriented (e.g., a challenging puzzle) compared with when that task is presented as fun-oriented (e.g., a fun game). The reverse pattern—better performance when a task is presented as fun-oriented—is observed for individuals who are not typically motivated by achievement goals. These results highlight the importance of goal-state in teaching and learning: both student groups can perform well with the appropriate kind of motivation. For underachieving children, learning activities in which the students feel they are having fun, such as in a learning game or arts activity, may be important for motivation for learning and to foster emotional connections to the content.

> ◎ For underachieving children, learning activities in which the students feel they are having fun, such as in a learning game or arts activity, may be important for motivation for learning and to foster emotional connections to the content.

EMOTIONS AND THE ADOLESCENT

Ask any parent or teacher of an adolescent how behavior changes in those important years, and you are sure to get a laundry list of the difficult issues that come with this important time of life. Scientists are now demonstrating what teachers and caregivers have long known: adolescence is a time of rapid physical and emotional changes paired with challenging social changes; together, these factors lead to variations in behavior. Most notably, the peer group typically replaces the adult as the source of approval, and the tendency for risk-taking and thrill-seeking behaviors increases from the onset of puberty into early adulthood (Giedd, 2009; Steinberg, 2008).

In addition to physical, social, and emotional changes, sleep patterns change during adolescence. In fact, at the onset of adolescence, there are important changes to the neural systems of sleep and circadian rhythms (Dahl, 2004). Moreover, as technology facilitates increased social opportunities in the evenings coupled with physiological changes leading to later onset of sleepiness, adolescents are at risk of sleep deprivation. Understanding and preventing such sleep deprivation is critical as growing evidence demonstrates that lack of sleep can create emotional as well as cognitive and physical health problems (Steinberg et al., 2006).

> ◎ As technology facilitates increased social opportunities in the evenings coupled with physiological changes leading to later onset of sleepiness, adolescents are at risk of sleep deprivation.

Though adolescence brings a number of potentially negative effects on emotions (and therefore on learning), at the same time, educators who enjoy working with adolescents cannot help but notice the many benefits of the high-intensity feelings that are part of this developmental period. The challenge and reward is the process of sculpting that passion through exciting learning activities, self-expression in the arts, and collaboration on sports fields, in special interest clubs, and with human service projects.

IMPLEMENTING BRAIN-TARGET ONE

ESTABLISHING THE EMOTIONAL CLIMATE FOR LEARNING

Whether working with young children, adolescents, or young adults, educators must be aware of their powerful role in establishing and maintaining a positive and productive environment in the school and classroom. As our examples at the beginning of this chapter demonstrate, even the best of teachers may inadvertently engage in a teaching or disciplinary practice that induces stress and inhibits learning. If teachers are armed with a basic understanding of the effects of stress on learning (as presented in this chapter), they will be better able to avoid such stress-inducing practices.

> ◎ Educators must be aware of their powerful role in establishing and maintaining a positive and productive environment in the school and classroom.

Research from biological and behavioral studies clearly informs educators of the importance of purposeful activities to establish a positive emotional climate in a classroom. As we begin to design learning units in the Brain-Targeted Teaching Model, Brain-Target One contains the following goals: (a) to establish and revisit practices that promote a positive environment and (b) to design activities that engage students emotionally in the content or skills of the lesson. Below I address each of these goals in turn and present areas to consider in creating the kind of classroom environment that will support learning and will be long remembered by students as a time and place of joyful learning.

Strategies for Promoting a Positive Learning Environment

Positive Language: Praise and Veiled Commands

Praising students for positive behaviors often comes naturally to teachers. But is all praise equal in its effect on learning and is it always productive? Research tells us that behavior-specific praise is more effective in reinforcing and shaping behaviors than generalized praise (Mueller & Dweck, 1998). For example, it is more effective to call attention to a

> ◎ Behavior-specific praise is more effective in reinforcing and shaping behaviors than generalized praise.

specific behavior such as, "You are each assuming full responsibilities in your cooperative learning group" rather than simply saying "Good job today, class."

Positive language through praise of effort (e.g., "you must have worked hard on this task") has also been shown to be more productive than praise of ability (e.g., "you must be smart on this task"). To assess the effects of these two approaches to praise, Carol Dweck (2008) conducted multiple studies in a variety of settings with students from age four through adolescence. Results indicated that students who were praised for ability on a task were less successful on subsequent tasks than those praised for their effort on the task. For example, students who were told they were successful on math problems because they were smart were less confident and motivated to complete harder problems than those who were told that their suc-

> ◎ Students who were praised for ability on a task were less successful on subsequent tasks than those praised for their effort on the task.

cess was due to hard work. Thus praising students based on intelligence appears to reduce confidence when they encounter a difficult task whereas praising effort enhances perseverance and engagement.

We should, in communicating with students, avoid using "veiled commands" (Delpit, 1988, p. 289) that disguise the intent of the communication. For example, the teacher may intend for the question "*Is that where your scissors belong?*" to be a command to put the scissors away in a box. The child may interpret the question literally as a question and not respond to the indirect command. Delpit points out that cultural background may influence whether children understand the intended meaning of an indirect or veiled command.

We should work toward developing a classroom culture in which positive language between the teacher and students as well as among students is the expectation at all times.

Predictability: Classroom Routines, Rituals, and Celebrations

Establishing classroom routines lets students know what is expected of them academically and socially in the context of the classroom. For example, using quick review drills or journal writing is an activity that many teachers use daily to get the lesson started while they are engaged in the "housekeeping activities" of recording attendance and distributing materials. Many teachers effectively use work stations to provide students with information and materials they need on a regular basis such as a notebook of homework assignments, makeup work for absentees, work for extra credit, forms needed for fieldtrips, or other administrative tasks.

Rituals that are quick and fun such as chants, hand signals, clapping patterns, songs, movements, or relaxation exercises help to motivate and engage students and build a sense of group identity. Rituals can also serve as powerful social messages that become the standard for peer social interactions and work expectations.

◎ Rituals that are quick and fun such as chants, hand signals, clapping patterns, songs, movements, or relaxation exercises help to motivate and engage students and build a sense of group identity.

Celebrations for academic success, special cultural events, or reaching academic or social goals often go a long way in giving children a sense of belonging and building group cohesiveness.

From the Expert Teacher

To Make a Friend, Be a Friend

As I began to implement components of Brain-Targeted Teaching, I realized how important it is for students to experience caring friendship from classmates to support a healthy emotional environment. Some kids are "naturals" at making friends while others, unfortunately, are not. When it comes to developing my students' social skills, I've learned that "showing" is a lot better than "telling." A great place for my kids to "see" friendship in action is at our class Communication Center.

Like many successful projects, a Communication Center is very easy to set up and to use. It is just a bulletin board covered with empty envelopes—one for each student and one for the teacher. Nearby are a can filled with pencils and a box containing notepaper. In September before I attach the envelopes to the board, the students personalize them with their names and decorations. After the center is created, we have conversations about when and why friends communicate. For example, friends notice when their buddies do something well. They say thank you. They ask for help. They honor birthdays and offer get-well thoughts. They tell jokes. They chat. I also point out that this year we will be communicating with one another by writing and reading as well as by speaking and listening.

Every day I allow a few minutes for our note-writing. My "envelope" serves double duty as the class Suggestion/Complaint Box. Interestingly, I have found that this helps us stay on schedule. For example, if a student has an "issue," I may ask the child to write it down for me to address later (which I always do). This can stop a mid-lesson distraction.

The Communication Center becomes a friend-making machine when it is used often by everyone—especially the teacher. As an advocate and friend to all my students, I keep a very close eye on the envelopes. Despite all my efforts, there are always some that are empty while others seem stuffed. When this happens,

(Continued)

I very quietly and privately help my socially awkward students realize that the best way "to make a friend is to be a friend." It's important to remember that children often don't understand this simple rule and that they may need a little additional guidance in this area.

Helping my students reach high academic standards is one of my paramount objectives. However, in the last decade there have been incidents in schools when kids who have felt "left out" have "acted out"—sometimes in very destructive ways. Helping my students feel emotionally safe and socially accepted is as important as helping them achieve their intellectual goals.

Sharon Delgado
Teacher, Elementary School, Special Education

Emotional Events: Engagement Versus Disengagement

While working toward promoting a positive environment within the classroom, most teachers experience any number of factors outside of the classroom that are beyond their control, including home life, peer interactions, and societal and community stressors. Coping and managing these inevitable factors is necessary for creating and maintaining a positive classroom environment.

One decision that teachers are often faced with is how to deal with an emotionally charged event that students experienced before entering the classroom. A common scenario involves a student who enters the classroom distraught because of a situation at home, an altercation with a peer, or a multitude of other causes. The teacher can decide to allow the student to process the emotion through dialogue, he or she can redirect the student through engagement in an academic task, or the teacher can simply ignore the student's emotion. Recent research may provide some answers as far as which decision will optimize subsequent learning. Rice, Levine, & Pizarro (2007) assessed students' performance in an academic task following a negative emotional event. After viewing segments of a sad film, students were tested in one of the following three ways: (a) students were asked questions that engaged them in processing the feeling of sadness, (b) students were told not to feel sadness from the emotional scene and were redirected to analyzing neutral information, or (c) students were given neutral information to analyze without any mention of the emotional scene. Results showed that children who were instructed to disengage performed better on educational tasks than those who were instructed to process their feelings or those who received no acknowledgement of the emotional event.

◎ Children who were instructed to disengage performed better on educational tasks than those who were instructed to process their feelings or those who received no acknowledgement of the emotional event.

These findings may help to inform those quick and important decisions that teachers are frequently faced with when dealing with students' emotional stress. Although certainly some situations will require immediate interventions from the teacher or support personnel, it appears that acknowledging the emotion and redirecting the student may be the most effective approach.

Testing the Emotional Temperature

These findings address how to deal with an emotionally charged event that a student has encountered. But in order to manage such emotions, teachers must first discern whether or not each child has experienced such an event. In a busy classroom environment, teachers, and especially those who teach multiple groups of students for short periods each day, may find it challenging to check the "emotional temperature" of each child. Creative teachers, however, find a way to assess how students' emotions might influence their engagement in classroom activities. One such teacher, Marian, who taught in an inner city school with high levels of poverty solved this problem with a simple strategy. Each day her first graders would come into the classroom with various issues that were affecting their performance and as a result impeding her ability to teach the class and maintain order. To address this difficulty, she designed a simple "emotional temperature form" with a row of emotions and corresponding adjectives (e.g., good, bad). Students were asked to circle how they felt that day and to write a word or sentence or draw a picture that expressed his or her emotion. This activity became a daily routine for the children as they entered the room. They would take the form, complete it, and then return it to a basket before beginning their work. The teacher reported two significant results of this activity. First, it served to acknowledge the emotions students were feeling, consistent with research findings described above, which then allowed them to disengage and redirect to an academic task. Second, in reviewing their responses, the teacher had better insights into the world of each child and therefore could make better decisions about the need for any follow-up activity or intervention services.

Connectedness in School With a Caring Adult

Taking the emotional temperature of a group of students allows a teacher to know which children may need more support from adults within the school and community. Research demonstrates the importance of a connection to a caring adult for learning and social development. In an extensive analysis of literature related to children's temperament and their relationships with adults, Shonkoff and Phillips (2000) stress the importance of secure emotional relationships with caring adults in emotional regulation and development (p. 237). For example, Nachimas, Gunnar, Mangelsdorf, Parritz, and Buss (1996) exposed toddlers to a live clown who entered a room and invited the toddlers to play. The children who had been shown to have secure relationships with a caregiver had no rise in stress hormones, even if they demonstrated that they were fearful of the clown. In contrast, the children with insecure relationships with adults showed a significant rise in stress hormones. Evidence also exists that adult nurturing actually alters brain physiology and structure. In animal studies, frequent licking and grooming of a pup by its mother altered hippocampal plasticity and resulted in increased learning and memory, even in high-stress environments (Champagne et al., 2008). In analogous human studies, infants who received parental nurturance in the form of massage therapy showed reduced cortisol levels (Field et al., 2004). In addition, the body massages stimulated food-absorption hormones that helped the infants gain weight.

> ◎ Taking the emotional temperature of a group of students allows a teacher to know which children may need more support from adults within the school and community. Adult nurturing actually alters brain physiology and structure.

The importance of connecting with a caring adult extends far beyond early childhood. The National Longitudinal Study of Adolescent Health surveyed over 12,000 students in Grades 7–12 and found that those who reported a feeling of connectedness through the presence of a caring adult in school were less likely to be involved in every risk behavior studied, including drug use, cigarette smoking, early sex, violence, and suicidal thoughts (Resnick et al., 1997). With regard to connectedness and education, students who report having personal connections with adults in school have stronger academic performance (Wilson, 2004), attendance (Croninger & Lee, 2001), and school completion rates (Connell, Halpern-Felsher, Clifford, Crichlow, & Usinger, 1995; Finn & Rock, 1997). They also are less likely to engage in disruptive behavior and violence in school (Goodenow, 1993; Lonczak, Abbott, Hawkins, Kosterman, & Catalano, 2002). Finally, positive student-teacher interactions correlate with students' reports of liking school (Valeski & Stipek, 2001) and predict social and academic outcomes (Hamre & Pianta, 2001).

> ◎ Students who reported a feeling of connectedness through the presence of a caring adult in school were less likely to be involved in every risk behavior studied.

Fostering a nurturing environment where all students feel connected to a caring adult must be a priority in every classroom in every school. Teachers promote the connectedness of children in school by

- Providing consistent classroom expectations and fair, nonaggressive strategies to manage disciplinary processes;

- Designing instructional activities that are rigorous, engaging, differentiated, and meaningful;

- Involving all students in the care of the classroom;

- Creating opportunities for peer-tutoring and cooperative group work;

- Communicating positive messages to children and parents through notes, awards, and phone calls or e-mails home;

- Creating individualized learning goals for each student;

- Assuring that each child has an opportunity to be called on during class and/or participate through a unique contribution such as designing a bulletin board or decorating work space;

- Role-playing ways to resolve conflicts, especially through content-based activities such as literature or social studies lessons;

- Establishing opportunities for cross-age interactions such as content-based tutoring, theater and other arts programs, and library or study skills sessions; and

- Modeling warmth and kindness in the classroom.

> ◎ Fostering a nurturing environment where all students feel connected to a caring adult must be a priority in every classroom in every school.

From the Expert Teacher

Calamity Jane and Positive Emotions

I always prided myself on being sensitive to my students' feelings, but I never consciously associated emotions with pedagogy in any meaningful way—that is, until I learned about Brain-Targeted Teaching. Jane (not her real name) was a calamity. It seemed her sole purpose in coming to school was to engage her teachers in battle. She would defy from the principal right down to the school resource offices. School rules meant nothing to her. Jane would be in class with her iPod on. During class, she would leave without permission and chat on her cell phone in the hallway. An unsuspecting teacher just had to ask, "Aren't you supposed to be in class young lady?" and immediately a barrage of expletives would spew forth. Routine disciplinary measures were largely ineffective since her behavior was invariably determined to be a manifestation of her disability. Armed with my new knowledge of "setting a positive emotional climate," I decided to engage my students in a little experiment. We would be unconditionally nice to Jane for 1 week. Regardless of how infuriating she was, regardless of what she said or did, regardless of how much she put her emotions into motion and created a

(Continued)

commotion, we would be nice to her. The first person to respond with hostility to Jane would have lost the bet. Of course, the class was hooked and the bet was on.

At first, Jane hardly seemed to notice that students and I were ignoring her outbursts and confrontational behaviors and continued her maverick ways. Then, on the second day, she became cynical. "What is with you all not getting mad at me?" she demanded. By this time, her escapades from class had decreased from an average of 4 to 0. Use of expletives and other disruptive behaviors as charted on her behavior point sheet had fallen by as much as 60% in my class. Of significance, there were no notable changes in her behavior point sheet for her other three classes. By day three, I had called home to comment on the dramatic turn-around in Jane's behavior. Jane had actually begun to participate in some class activities and even removed her headphones after being asked without her usual tantrum. On the fourth day, Jane was engaged in class to such an extent that she no longer ostensibly stood out as a disruptive student. On the fifth day, the experiment was finally revealed to Jane. She seemed flattered that she was the object of so much positive attention. There can be no denying the power of setting a positive emotional climate. Students' attitudes can definitely transform from hostility and cynicism to enthusiasm and intrinsic motivation; consequently, their academic performance increase when there is a purposeful attempt to establish a positive emotional climate within the classroom. This little experiment instilled in me a profound respect for the tenets of Brain-Targeted teaching.

Dev Sharma
Teacher, High School Special Education

Control and Choice

Offering students choices relating to the content and process of learning has been shown to provide a sense of agency or control over outcomes and is associated with increased levels of motivation and achievement (Wentzel & Wigfield, 1998). Given appropriate guidance and structure, teachers can motivate performance by allowing choices in content, methods, and assessment. Below are some examples in each area:

Choices in Content:

- Students have access to activity centers that reinforce skills through multiple content choices.

- Students are given a choice from a selection of reading material or genres of literature that address curriculum objectives.

> ◎ Teachers can motivate performance by allowing choices in content, methods, and assessment.

- In subjects where content is flexible, groups of students choose a topic, research elements, and present findings to the class.

Choices in Methods:

- Given a specific assignment (e.g., responding to a story or reading a historical document) students choose one of several ways to demonstrate understanding such as a summary where they highlight key points of the assignment, an analysis where they compare and contrast details with other similar genres, or an application where they create a plan of action based on the content.

- Given one response strategy (e.g., summary), students pair it with an additional response mode, such as a project using an art form such as music, visual arts, role playing, poetry, or rap.

Choices in Assessment:

- Demonstrating understanding of learning objectives through traditional methods may be required in many school districts through standardized assessments and regular benchmark curriculum-based assessments. However, teachers can supplement these assessments by allowing students to choose an art form or technology to demonstrate understanding of content, skills, or concepts.

- Assessment activities that require students to move beyond the mere acquisition of knowledge and apply content in authentic ways will allow for deeper thinking and provide choices for students to identify a problem, analyze strategies, and design action plans.

Social and Emotional Learning

The proliferation of formal social and emotional learning programs in schools demonstrates the growing acceptance that schools can no longer focus solely on students' academic performance without also addressing their emotional and social needs (Zins, Weissberg, Wang, & Walberg, 2004). As highlighted in this chapter, neuro- and cognitive sciences have shown us that cognition and emotions are not separate systems but are intricately connected in terms of brain structure and function.

> ◎ Schools can no longer focus solely on students' academic performance without also addressing their emotional and social needs.

Research suggests that a child's ability to recognize and interpret emotional cues has long-term effects on social behavior and academic competence (Izard et al., 2001). In recent years, social and emotional learning programs (SEL) have been designed to help children recognize and manage emotions within the context of the learning and social environment. Recent research findings show that SEL programs improve students' academic performance and general school performance. In a meta-analysis involving more than 200 studies of social-emotional learning programs in schools, Payton and colleagues (2008) found that students scored more than 10 points higher in academic achievement and also had better school attendance, grades, and social interactions within the classroom. SEL programs include fostering awareness of emotions, regulation of emotions through stress management, developing understanding and empathy toward others, building relationships, and responsible decision-making.

Reflection and Mindfulness Training

Similar to social and emotional learning programs, the growing practice of mindfulness training to help students manage stress and improve attention is gaining popularity in schools and classrooms (Brown, 2007). Mindfulness interventions provide explicit instruction in secular meditative-type relaxation exercises and quiet sitting while observing one's thoughts and feelings. Research findings with school-aged children point to improvement in subjects' attention regulation as well as reduction of anxiety and depression after receiving mindfulness training (e.g., Biegel, Brown, Shapiro, & Schubert, 2009; Zylowska et al., 2007). In a pilot randomized controlled trial of school-based mindfulness and yoga training for urban youth, Mendelson and colleagues (2010) suggest that such training reduces negative physiological and cognitive reactions to stress and improves self-regulation. Specifically, they found that children who received the mindfulness training reported significant reductions in rumination (negative, brooding, or obsessive thoughts), intrusive thoughts that divert attention, and negative emotional arousal. A recent study of mindfulness training has also shown changes in brain structure. Hölzel and colleagues (2011) conducted a longitudinal study of a program designed to teach mindfulness strategies to students. They found that participation in the practice of mindfulness is associated with increases in the density of brain regions involved with cognitive processes important to learning such as memory and emotion regulation. Given the growing evidence of the efficacy of mindfulness and yoga training, teachers might consider adding moments during the school day to allow students to have the opportunity for calm attention, awareness, and quiet reflection such as paying attention to breathing, or thinking good thoughts about positive experiences or loved ones and friends. This approach to social development and emotional regulation appears to be consistent with recommendations to focus on positive interventions rather than those aimed at specific negative behavioral symptoms (Guerra & Bradshaw, 2008).

◎ Participation in the practice of mindfulness is associated with increases in the density of brain regions involved with cognitive processes important to learning such as memory and emotion regulation.

Humor

We all enjoy a good laugh. But what does that have to do with learning? Research has shown that students score significantly higher on a test when the class was presented with humor compared with when the teaching did not include humorous comments (Schmidt, 1994; Ziv, 1988). In addition, Masten (1986) found that children who were better able to describe humorous cartoons had higher levels of academic and social competence. Strick, Holland, van Baaren, and van Knippenberg, (2009) also found positive effects of humor. When participants were given negative or neutral input followed by humorous material, humor was shown to significantly reduce participants' negative emotions.

◎ Humor was shown to significantly reduce participants' negative emotions.

For teachers who worry that they cannot tell jokes or do not have a natural humorous disposition, there are alternative ways to insert humor in the classroom. Numerous books on humor in the classroom (e.g., Droz & Ellis, 1996; Morrison, 2008) provide guidance in how it can be embedded into lessons across content areas. Teachers must be cautious, however, to avoid sarcasm or teasing that may seem good-natured but can be hurtful and elicit peer teasing or bullying.

Engagement in the Arts

A growing body of research is pointing to the positive effects of the arts in students' school experiences. Troubled youth, for example, demonstrated more positive prosocial behaviors after receiving instruction in the visual and performing arts (Psilos, 2002). And simply listening to music for just over 20 minutes significantly reduced subjects' levels of the stress hormone, cortisol, in blood levels (Field et al., 1998). The visual and performing arts engage students in the fabric of the school, but they also appear to provide students with skills that support academic areas such as persistence to task, visual thinking, collaboration, and improvisation (Deasy, 2002). In addition,

◎ Embedding arts activities into instruction in content areas provides a natural vehicle for enhancing long-term retention of content and deeper learning.

in our study of Brain-Target Four, we explore how embedding arts activities into instruction in content areas provides a natural vehicle for enhancing long-term retention of content and deeper learning.

From the Expert Teacher

Visual Symbols and Emotional Connection

Since I began teaching, I've tried to present curriculum through meaningful and effective methods that shape my instruction to reach all students. Brain-Targeted Teaching, with its emphasis on arts integration, continues to influence my units and lessons to improve learning outcomes and engage all students. Recently, I taught a unit with my eighth-grade Language Arts class on The Giver, *by Lois Lowry, in which symbolism is present throughout. I expanded this notion of symbolism to give students an emotional connection with the content through arts-integrated activities.*

For example, at the beginning of our study of this novel, each student was asked to create a visual symbol to represent his or her personality. The symbols were displayed in the hallway (without naming the students they represented) and anonymous feedback was solicited from members of the school community. Administrators, teachers, fellow students, and guests were encouraged to react to one of the student's symbols by completing an evaluation slip identifying at least two characteristics of the person that they interpreted from the symbol and explaining their interpretation of its meaning.

During the time projects were displayed, my students looked forward to receiving this anonymous feedback. Engaging the school community in the students' work was successful. The attention motivated students to have a fuller connection to our study of symbolism, and deeper engagement with the characters and conflict represented in the novel. The activity resulted in the students' greater emotional connection to the content, and most of all, created an emotional connection among members of the class as students shared feedback from outside observers and evaluated their use of visual symbols to portray their personalities and interests.

Scott Williamson
Teacher, Middle School Language Arts and Latin

Emotional Connection to Learning Goals and Objectives

In our study of the elements of Brain-Target One, we have focused on fostering a positive emotional climate in the classroom. The second element of Brain-Target One is designing activities that purposefully connect students emotionally with the content, skills, and concepts taught within the learning unit.

Embedding activities into lessons that connect students on an emotional level to the content can take on many forms. Our descriptions of activities from our expert teachers in this chapter are just a few examples of ways teachers can purposefully target positive emotional connections in the classroom and within content. In the following section, we begin looking at two field-tested Brain-Targeted Teaching learning units described in our overview of the model in the previous chapter. Clare and Suzanne begin by sharing examples of how they establish a positive learning environment and make explicit emotional connections to the content through Brain-Target One activities.

> ◎ Embedding activities into lessons that connect students on an emotional level to the content can take on many forms.

WHAT DOES A BRAIN-TARGETED TEACHING UNIT LOOK LIKE IN THE CLASSROOM?

Learning Unit: Surviving Alone in the Wilderness: A study of the novel *Hatchet* by Gary Paulsen

Grade/Content: Fifth-Grade/Language Arts

Author: Clare O'Malley Grizzard

Overarching Goal of Unit: Students will increase language arts skills of reading for understanding through analysis of character, plot, main idea, and symbolic language.

Brain-Target One: Establishing the Emotional Climate for Learning

Reinforcing the positive emotional environment was a residual process throughout the teaching of this unit. Exploring *Hatchet*, an enticing action-packed adventure that also offers quiet, reflective moments, was rich in opportunities to do so. All activities and assessments throughout the learning unit were designed through the lens of the emotional climate.

> ◎ All activities and assessments throughout the learning unit were designed through the lens of the emotional climate.

To encourage a deeper connection through perspective taking, we retitled the unit "Surviving in the Wilderness"—in order to make the students *a part of the story* rather than just a passive audience. This journey was going to be *theirs* as well as Brian's (the main character in the book).

Visualization and guided-imagery exercises furthered the connection with the novel. Tapping into children's natural ability to visualize vivid images and detailed action, the students followed the narrative of Brian's story more closely with their feelings leading the way. They began to recognize themselves in the book and identify with the action.

> ◎ Tapping into children's natural ability to visualize vivid images and detailed action, the students followed the narrative of Brian's story more closely with their feelings leading the way.

Our activities led students asked, "What does the character think, believe, want, or feel? And how would I show it if it were me?" They made self-portraits of what they would look like if they found themselves in Brian's situation (stranded alone in the wilderness). This exercise required that they put themselves into the story rather than simply illustrate a scene from the book as an outside observer.

We used several drama exercises throughout the unit to study character, setting, and even vocabulary. We used tableau to describe a "frozen moment" in the story. To build empathy we found role-playing allowed students to look at issues from another perspective—Brian's—and to build a deeper emotional bond with his fate.

In creating a nurturing emotional environment, Linda Bluth, my coteacher, and I constructed ongoing positive supports throughout the year, not just during this particular novel study. These activities ranged from greeting each student by name at the door to noncompetitive discussion and class critique using positive, supportive language.

Mrs. Bluth was a practitioner of yoga, and she used it daily to help students disengage from the outside into a new state of mind in the classroom and as a means to teach children to relax, encourage their creative imagination, and invoke their imagery skills. It also changed the rhythm of a typical school day routine, which often is rife with distraction. Criteria for excellence were clearly displayed and discussed to reduce anxiety. For artwork especially, we used exemplars to make expectations clear and to inspire so that all students could succeed.

This journey was going to be *theirs* as well as Brian's.

Students make a personal connection with the main character by visualizing themselves stranded alone in the wilderness.

Learning Unit: Genetics and Heredity—Thinking Outside the Punnett Square

Grade/Content: Tenth-Grade/Biology

Author: Suzanne P. McNamara

Overarching Goal of Unit: Students will apply their understanding of genetics and heredity in discussions centered on current medical and social issues as well as an appreciation for human diversity.

Brain-Target One: Establishing the Emotional Climate for Learning

Biological Family Histories

Although often ignored, emotions play a vital role in the learning process. A "great lesson plan" can be completely useless if children do not feel comfortable in their classroom. For many of my students, safety is a central part of a positive emotional classroom environment. Every day, I see that before a child can learn, she needs to be confident that my classroom culture is welcoming, engaging, and supportive. All students should feel a sense of belonging in their classroom. Most teachers would agree that it is impossible to separate a child's emotions from the learning process. A positive emotional climate sets the tone for high levels of learning and performance.

> ◎ A "great lesson plan" can be completely useless if children do not feel comfortable in their classroom. All students should feel a sense of belonging in their classroom.

For a variety of reasons, I have seen many students becoming disenfranchised, feeling as if they are not connected to their school and perpetuating a cycle of failure. For some, life outside the classroom is so filled with hardship, stress, and, often, despair, that it can be challenging to find purpose in their schooling. For others, school is not an exciting place that engages students, but rather a worn-out institution that fosters low expectations. Reconnecting these students to a meaningful and supportive school experience may require drastic measures to break this cycle of failure.

When creating a positive emotional classroom environment, I see how important it is to provide opportunities for *all* students to feel comfortable and confident. At the beginning of this unit, students were encouraged to bring in pictures of biological family members. (Students had the option to bring in pictures of their own biological family members, or nonbiological family members with whom they live.)At the beginning of each class period, a picture was projected. Students had to figure out the biological family member of the person in the picture. In order to offer a guess, a student had to identify three genetic similarities between the person in the picture and the suggested family member. When the class determined who supplied the picture, that student had an opportunity to share more information about her family with the rest of the class.

In high school, students are not often asked to share information about their families with their classmates. This ongoing activity provided an opportunity for all students to feel confident that they have background knowledge about genetics. It encouraged students to talk about and share information about genetics with family members and friends outside the classroom. Throughout the unit, students continued to bring in pictures and share them with their peers during the school day, which helped to strengthen positive friendships at school. It also helped to set the tone for mature conversations in a high school biology classroom. When learning about various genetic disorders later in the unit, for example, students were reminded of the personal information that classmates volunteered about their families.

Students developed a sense of tolerance and appreciation for diversity throughout the genetics unit. The family picture activity helped to establish a culture of respect and encouraged students to be confident in sharing their thoughts and ideas.

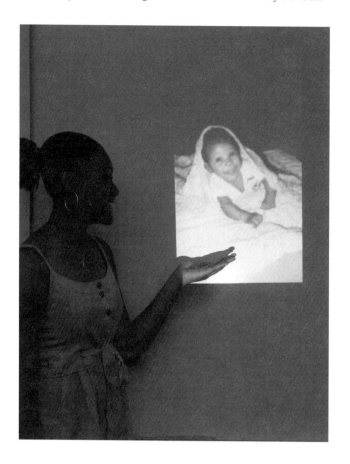

Brain-Target Two

Creating the Physical Learning Environment

The child, left at liberty to exercise his activities, ought to find in his surroundings something organized in direct relation to his internal organization which is developing itself by natural laws.

—Maria Montessori

Shira could not believe her eyes when her mother's car pulled into the loading zone in front of her new school. Recently relocated from another city, Shira dreaded the move. But as she looked at the school in which she would now enroll, her attitude quickly changed. The front of the school was filled with beautiful gardens, a fanciful sculpted fence, a playground full of inviting equipment, and, flanking the front door, barrels of brightly colored potted flowers. Walking into the school's lobby, she saw a kaleidoscope of colors from murals, artwork, sculptures, and award certificates as well as posters advertising a school play and signs welcoming visitors. She heard soft music coming from a kindergarten classroom and singing coming from the auditorium. The physical environment of the school delivered an unspoken but strong message to Shira; she couldn't wait for this school to become her own.

The physical environment of a school is indeed an unspoken but powerful messenger. From the curb to classroom, halls to lavatories, offices to cafeteria, the physical environment not only influences how children feel about the school but also affects their learning (Lyons, 2001). In the last chapter, our study of Brain-Target One led us to review how the emotional climate shapes social behaviors, cognition, and learning. Building from those concepts, this chapter focuses on how various elements in the physical learning environment influence students' attention and engagement in task-oriented activities.

> ◎ The physical environment of a school is indeed an unspoken but powerful messenger.

Our study of Brain-Target Two, Creating the Physical Learning Environment, begins with a look at attention, the portal to learning, and how the classroom environment can be engineered to help engage and sustain students' attention and interest in learning. We will look at novelty as a tool to engage attention. We will also examine how the classroom environment can enhance learning and engage students through the physical features of lighting, sound, and scent, as well as through movement, order, and beauty.

ATTENTION AND NOVELTY

Attention is cognitive selection to a sensation, thought, or event. From a myriad of sensory stimuli, attention systems selectively choose which stimuli are filtered out and which become part of the conscious response system (Posner & Patoine, 2009). As discussed in Chapter 1, Posner and Rothbart (2007) identify three neural networks or systems of interconnected brain regions underlying aspects of attention. The *alerting network* engages children in the task at hand and is important for capturing their attention to learning; the *orienting network* keeps attention attuned to external events rather than internal thoughts; and the *executive attention network* inhibits extraneous thoughts, shifts the attention system to focus on stimuli, and regulates emotions.

> ◎ Attention is cognitive selection to a sensation, thought, or event.

Selective attention to conscious thought is an important filtering mechanism as the brain discards information that it perceives as neither relevant nor useful. It is unlikely that you are aware, for example, of your clothes touching your skin, the hum of electrical lights and appliances, or the chair you are sitting on until it is called to your attention. The brain's attention system ignores these physical and sensory bits of information in order to tune into what it perceives as more meaningful and enticing.

> ◎ The brain's attention system ignores these physical and sensory bits of information in order to tune into what it perceives as more meaningful and enticing.

One feature that the attending system is not likely to ignore is novel objects or events. Novelty in the environment triggers the alerting and orienting systems (Posner & Rothbart, 2007). Teachers see this attending system at work every day when they note how even small changes in the classroom environment generate students' comments or questions. But how long is that stimulus novel? Regrettably, although novelty grabs attention, it does not help to sustain it, as maintaining attention involves more complex executive function processing (Posner, Rothbart, & DiGirolamo, 1999). The new poster a teacher puts on the wall, for example, may interest students at first, but if it remains there for a lengthy period of time, it becomes like wallpaper, blending into the background environment and even cluttering the space rather than enhancing it. Unchanging visual environments create *habituation*, a term used to describe how the same stimulus presented for a long period of time produces a reduction of interest or even boredom (Ariga & Lleras, 2011).

> ◎ Novelty in the environment triggers the alerting and orienting systems. Unchanging visual environments create *habituation*.

Some studies, however, demonstrate a positive influence of novelty not only on attending to information but also on retention of information. Smith, Glenberg, and Bjork (1978), for example, found that alternating the room where a person studies improves retention. They conducted a study in which one group of students studied vocabulary words in one room and a second group studied the words in two different rooms. Those who studied in two rooms performed better on measures of memory for the words than those who studied in the same environment. This study and others demonstrate that when the outside surroundings are varied, information is enriched and retention of content is improved. What is more, Sidney Zentall (1983; see also Zentall & Zentall, 1983) argues that children exposed to bland, unchanging environments become stimulus adapted and appear to seek out their own novel stimulation, often leading to nonoptimal behavior. In studies comparing unchanging environments with ones that provided novelty, children were generally off-task and out of seats more often in bland environments. In particular, children with attention deficit hyperactivity disorder (ADHD) were less efficient learners in classrooms where

> ◎ When the outside surroundings are varied, information is enriched and retention of content is improved.

environments and teaching techniques were monotonous and predictable. They tended to seek out their own stimulation through off-task behaviors.

Regular changes in the learning environment seem to be an effective tool for capturing attention and providing visual stimulation. This can be accomplished in a multitude of ways, such as changing seating arrangements, rotating visual displays, and adding objects that connect to themes of content instruction. With all of the tasks on a teacher's daily list of chores, we understand that purposeful changes to the physical environment may well drop to the bottom of the list. However, if we consider the importance of novelty to capturing students' attention, it is worth taking the time to make even simple changes that help engage students.

> ◎ If we consider the importance of novelty to capturing students' attention, it is worth taking the time to make even simple changes that help engage students.

It must be noted, however, that while novelty is a powerful and important instructional tool, teachers should find a balance between the need for a climate that demonstrates predictable routines and providing novel experiences and environmental changes. Teachers should make these instructional decisions based on what is appropriate for their students.

Here one of our expert teachers describes how she believes that changes in seating arrangements make learning more interesting and engaging for her students:

From the Expert Teacher

Novelty in the Classroom

When I first started using the Brain-Targeted Teaching (BTT) Model, I was intrigued by the idea that novelty in the environment was important, that I could possibly increase students' attention to learning activities by changing seating or displays. As I wrote my first BTT unit, I thought about the various ways I would change seating for my sixth-grade students based on the activity I had planned for the day. During one 2-week unit, the seating changed from traditional rows, to a large circle, to clusters, to theater-style. I brought in a different object related to our unit every few days. There was no question that changing the classroom piqued my students' interest. As soon as they entered the room, they would make the connection between how the room was arranged and the work they would be doing that day. One day as students were lining up to enter the room, I heard several students

(Continued)

> debating how the room would look when they entered. I observed students becoming more interested in what I was teaching because of these changes. Now, for every unit that I teach, I become even more creative about changes to the environment to grab students' attention and make them more interested in the lesson.
>
> Alexandra Fleming
> Teacher, Middle School Social Studies

THE EFFECTS OF ENVIRONMENTAL FEATURES ON ATTENTION AND LEARNING

Lighting in the Classroom

Lighting the fire of learning can sometimes be as simple as lighting a classroom with natural daylight and providing outside views. Visiting schools, one is likely to see some classrooms with no windows, clouded plastic-like windows that provide only filtered light, and no views of the outside, or window shades pulled down to eliminate all natural light and outside views. Perhaps teachers believe that lowered light levels calm students or make them more attentive. Perhaps the thinking is that outside views distract children. Alas, it is not uncommon to see students sitting in dark rooms with drooping eyes and heads on desks. Such poorly lit rooms influence pineal gland activity of synthesizing melatonin, which plays a role in arousal and the production of serotonin, the neurotransmitter that regulates moods (Ott, 1973). Alexander and colleagues (1977) posit that low levels of light in classrooms may also affect students' ability to regulate circadian rhythms, the body's natural cycle of sleep and arousal.

> ◎ Lighting the fire of learning can sometimes be as simple as lighting a classroom with natural daylight and providing outside views. Low levels of light in classrooms may also affect students' ability to regulate circadian rhythms, the body's natural cycle of sleep and arousal.

Windows in a classroom are important for more than merely providing natural light. Tanner (2008) argues that students whose classrooms allow for outside views through window gazing are better able to redirect attention to academic tasks than if their attention strays to other activities such as doodling in a notebook. He characterizes window gazing as requiring "soft attention," which is cognitively less consuming than other types of distraction that may capture students' more focused attention (p. 455).

Research now has "shed light" on the importance of lighting in learning in a classroom environment. In a study of more than 21,000 students across three states, Heschong (1999) studied the effect of natural light on student achievement. Results showed that students who studied in classrooms with the most day lighting demonstrated 20% better scores on mathematics assessment and 26% on reading assessments. Similarly, Hathaway (1995) examined students' performance under varied conditions of artificial light. He found that children who were in classrooms with lighting that most mimics natural sunlight—full spectrum fluorescent lights with ultraviolet supplements—had significantly better health, school attendance, and achievement than subjects whose classrooms had cool white fluorescent or sodium vapor lamps.

◎ Students who studied in classrooms with the most day lighting demonstrated 20% better scores on mathematics assessment and 26% on reading assessments.

As a growing number of studies show the positive effects of optimal lighting on learning (Edwards & Torcellini, 2002), those making decisions regarding school construction and classroom practices should take note. As one expert teacher recounts below, teachers may not always have optimal conditions in their classrooms for lighting, and they may need to engage in some creative problem-solving to make the classroom lighting more comfortable and effective.

From the Expert Teacher

Let the Light Shine

The lighting in my classroom was "upgraded" as part of the school district's measures for efficiency and cost savings. The fluorescent lights, previously embedded in the ceiling tiles, were now hung several feet from the ceiling in long rows. The minute I saw the room, I was startled at the difference in ambiance and light levels. The top walls of the classroom were now barely lit. The new lights created glare for the children sitting directly under them and shadows for those between the rows of florescent lights. The room appeared dimmer now and I could feel the loss of light affecting my own mood and I believe the moods of the children too. I decided to counteract this effect by bringing as much light into the classroom as I could. Shades were pulled all the way to the top to allow for more natural light and I added three standing lamps in various sections of the room. Manipulating the levels of light in the room is critical; I see every day how lighting affects my students' attention and their moods.

Amanda Kowalik
Teacher, Elementary School

Sound in the Learning Environment

Imagine driving on a highway going on a long trip. You are relaxed and listening to your favorite song on the radio. You suddenly find yourself in the wrong lane and are forced to exit onto another highway. Cars are speeding by you on both sides, and your brain is now on high alert trying to figure out how you are going to get back on the right course. What is the first thing you do?

If you said, turn down or turn off the radio, you would join the majority response. But wait, this is the auditory system, what does that have to do with your visual tracking? Obviously, the answer is "a lot"! Background sounds, even relaxing music, can become a distraction when higher mental processes are needed (Howard, 2000).

Most teachers would agree that they have greater control of the visual environment in the classroom than they do the acoustical. Classrooms are often bombarded with white noise such as the buzzing of electrical lights and hums from heating and cooling systems, audiovisual equipment, and computers. Noise may also come from hallways, other classrooms, and outdoor sounds from traffic, sirens, and playgrounds. Finally, at times the school's public address system could be a distraction to learning, especially if it is used inappropriately or too frequently during instructional time. Unlike the driver on the highway who might turn off the radio, these distractions are not as easily extinguished.

> ◎ Most teachers would agree that they have greater control of the visual environment in the classroom than they do the acoustical.

And in reality, most schools have higher levels of background noise than they should. This is unfortunate as young children are especially vulnerable to distractions created by noise (Nelson & Soli, 2000). Smyth (1979) studied the effects of noise on children's ability to retrieve information by comparing their performance in noisy classrooms with that in quiet classrooms. He found that children in noisy classrooms had significantly poorer performance than those in quiet classrooms, with the greatest disparity occurring with younger children. Similarly, Hygge (2003) found that adolescents had significant impairment on information recall and recognition tasks after exposure to levels of noise simulating typical environmental sounds.

Background sounds, however, are not always harmful. Music has been shown to have relaxing effects on adults in experimental studies (e.g., Giles, 1990). Consistent with this research, sounds in the environment can be soothing for students and even mask ambient noise in the classroom. When children are at work in routine tasks, sounds can add a texture of peace and relaxation to the classroom environment. Some ideas for sound elements include the following:

- Playing background music that will relax students; classical music is often used in this way, but other musical genres can serve the same purpose;

- Hanging wind chimes in a window or just above air vents so that they tinkle when air systems come on;

- Playing recordings of sounds of nature such as waves, waterfalls, bird chirps, seagulls, or dolphins;

- Adding waterfall fountains that provide the sound and view of falling water;

- Adding materials that produce gentle sounds such as rain sticks or small bells to sensitize children to different sounds.

> ◎ Music has been shown to have relaxing effects on adults in experimental studies.

Finally, although we all love the delightful sounds that emanate from classrooms where children are engaged in active learning tasks, teachers at times may want to consider reserving some moments during the school day for quiet reflection. A good example of this practice is in a Montessori classroom. Maria Montessori promoted the regular practice of silence because she believed that it helped children regulate attention, develop inhibitory control, and become more sensitized to sounds in the environment (Lillard, 2005, p. 316).

> ◎ Teachers at times may want to consider reserving some moments during the school day for quiet reflection.

Sounds in classrooms can and should vary widely from the purposeful chatter that comes from cooperative learning or project-based learning tasks to the quiet necessary while students are engaging in learning a new skill that requires concentration, and from relaxing background sounds during routine tasks to periods of quiet that promote purposeful control and reflective practices.

From the Expert Teacher

Montessori and the Silence Game

Montessori classrooms are a buzz of activity. Children are engaged in meaningful learning—some learning by themselves and others in groups. Some children are receiving direct instruction from the adults and others are learning by watching their older peers. With all this activity, one can imagine all the synapses in the brain being formed!

Maria Montessori recognized the benefits of engaging children in activities of their own choosing. She also appreciated the need for creating pauses in the child's

(Continued)

day for consolidation. One of the ways she helped children learn the importance of quiet time was through the exercise called "The Silence Game." The Silence Game gives children deliberate practice in controlling their impulses and their movement. It can be practiced as a group activity or individually by choosing materials from the shelf that guide the child to silence. In either form of the game, children are learning self-control.

While observing a Montessori classroom in Beijing, I saw a child sit in the middle of a busy classroom on a mat, his eyes cast downward on the hourglass placed in front of him, practicing silence. Montessori understood that whether the game is performed as a group exercise (children collectively have to choose to be silent or the game stops) or is chosen individually, developing self-control and willpower through silence was worth the time spent practicing these skills.

Michelle Hartye,
Montessori Teacher, Administrator, and Teacher Educator

Scent in the Classroom

Of all sensory perceptions, scent has a unique role in human development. As explained in Chapter 2, the thalamus sorts sensory information then relays the signal to brain structures for processing. The exception is olfactory input, which bypasses the thalamus and takes a direct path to the brain's limbic system for processing by structures associated with emotion and memory (Gazzaniga, Ivry, & Mangun, 2009, p. 171). This may explain why certain scents produce vivid memories such as the smell of grandmother's apple pie or the scent of a cologne connected with a person from the past.

> ◎ Of all sensory perceptions, scent has a unique role in human development.

Research on the effects of scents on human behavior suggest that scents play a role in emotion and memory (Herz, Eliassen, Beland, & Souza, 2004; Herz, Schankler, & Beland, 2004). For instance, findings showed that certain scents such as orange and lavender reduced anxiety (Lehrner, Marwinski, Lehr, Johren, & Deecke, 2005). Similarly, subjects showed improvement in performing an attention-related task in an environment with scents such as lily of the valley and peppermint compared with a nonscented environment (Barker et al., 2003; Warm, Dember, & Parasuraman, 1991).

> ◎ Subjects showed improvement in performing an attention-related task in an environment with scents such as lily of the valley and peppermint compared with a nonscented environment.

Studies of the effects of scents in classroom environments demonstrate similar results. Gabriel (1999) reported a 54% reduction in off-task behaviors after adding scented oil to the classroom. Epple and Herz (1999) found that odors can condition emotional experiences influencing subsequent performance. They introduced a particular smell to students while they were performing a frustrating task, thus associating that scent with frustration. When performing a different task, they introduced the same scent. Students performed significantly worse on the second task when the scent was introduced compared to that same task under the conditions of no scent or a different one.

These studies suggest that scents influence emotion and performance and may provide an additional environmental asset to enhance students' attention and memory. When scenting classrooms, however, caution should be taken not to introduce artificial chemicals that might trigger allergies. Natural products such as oils may be safer for use with children.

> ◎ Studies suggest that scents influence emotion and performance and may provide an additional environmental asset to enhance students' attention and memory.

Let's hear how one of our expert teachers uses scent to gain students' interest, attention, and performance. We will hear from eighth grader, Angela, as she describes her language arts teacher's classroom.

From the Expert Student

Vanilla Makes Me Happy

My favorite class that I go to each day is definitely language arts. I like the subject and the teacher, but I also just like the feeling of being in the room. This may sound funny, but that room is not like any ordinary classroom. The walls are painted a copper color, burgundy curtains drape the windows, and the room smells like vanilla. It makes me feel good to be there, sort of like home when my mom makes vanilla pudding. I like doing my work in the room because I feel relaxed and happy. Everyone in the class feels the same way and no one really goofs off during that class. It is just fun to go there. I wish more teachers would do what Mr. Hallam has with his classroom. It really makes us know that he cares about how we feel as much as what we learn.

Angela
Eighth-grade student in David Hallam's class

The Effects of Movement on Attention

Few would argue with those in the popular media who cite the growing problem of obesity and lack of movement in the lives of children. With advances in modern technology, physical activity has ceased to become a natural part of everyday lives. Yet as John Ratey (2008) points out, exercise is in the roots of our biology and strongly influences cognition; moving muscles produces proteins in the blood that affect learning. Ratey and others (e.g., Hillman, Buck, Themanson, Pontifex, & Castelli, 2009) also note that exercise improves certain mental processes that regulate alertness, attention, and motivation.

◎ Exercise is in the roots of our biology and strongly influences cognition.

Getting students moving in the school environment may be increasingly difficult as schools continue to engage in the unfortunate practice of reducing physical education and recess programs to allow for more instructional time in tested areas. Still, teachers can provide students with opportunities for movement within the classroom and during content instruction. Purposeful movement can be created within the physical features of the classroom through the use of workstations, research space, special nooks, and alcoves for reading or other group or individual activities. In addition, movement during learning can occur through arts integration such as theater, dance, tableau, yoga, and other forms of creative movement. We will discuss arts integration strategies further in our study of Brain-Target Four.

Order and Beauty in the Classroom

The philosophies and practices of schools such as Montessori, with its focus on the prepared environment, and Reggio Emilia, with its arts studio-like educational setting, can provide wonderful models of purposeful use of the physical environment to promote engagement in learning. In both models, order and beauty are key components of a classroom. Maria Montessori, for example, strongly advocated that learning is optimized when children are in environments that are free from clutter and are aesthetically pleasing (Lillard, 2005). Reggio Emilia promotes the environment as a critical component for allowing children to develop and grow, and for facilitating communication, interaction, creativity, and discovery (Cadwell, 2003; 1997).

◎ Learning is optimized when children are in environments that are free from clutter and are aesthetically pleasing.

My experience in schools leads me to believe that not all teachers understand the importance of order and beauty. Although I could site many examples of lovely classroom environments, I've also witnessed classrooms in which vertical spaces were cluttered with posters that never changed, and horizontal spaces piled with stacks of books, papers, projects, and a myriad of other objects. Let's hear from one of our expert teachers about how she organizes the classroom to reflect order and beauty and how that affects her students.

From the Expert Teacher

A Taste of Spain

When Grace walks into the Spanish classroom she picks up a pleasant smell that is a blend of calming essential oils. As she takes a deep breath, she comments that she "loves" this room. Sheer linen fabric is suspended over the fluorescent ceiling lights to diffuse the harsh glare that can compromise a student's concentration.

Dictionaries, classroom supplies, Spanish magazines, and the classroom Spanish library are neatly arranged in the green and blue bookshelves. There is one tall, yellow display bookcase that holds student's projects and a variety of objects/artifacts gathered from Spain. There are two floor-to-ceiling windows that look out into a side garden and a pathway. The window seats are filled with large green and brown sitting pillows that allow students to gather on the floor for Spanish conversation, reading, or partner work.

The side walls each have a bright decal with a Spanish saying and the top left front of the room has a deep maroon decal of an owl on a branch that is the classroom mascot. The front of the room demands student attention and is simply white with green accents. There is a high-frequency word wall on the gray cabinet to the right in addition to a few phonetic and grammatical charts along the top of the white-board. When a student's eye wanders, there is a poster of the Alhambra, the Spanish calendar, and the Spanish word of the day to focus on until they return to the lesson at hand.

Environment matters; nothing in this room is done without intention. There are no piles of papers, dated displays, or dusty stacks of books. I know from research and practice that sensitivity to a student's environment can positively impact the learning experience.

◎ Environment matters; nothing in this room is done without intention.

The unit is Islamic Spain, and there is a clementine on each student's desk today. Students describe the color and smell in Spanish as they are introduced to Andalusia, Spain. They hold their clementines and feel the texture as they view a series of photographs taken in Southern Spain. The narrow streets, the open markets, and most importantly, the Islamic, Christian, and Jewish sections of Seville.

(Continued)

They see clementines growing in many of the photographs. As they begin to eat, the room fills with a clean smell of citrus and they describe the taste in Spanish. How can they ever pick up another clementine without thinking of Andalusia?

This "saturation" of the senses allows students to have multipronged entry points to engage in the learning process. Lessons that go beyond the audio and visual senses can be powerful in grasping student interest and building connections throughout a lesson. Including smell, taste, and touch can increase the learning experience exponentially for the student.

Elizabeth Levy
Teacher, Middle School Spanish

In summary, features of the physical learning environment can attract students' interest in the lesson, give them a sense of comfort and belonging, and ultimately help to influence attention and engagement in learning. As one more tool to facilitate the teaching and learning process, teachers should deliberately plan the physical environment as they establish the goals and objectives for each new learning unit, a component described in more detail in Brain-Target Three in Chapter 6.

> ◎ Teachers should deliberately plan the physical environment as they establish the goals and objectives for each new learning unit.

We now leave our study of Brain-Target Two with descriptions of how Clare and Suzanne addressed the physical learning environment in their units on *Hatchet* and Genetics.

What Does a Brain-Targeted Teaching Unit Look Like in the Classroom?

Learning Unit: Surviving Alone in the Wilderness: A study of the novel *Hatchet* by Gary Paulsen

Grade/Content: Fifth-Grade/Language Arts

Author: Clare O'Malley Grizzard

Overarching Goal of Unit: Students will increase language arts skills of reading for understanding through analysis of character, plot, main idea, and symbolic language.

Brain-Target Two: Creating the Physical Learning Environment

Brian's adventures in the Canadian wilderness and our journey through the novel gave us many opportunities to expand the boundaries of the typical classroom. Because the main setting of this novel is the natural environment, we pursued the question of how Brian used that to survive. Since the unit was taught both in the language arts room and the art studio, we were able to express the theme of the novel in both "environments." We structured the students' encounter with the novel to be multisensory—engaging them through sight, sound, touch, and smell. Below are some of the activities that transformed our classroom during this unit.

> ◎ We structured the students' encounter with the novel to be multisensory—engaging them through sight, sound, touch, and smell.

- We brought the natural environment into the classroom and went outside for short field trips to encounter the school environment in broader terms. On walks around the campus, we focused on a new sensory awareness of our surroundings. We took field notes, drew maps, carried sketchbooks, and did observational drawings of plants and insects, which were displayed and used as points of references for other activities.

- We revamped bulletin boards and room displays to reflect the theme of our journey through the novel and displayed Canadian landscape paintings that became a focal point in dialogue and descriptive writing activities. Students decorated the room with observational drawings of natural specimens, personal visualizations of scenes from the novel and events from the plot, and displayed their self-portraits.

- A guest artist created a mural of a wilderness scene that became the background for many activities, including theater strategy creating a sound poem.

- Students did field study drawings of what they encountered outside the building. They *observed* and *documented* their environment in a new way, which mirrored the main character's development as a more acute observer of his environment.

> ◎ Students did field study drawings of what they encountered outside the building.

- Students collected items from our nature walks to create a naturalist station in the room. Plants (including edible ones) lined the windowsills throughout the year.

Learning Unit: Genetics and Heredity—Thinking Outside the Punnett Square

Grade/Content: 10th-Grade/Biology

Author: Suzanne P. McNamara

Overarching Goal of Unit: Students will apply their understanding of genetics and heredity in discussions centered on current medical and social issues as well as an appreciation for human diversity.

Brain-Target Two: Creating the Physical Learning Environment

Creating a Classroom Art Gallery

I used to think of decorating my classroom in the same way I thought about decorating my home. I would try to fill open walls with pictures, windowsills with plants, shelves with books, and bulletin boards with fly- ers. My classroom looked wonderful at the beginning of the year, but the environment remained static until I took everything down to pack up for the summer. Although it is helpful to keep consistency and order so that children know what to expect, it is also important to create a dynamic environment aligned with the curriculum. I was using the same posters, hung the same pictures, referenced the same signs, and showed the same images. Although my students knew what to expect each day, their environment did not impact their learning experience. I have come to recognize the importance of a visually appealing, novel classroom.

Teachers can take advantage of the brain's natural propensity to seek novelty by providing visually stimulating environments that support learning objectives. Capturing students' attention helps to keep them engaged and interested in what's next. There are not many other professions that allow (and encourage!) employees to occupy and decorate a fairly large space and call it their own. In some cases, however, there are strings attached to this privilege, including mandated word walls and posted standards. Furthermore, some teachers are not given their own room, but are forced to travel. Although these obstacles present challenges, it is important to incorporate as many visually appealing learning aids as possible.

> ◎ Teachers can take advantage of the brain's natural propensity to seek novelty by providing visually stimulating environments that support learning objectives.

Keeping walls clear at the beginning of each new unit, I was able to create an atmosphere that marked a change in focus and invited student participation. Many of the work products from student groups would be hanging on the wall the very next day. Not only could students see their own work and that of their classmates, but they also could see the work from other class periods. Each time there was a change to the walls, students wanted time to walk around the classroom to see all of the work samples, almost as if they were viewing artwork in a gallery. As the unit progressed, student groups reflected on their work and wrote captions so that other students could learn more about each sample. This process helped me hold groups accountable for their work because they knew that other students would be learning from them. The captions helped often answer questions from observing students, similar to captions in a museum.

> ◎ Each time there was a change to the walls, students wanted time to walk around the classroom to see all of the work samples, almost as if they were viewing artwork in a gallery.

When learning about mitosis and meiosis, student groups were required to create models of a particular stage and answer questions about the stage. These models were collected at the end of the period, and by the next day they were up in sequence in the classroom. Students were amazed to see how all the pieces fit together and were easily able to identify similarities and differences among the stages. The next day, students entered the classroom with some of the models removed and had to determine which ones were missing and sketch them.

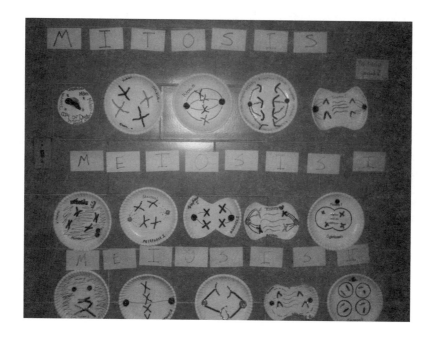

Students gained ownership of their classroom and started bringing in relevant items to include. Newspaper articles, pictures of twins in a student's family, cartoons and sketches of a DNA molecule, and many more items were brought into class to be included among the work on the walls. I began to think of my classroom more like an art gallery and less like a living room. The walls displayed deliberate pieces of student work that reflected the learning objectives of a particular unit. I focused more on quality artifacts and less on filling blank walls with posters. When the students became a part of creating their physical classroom environment, they started to treat it like their own. Cleaning up after themselves and re-hanging fallen student work became part of the classroom culture. The science classroom turned "art gallery" was a dynamic, visually appealing place of learning.

◎ The science classroom turned "art gallery" was a dynamic, visually appealing place of learning.

Brain-Target Three
Designing the Learning Experience

*Here is an essential principle of education: to teach details
is to bring confusion; to establish the relationship between
things is to bring knowledge.*

—Maria Montessori

The previous two chapters highlight research and practice focused
on establishing a classroom setting that enhances a positive emotional climate for learning (Brain-Target One) and creates a physical
learning environment for promoting attention and engagement in
learning (Brain-Target Two). Progressing through the stages of the Brain-
Targeted Teaching (BTT) Model, we now look at designing the learning
unit, the road map for instruction. In this next target, teachers use
content standards and curriculum guides to determine learning goals,
activities, and assessments. These key elements are presented to students

in a form of visual representation (e.g., concept maps or various graphic organizers), in order to display the big picture of how new learning connects with prior knowledge, how activities result in achieving learning goals, and how evaluations are designed to be able to demonstrate students' understanding of concepts, skills, and content.

Imagine trying to put together a large jigsaw puzzle without ever having seen the completed picture usually displayed on the outside of the box. Without a doubt, having an image of the whole picture gives each individual piece of the puzzle more meaning. Likewise, when we guide learning by providing students with broader view or "big picture," we promote an understanding of the connections between prior knowledge and new learning and also demonstrate the relationships among learning goals. This is consistent with the brain's propensity to look for patterns and associations between information at the forefront of thought and information stored in memory (Posner & Rothbart, 2007, p. 205).

In traditionally organized instruction, teachers typically follow a sequential list of skills, chapters from a text, or topics from curriculum outlines. This kind of instruction often moves from one objective to the next without a broader context. Although this instructional approach may promote learning specific pieces of content, students

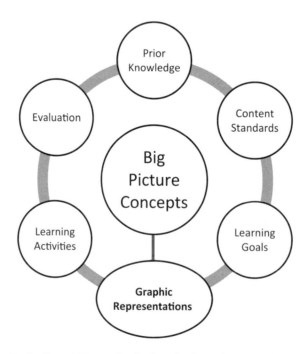

Brain-Target Three: Designing the Learning Experience

are likely to miss the larger concepts or the "big picture" essential for deep understanding and memory. Although some students might make such connections on their own, too many times they are just learning isolated facts with little connection to their prior knowledge or other content.

> ◎ When we guide learning by providing students with broader view or "big picture," we promote an understanding of the connections between prior knowledge and new learning and also demonstrate the relationships among learning goals.

In contrast to typical practice, we have known for some time the efficacy of explicitly teaching global concepts through visual representations such as concept maps (e.g., Ausubel, 1960; Luiten, Ames, & Ackerson, 1980). Studies have demonstrated increases in conceptual understanding, memory, and academic achievement when using concept mapping to demonstrate connections among learning goals and activities (Boon, Burke, Fore & Spencer, 2006; Chiou, 2008; Osmundson, Chung, Herl, & Klein, 1999; McAleese, Grabinger, & Fisher, 1999).

The ability to understand how ideas are connected is only amplified if students already have some prior knowledge to which new information can be related. For example, Chiesi, Spilich, and Voss

> ◎ We have known for some time the efficacy of explicitly teaching global concepts through visual representations such as concept maps.

(1979) demonstrated that students who had more prior knowledge about a content area—in this case baseball—were better able to relate and remember pieces of information. Moreover, having prior knowledge seems to be particularly important for students with reading difficulties. In one study, Recht and Leslie (1988) compared content memory in poor readers and strong readers with or without high prior knowledge in the content area. The results showed that despite their weak reading comprehension ability, poor readers with high prior knowledge remembered more than strong readers without prior knowledge. Taken together, these studies suggest that, in addition to presenting a global picture of the learning, teachers must also ensure that learning units build on what students already know.

> ◎ Studies suggest that, in addition to presenting a global picture of the learning, teachers must also ensure that learning units build on what students already know.

COGNITIVE DEVELOPMENT AND BIG-PICTURE THINKING

Bransford (2000) explains that knowledge is not a list of facts and formulas; rather, knowledge is organized around core concepts or big ideas that shape thinking. This view of learning is consistent with a type of cognitive structure known as *schema* (*schemata* in plural form) or "mental representation of what all instances of something have in common" (Byrnes, 2008, p. 26). According to proponents of schema theory, having global understanding of common elements in different pieces of information helps us to categorize content, remember information more effectively, comprehend concepts more deeply, and solve problems more efficiently. In addition, understanding connections among elements assists with abstract thinking and understanding relationships among disparate chunks of information (Byrnes, 2008).

◎ Understanding connections among elements assists with abstract thinking and understanding relationships among disparate chunks of information.

Byrnes (2008) points out that, unlike some other theories of learning such as Piaget's theory of cognitive development, schema theory does not account for developmental stages of learning. It does not address, for example, how the novel or younger learner may process global understanding differently from older or expert learners. Recent research, however, provides a fuller picture of developmental stages regarding the development of global thinking. Poirel, Mellet, Houde, and Pineau (2008) investigated how visual processing evolves during childhood by comparing global visual processing (whole picture) to local processing (component parts). Results showed that children at the age of 4 tend to focus more on component parts of a picture—or local processing—than on the whole picture. However, findings also showed that beyond age 4, children progressively demonstrated a tendency to process the picture globally. By the age of 9, subjects had an adult-like tendency for global processing—they more frequently identified a picture by its overall image and ignored the components that made up the picture. These results suggest that presenting visual information through global representations such as graphic organizers is most effective for children beginning in early elementary school, after the preschool and kindergarten years.

PLANNING A BRAIN-TARGETED TEACHING LEARNING UNIT

In the BTT Model, Brain-Target Three encourages teachers to design graphic organizers that include the overarching themes, content, activities, and evaluations that students will experience during the unit (Hardiman, 2003). This type of global planning allows students to see connections among topics, how activities relate to learning objectives, and how they will demonstrate understanding of the lesson's goals. From the teacher's perspective, planning BTT learning units necessitates having a thorough grasp of the content while also promoting interdisciplinary planning and creative teaching activities. It is consistent with the idea of "planning backward" advocated by Tomlinson and McTighe (2006, p. 27) in which teachers are encouraged to identify the essential content that should result in enduring learning, determine how students will demonstrate understanding, and plan instructional activities to meet instructional goals.

Here I briefly describe various areas to be considered in developing and planning a BTT learning unit, including choosing the learning goals and objectives, designing activities, creating evaluations, and displaying key concepts through graphic organizers.

> ◎ Global planning allows students to see connections among topics, how activities relate to learning objectives, and how they will demonstrate understanding of the lesson's goals.

From the Expert Teacher

How to Start a Learning Unit: Concept Mapping

Brain Targeted Teaching has become the tool that I use to drive each unit, even each lesson that I write and teach. When beginning the initial writing phase of a unit, I always begin with a concept map. I first make one for myself, with paper and pencil, which essentially conveys my thought process in print. Once the map is complete, I then make the same map again using large chart paper and colored markers to display for my students at the beginning of the unit. This allows them to see where we are heading throughout the unit and make connections between concepts and across content areas. Instead of wondering what they will do in class each day, how it all fits together and makes sense, they have a clear map to guide them. I refer to the map throughout the unit and so do my students. At the end of the unit, I give each student their own small concept map to keep. We go through each part of the map to form a discussion of how we covered each concept. The discussion always ends with students having moments of self-discovery about what they accomplished. As a result, they show greater confidence in the content they have mastered.

Amanda Kowalik
Teacher, Elementary School

Instructional Decision-Making: Content Choices for Learning Goals and Objectives

As teachers begin to plan BTT learning units, the first decision is to determine the essential concepts, content, and skills that students will need to know, not only to pass the unit test but also for long-term learning. This instructional decision-making is not always easy. Many teachers lament that they are expected to cover too much material in too little time. Unfortunately, this "inch deep mile wide" approach to curriculum has forced some teachers to move quickly through the content and avoid interactive and problem-solving activities that would lead to long-term retention of content as well as make learning more engaging for students. High-stakes testing in reading and mathematics, curriculum-based benchmark testing, preparation for high school assessments and Advanced Placement tests can certainly shape curriculum decisions for teachers and school administrators. Still, it is often left to teachers to make instructional choices for learning goals and objectives, which may require sifting through content standards, curriculum guides, and textbooks to determine the knowledge and skills that students will need in order to be successful in the educational environment and become life-time learners.

> ◎ First decision is to determine the essential concepts, content, and skills that students will need to know.

Learning Activities

After teachers determine the learning goals and objectives for the lesson, the next stage of planning is to determine activities to engage students in learning that will lead to long-term retention of content. Teaching activities take on many forms, from teacher-directed instruction to problem-based inquiring learning. In the BTT model, teachers are encouraged to use a variety of teaching practices—more traditional forms of teaching might work for some objectives while in other cases teachers will want to engage students in more interactive tasks such as arts-integrated learning (see Brain-Target Four) or creative problem-solving (see Brain-Target Five). The most important consideration in planning learning activities is to be sure that they are purposeful and relate to learning goals. As Tomlinson and McTighe (2006) point out, teachers should avoid activities that are like "cotton candy—pleasant enough in the moment but lacking long-term substance" (p. 28).

> ◎ Teaching activities take on many forms, from teacher-directed instruction to problem-based inquiring learning.

From the Expert Teacher

Mapping the Journey of Learning

Before I finished my teacher education, I used to fantasize about a "road school," where another teacher and I would have 12 students and a big RV and we would essentially take the students on a 40-week-long road trip; the ultimate experiential education. Of course, that would be completely impractical, but I have come to see my 180 days with my students as a journey. And just as I wouldn't have taken them across the country without maps, I don't teach without curriculum maps.

The curriculum maps I create for each unit detail all of the main skills and concepts I will include. Key vocabulary is also included. I use the maps to plan how I will integrate multi-arts and multi-sensory strategies for learning objectives. I also use curriculum maps (or webs) to determine the most efficient way to scaffold prior knowledge. Planning in interdisciplinary teams enriches this exponentially, and allows for multidisciplinary activation of schemata. I use the web as a part of my syllabus for each class as well and have found that parents really appreciate having this scope of what their children will learn.

When beginning a unit, I present the map to the class, and we review any prior knowledge they might have. This also helps me to be more analytical in the planning of individual lessons. As a special educator, task analysis has become a huge part of my planning. Within the skills and strategies I am planning, what skills do I assume my students have previously mastered? For instance, when I teach Renaissance-era geography, I know that cartography will be a big part of the learning experience. For the group I have, how much time will I have to spend on key concepts, such as cardinal and intermediate directions, absolute and relative location, and finding accurate scale?

Some things I think about when creating these curriculum webs are: How can I make the curriculum web visually interesting without cluttering it? Where can I post it prominently in the room so that it can also be used as a checklist for mastery of skills and content? How can I include my students as part of the learning design process?

Finally, having a clear visual representation of everything that will be included in a unit of study is an important way for me to be objective about the efficacy of my teaching. I can analyze and prioritize content based on mandated content standards.

> ◎ Having a clear visual representation of everything that will be included in a unit of study is an important way for me to be objective about the efficacy of my teaching. I can analyze and prioritize content based on mandated content standards.

Susan Rome
Teacher, Social Studies Middle School

Evaluating Learning

At this stage in the planning process, teachers should consider what evaluations are required in the lesson such as district-based benchmark assessments or end-of-chapter tests. In addition to those traditional forms of tests, teachers should consider how alternative forms of assessments such as performance-based assessments will be included in the unit, including rubrics for how various activities and assignments will be graded. Our study of evaluation in Brain-Target Six will consider the role of evaluation in learning as well as examine different forms of evaluation.

USE OF GRAPHIC ORGANIZERS IN THE BRAIN-TARGETED TEACHING MODEL

The use of graphic organizers in instruction is not new; in fact researchers established the important role of organizers for learning and memory as early as the 1960s (Ausubel, 1960; see Mayer, 1979 for a review). Consistent with these findings, many teachers include some form of graphic representations of various forms including Venn diagrams, cause/effect charts, linear or cyclic sequences, spiderwebs, or concept pattern organizers. What may be different for some teachers as they consider the BTT Model is the use of a graphic organizer as a framework for a defined unit of study (e.g., a 2- or 3-week unit on a topic) or a sequence of skills that might extend for the school year. Sharing this advanced organizer with students also can take many forms. Sometimes teachers give students a finished product; other times they provide the beginning of an organizer that students complete as the unit progresses. Hyerle (2011) described "Thinking Maps" as a tool for presenting a "common visual language for thinking and learning across whole learning communities [and] are taught to students in order for them to improve their unique cognitive abilities and to transfer these processes deeply into academic fields" (p. 3). Below we will see examples of how teachers use concept maps in their classrooms and hear from Clare and Suzanne as they demonstrate the use of concept maps as an important part of their teaching repetoire.

◎ What may be different for some teachers as they consider the BTT Model is the use of a graphic organizer as a framework for a defined unit of study.

From the Expert Teachers

Classification of Two Dimensional Shapes

Because students have been identifying shapes since their earliest years, they may consider geometry to be "kid stuff," and fail to pay close attention when more sophisticated information is introduced. This concept map allows the students to "see" instantly that they will now be doing more than just naming shapes. Not only does it offer an overview of the two dimensional shapes presented in fourth grade, it also includes identifying characteristics for individual shapes. In addition, the concept map provides space for the students to draw their own representations for each named shape.

Meredith Adelfio, Victoria Douglas, Vicky Krug,
Kelly Murillo, and Jeremy Mettler
Johns Hopkins University, Mind, Brain,
and Teaching Certificate

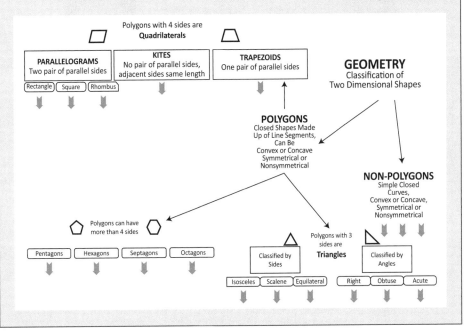

How to Grow a Democracy: The Three Branches of Government

Every youngster understands that our form of government provides all citizens with the right to vote, but our freedom depends on more than just elections. Our democracy is also fostered by the balance of powers between the three branches of government. This is a complicated idea even for high school students. This concept map helps students visualize the relationships between and organize the characteristics of the three branches. During this unit of study the students will

(Continued)

find and discuss current newspaper articles about each branch. On this concept map in the space below each description the headlines of their articles will be recorded.

Carol Lautenbach, Harriett Saviello,
and Misty Swanger
Johns Hopkins University, Mind, Brain,
and Teaching Certificate

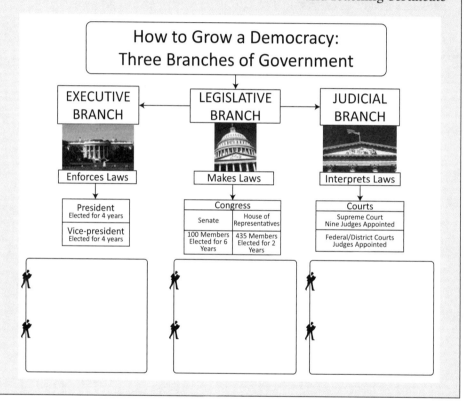

Fables: Learning to Make Wise Choices

In addition to identifying the structure and features of fables, during this literature unit students will consider the morals learned by the animal characters and reflect on similar experiences in their own lives. This concept map is designed to remind students that they, too, have personal traits just like the characters in the fables do; and just as with the animals, these traits may lead to situations where lessons are learned.

Amy Cotugno, Marian Derlet, Emmalie Dropkin,
Dev Sharma, and Juliet Stevens
Johns Hopkins University, Mind, Brain,
and Teaching Certificate
(Continued)

Fables
Learning to Make Wise Choices

Reading About the _____	Learning About Who I Am
Animal Character Traits _____ = _____ _____ = _____	An Interesting Trait of Mine
Moral or Lesson Learned By	Moral or Lesson Learned By Me

Native Americans in Pre-Colonial Maryland

Fortunately Brain-Targeted Teaching has helped me realize the value of a well-designed concept map. These visual representations enable us all to stay focused on the big ideas while helping us attend to the many small details that enrich the learning process.

For example, an essential understanding for this particular unit was: We use information about how we live today to understand how people lived long ago. Because this big idea is interwoven throughout the unit, I placed it prominently in bold type at the very top of the unit concept map. Thus it becomes easy to reflect briefly on the theme every time we take out our maps to check off an activity or to find out what we're going to do next.

*In every instructional unit students obtain knowledge or skills about a topic. They will also have opportunities to apply their new understanding to different situations. Young students don't always make the connection between these two types of learning experiences, so to push this connection between knowledge and application further, I placed special "donut" icons next to each **"You'll Need to Know/So That You Can"** activity pair. When the students first acquire concept information or skills, they color in the outer ring of an icon. When they later apply the information, they color in the inner circle.*

In this interdisciplinary unit during a math class, the students learn how to locate positions on a coordinate plane. Later they apply this skill when

(Continued)

they attempt "to preserve a site" of a Native American settlement as archaeologists sometimes do by plotting on a grid where artifacts are located in situ. Because some activities in multidisciplinary units can be very "hands on" (during the archaeological activity the students are literally digging in dirt), parents might wonder if we're having a bit too much fun. To head off any misunderstandings, I like to send home a copy of the unit concept map along with a second paper that includes some of the matching learning objectives. This allows the parents to follow along at home and, perhaps, it might also stimulate some dinner table discussions about "what I learned in school today." Brain-Targeted Teaching stimulates all the senses, inspires active experiences, and promotes higher-level thinking. With so much learning going on at so many levels, a good concept map helps to keeps us all—students, teacher, and parents—purposefully moving along toward our common learning goals.

◉ With so much learning going on at so many levels, a good concept map helps to keeps us all—students, teacher, and parents—purposefully moving along toward our common learning goals.

Sharon Delgado
Teacher, Elementary School, Special Education

We use information about how we live today to understand how people lived long ago.
Native Americans in Pre-Colonial Maryland

You'll Need to Know	So That You Can
◉ How to locate positions on a coordinate plane ◉ What is the geography of the three regions of MD	During the "Archaeological Dig" • Preserve your site • Interpret your site
◉ What human, natural, & capital resourses were available long ago ◉ How NA children contributed to their family's survival	During the "Family Improv" • Make a job list • Role-play your part
◉ What are a folktale's attributes ◉ How NA might have got goods & services ◉ What were some cultural activities of Pre-Colonial MD Native Americans	During the "Big Celebration" • Share your folktale • Barter for materials you need to create jewelry • Participate in a celebration

By Sharon Delgado

What Does A Brain-Targeted Teaching Unit Look Like In The Classroom?

Learning Unit: Surviving Alone in the Wilderness: A study of the novel *Hatchet* by Gary Paulsen

Grade/Content: Fifth-Grade/Language Arts

Author: Clare O'Malley Grizzard

Overarching Goal of Unit: Students will increase language arts skills of reading for understanding through analysis of character, plot, main idea, and symbolic language.

Brain-Target Three: Designing the Learning Experience

In approaching the design of the learning unit, we used graphic information displays from the beginning to the end of the planning process: in teacher planning maps, discussion guides for students, and global unit concepts maps that were referred to by students as we proceeded through the lessons.

The first step was to identify the common core standards in standards in English and Language Arts that our unit would address (www.corestandards.org/the-standards/english-language-arts-standards/reading-literature/grade-5/). Those standards included the following:

- Determine a theme of a story, drama, or poem from details in the text, including how characters in a story or drama respond to challenges or how the speaker in a poem reflects upon a topic; summarize the text.

- Explain how a series of chapters, scenes, or stanzas fits together to provide the overall structure of a particular story, drama, or poem.

- Describe how a narrator's or speaker's point of view influences how events are described.

In order to create a map of the unit, we decided on the essential questions or big ideas derived from the standards that deconstructed the themes of the novel and guided our investigation into "Surviving Alone in the Wilderness." We identified three aspects of Brian's ability to survive were ingenuity, keen observation, and use of the materials at hand. We used these three aspects to organize the unit into three big ideas:

- Learning to use the environment

- Listening to one's inner voice

- Becoming a different kind of an observer

We mapped supporting activities and strategies, meeting our curriculum standards, according to the three different themes. We used relevant guiding questions to create a unit map with students:

- How would you use the environment?

- What would you be saying to yourself?

- How would this experience change the way you look at the world?

Study of *Hatchet* by Gary Paulsen
Surviving Alone in the Wilderness

Surviving Alone in the Wilderness

Learning to use the natural environment

Listening to one's inner voice

Becoming a different kind of observer

Nature walks Collection of natural objects

Journal entries, diary, essays, reflection statements

Field studies, observational drawings

Guidebook and box for survival unit materials

As they engaged in various activities of the unit, students used relevant graphic icons, which they designed, to identify which big idea they were pursuing and to track their progress on unit maps.

Learning Unit: Genetics and Heredity—Thinking Outside the Punnett Square

Grade/Content: 10th-Grade/Biology

Author: Suzanne P. McNamara

Overarching Goal of Unit: Students will apply their understanding of genetics and heredity in discussions centered on current medical and social issues as well as an appreciation for human diversity.

Brain-Target Three: Designing the Learning Experience

The Big Picture

Using the concepts from Brain-Target Three is extremely important for my students when they are presented with new information. I see everyday how students must be able to use prior knowledge as a filter to establish the meaning and relevance of new information.

I also have found that providing my students with "big-picture" ideas, including the corresponding supporting concepts, helps them to organize the new ideas that I am teaching and better enables them to process, integrate, apply, and retain the key elements of the unit. It is clear that when my students are taught skills and concepts taught in isolation, they are often meaningless or confusing to them. Concept maps are critical to visually displaying key concepts that students will learn throughout the unit and how these concepts relate to prior learning.

> ◎ Concept maps are critical to visually displaying key concepts that students will learn throughout the unit and how these concepts relate to prior learning.

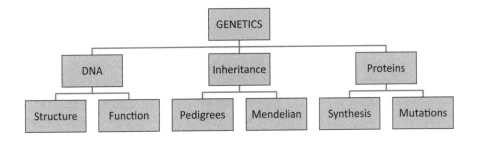

When first introducing this concept map, I encouraged students to start making connections with their prior knowledge. The students brainstormed any relevant words to add to the concept map in order to surface what they already knew about the various concepts. This activity helped to introduce the main concepts of the unit and provided a foundation upon which to build. This map was referenced constantly, and students were required to use it as a skeleton for adding new concepts. Manipulating this concept map to make it their own helped students to organize the new information learned throughout the unit.

Brain-Target Four

Teaching for Mastery of Content, Skills, and Concepts

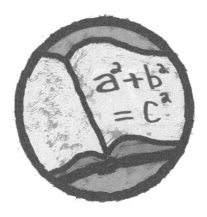

If teaching were the same as telling, we'd all be so smart we could hardly stand it.

—Mark Twain

Formal schooling is built on the assumption that students learn content, skills, and concepts that will help them throughout life. Although debates continue in the educational arena over the importance of acquiring knowledge versus "learning how to think," the Brain-Targeted Teaching (BTT) Model is built upon the assumption that the latter is in many ways dependent on the former. In other words, in order to be effective thinkers, children must possess the background knowledge needed to be literate in today's society and perform everyday tasks at a high level. Moreover, they also must strive to become lifelong learners—creative problem-solvers who can engage in inquiry and discovery. For the next two components of the model, we review ways that teachers can promote mastery of targeted learning goals (Brain-Target Four) and help students learn to apply knowledge in creative ways in real-world problem-solving tasks (Brain-Target Five).

> ◎ Children must possess the background knowledge needed to be literate in today's society and perform everyday tasks at a high level. Moreover, they also must strive to become lifelong learners—creative problem-solvers who can engage in inquiry and discovery.

In the discussion of Brain-Target Three in the last chapter, we focused on the "what" of teaching—the key goals upon which BTT learning units are built. We suggest displaying those goals and the activities that help students reach them in visual representations to promote big-picture thinking—both for the benefit of the teacher, who plans instruction, and for the benefit of the student, who learns from instruction. As we continue on our journey through the BTT Model, we now begin to focus on the "how" of teaching; that is, on strategies teachers can use to bring students to mastery in a given domain. In this chapter, we first consider how learning depends fundamentally on memory processes. We will review human memory systems and discuss how memories are encoded and retrieved. We then examine research from the neuro- and cognitive sciences on factors that improve long-term memory for material. Finally, we will discuss how these factors can be leveraged through the use of certain instructional strategies, in particular the integration of visual and performing arts into classroom activities.

LEARNING AND MEMORY

Like twin stars, learning and memory are intricately connected. Learning is the acquisition of new information, and memory allows this information to be stored and then recalled as needed at a later time. Lasting memories for some information are created after just a single exposure, while other times, memories form only after many repetitions. In 1890, William James' seminal work, *Principles of Psychology*, described memory as the recollection of "states of mind" that occurred in the past. Influenced by this early work, "information processing theory" emerged in the middle of the 20th century as a way to understand how information is received and processed through the senses, maintained in temporary memory systems, and potentially stored in long-term memory to be retrieved later for use in thought or action. The proto-typical model of information processing is depicted in the figure below.

◎ Like twin stars, learning and memory are intricately connected. Learning is the acquisition of new information, and memory allows this information to be stored and then recalled as needed at a later time.

Types of Memory Processes

Rather than being a "vessel" for information, memory is better thought of as a collection of systems and processes that serve a variety of functions. Certain "types" of memory often overlap with one another, and classifications employed by scientists are driven in many ways by dis-tinctions among the various kinds of information people can remember. Scientists have developed theoretical models for memory systems that deal with everything from unnoticed sensory input to information that is etched on our minds for life. Although there are differences between theo-rists regarding the details of these models, they generally address three different kinds of phenomena: (a) quickly fleeting memory for sensory

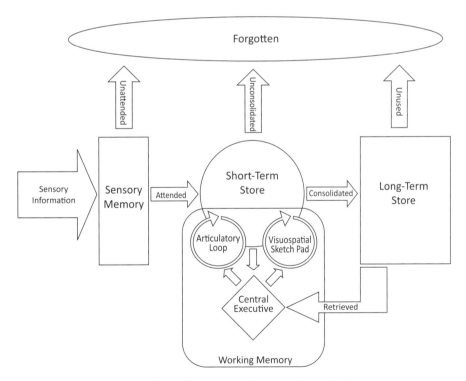

The Information Processing Model

information, (b) short-term and working memory (forms of temporary storage), and (c) long-term memory (the relatively permanent storage of information).

Sensory Memory

Sensory memory, which lasts from milliseconds to seconds, refers to the very brief storage of large amounts of visual, auditory, olfactory, or haptic input from the environment. The vast majority of this information never reaches other memory systems; our brains filter out about 99% of sensory information because it is irrelevant (Gazzaniga, 1998). However, as was first shown for visual information by Sperling (1960), we are able to retrieve sensory data for a short time after it is received, even if we are not consciously paying attention to it. For example, even when not actively listening, we might be able to repeat back the last word we heard from a television commercial, because auditory information briefly persists in our sensory memory as a kind of "echo" that we can reproduce. However, this type of memory is fleeting, and sensory information is not processed further by other memory systems unless some kind of meaning is attached to the stimulus (Gazzaniga, Ivry, & Mangun, 2009).

> ◎ Our brains filter out about 99% of sensory information because it is irrelevant.

Short-Term and Working Memory

"Short-term memory" and "working memory" are often used interchangeably in the memory literature to describe the temporary storage of information. Though these forms of memory likely share some of the same neural or cognitive mechanisms (Unsworth & Engle, 2007), short-term and working memory models are conceptually distinct and account for somewhat different phenomena (Nadel & Hardt, 2011). Fundamentally, short-term memory refers to the temporary storage of information that was just received for up to about 20 seconds (though this span can be increased if information is actively rehearsed mentally). Working memory, conversely, refers to a more complex cognitive system in which information is held in one's conscious awareness in order to perform computations or manipulate that information in some way. The first in-depth theory of working memory (and the best known) is that offered by Baddeley and Hitch (1974), who created a model to describe the basic processes through which information is received, maintained, and retrieved. Information held in working memory often comes from the environment—for example, prices that are kept in mind to do mental arithmetic and figure out how much is saved with a discount. However, working memory is also used to retrieve and manipulate information already stored in long-term memory. For instance, working memory is what allows one to bring to mind previously scheduled appointments in order to figure out when to schedule a new one.

> ◎ Short-term and working memory models are conceptually distinct and account for somewhat different phenomena.

According to Baddeley and Hitch (1974), working memory has three components: (a) a central executive that receives information from the senses or long-term memory, activating either (b) the "phonological loop" (for verbal information) or (c) the "visuospatial sketchpad" (for visual/spatial information). These latter two components of working memory serve to maintain information within conscious awareness so that the information can be acted upon. Repeated rehearsal of novel information within the phonological loop or visuospatial sketchpad can contribute to the formation of long-term memories, as can the deeper processing associated with performing mental operations on information. Usually, however, once information from the external environment has been acted upon, it is no longer needed and is lost from memory.

> ◎ Once information from the external environment has been acted upon, it is no longer needed and is lost from memory.

It is important here to address the popular belief that short-term and/or working memory has a capacity of approximately seven items. This belief was spawned by Miller's (1956) article about "the magical number seven," in which he noted that people's capacity for processing information appears in a variety of different cases to be limited to seven (plus or minus two) "items," where items include things like digits or words. Following Miller's work, many people subsequently drew the conclusion that short-term or working memory capacity *in general* is limited to seven items or "chunks." This conclusion is an overinterpretation of Miller's article, and, since its publication, numerous counterexamples and mitigating factors (e.g., expertise in a given domain, practice, etc.) have been recognized (Shiffrin & Nosofsky, 1994). Fundamentally, Miller meant only to highlight people's limited capacity for information processing. Yet the idea that working memory capacity is strictly limited to seven items still persists as a myth—despite more recent evidence (such as that offered by Cowan, 2001) that if it is reasonable to ascribe to working memory a general limit of this sort at all, this limit is probably closer to about four chunks. Complicating matters, this conclusion is based on the assumption that information can be readily divided into obvious chunks. In many practical situations, there is no one obvious way to chunk information and therefore little to no justification for carving instructional content into a preordained number of chunks. Instead, teachers should simply rely on their intuitions and seek out relatively natural ways to chunk information. For any given task, what's important is just that teachers think about the amount of information a student might need to maintain within his or her conscious awareness at one time, look for helpful ways to chunk that information, and avoid overwhelming students with too many isolated pieces of information.

Long-Term Memory

Long-term memory refers to the retention of information (without active rehearsal) for a significant amount of time, whether years or a life-time. Though information that is not retrieved every now and then tends to be forgotten over time, the total volume of information that can be retained in long-term memory is for all practical purposes unlimited. An important overarching distinction within long-term memory is the differ-ence between *explicit* and *implicit* memory. Further distinctions between different forms of memory can be considered within each of these broad headings.

Explicit memory. All explicit memory can also be described as *declarative* memory. This form of memory deals with knowledge that one is consciously aware of, such as events that occur in our lives or informa-tion we have knowingly acquired. When we recall events from our past, like performing in a play or winning a tennis match, this is referred to as *episodic memory.* Episodic memory does not function by storing and retrieving all the information associated with an event. As Squire and Kandel (1999) explain, unlike a video camera, we are not able to simply "mentally record" events exactly as they occur. Each time we remember an event, we use key pieces of remembered information to reconstruct the experience; this sometimes results in changes to details or more sig-nificant inaccuracies or embellishments. Episodic memory is generally contrasted with *semantic* memory, which refers to our ability to remember facts or concepts—propositions about the world, meanings of symbols and words, gram-mar rules, uses for objects, mathematical ideas, and so on. Both types of declarative memory, episodic and semantic, are criti-cal for allowing us to access and use our knowledge so that we can conduct our everyday lives.

> ◉ When we recall events from our past, like performing in a play or winning a tennis match, this is referred to as *episodic memory*. Both types of declarative memory, episodic and semantic, are critical for allowing us to access and use our knowledge so that we can conduct our everyday lives.

Implicit memory. Fundamentally, implicit memory refers to experi-ences that we remember without conscious awareness that learning is taking place. Though there are several types of implicit memory, the most important one to distinguish is *procedural memory*. Procedural memory is often contrasted with declarative memory and supports our ability to "know how" to do something without thinking about it. Procedural memory explains why we can learn to perform certain tasks without being able to say precisely how we're doing them. For example, when we learn how to ride a bike, there are a few relatively vague things that others might tell us to do (e.g., "push on the pedals," "steer," etc.), but for the most part we learn how to ride a bike through practice and trial and error. As we try and try again to ride the bicycle, a wide variety of motor processes are taking place, and movements and actions that lead to success are stored in our memory systems without our conscious awareness. Procedural memory is very important in school settings, but the ways in which children rely on procedural memory are not always easy to recognize. For instance, when learning to read, students acquire decoding skills through repeated exposure and practice—that is, through a largely hidden process of implicit, procedural learning (Gazzaniga, Ivry, & Mangun, 2009).

> ◎ Procedural memory explains why we can learn to perform certain tasks without being able to say precisely how we're doing them.

Memory Systems in Daily Life

In summary, although our sensory, short-term, working, and long-term memory systems are distinct from one another, they are interrelated in important ways. Further, memory is influenced by many factors, including our experiences, our senses, the importance we assign to information, and what we do with information once we receive it.

To consider how the memory systems work together, imagine the following scenario: An announcement is made in your school asking faculty to attend a special meeting. The meeting will be held in room 128, and, as you are walking down the hall, you pass by the lighted gym before reaching your destination. At the meeting, the principal announces that the school will receive a grant for 60 new computers from the Azzara Foundation. What might you remember from this experience, and for how long? What types of memory will be utilized?

First, following the announcement, you must initially rehearse the room number to yourself in order to maintain it in working memory; however, once the meeting is over and this information is no longer needed, it will likely be soon forgotten. As you head toward the meeting, the directions to the designated room must be retrieved and held in working memory long enough for you to get to the right location. As you pass by the gym, the light from inside would reach your visual system, but unless this has some importance or meaning that would lead you to pay particular attention, this sensory information would likely not be retained even in short-term memory, let alone long-term memory. The Azzara Foundation may be known to you, or it may have no meaning or significance at all—in which case the name may be retained only briefly in short-term memory. When you hear that the school will receive 60 computers, you must hold that information in working memory in order to figure out that since there are 6 teachers, you will be receiving 10 computers for your classroom. The total number of computers the school received might be forgotten but could perhaps be reconstructed based on what you know. The memories from the meeting itself that would be most likely to stay in long-term memory would be those having to do with the computers you now see your students using daily in your classroom.

NEUROBIOLOGY OF LEARNING AND MEMORY

As discussed in Chapter 2, the typical neuron shares information by "firing" an electrical impulse down its axon, where this impulse causes the release of various neurotransmitter chemicals at tiny junctions between neurons called synapses. On the other side of each synapse, a dendrite attached to another neuron takes up these neurotransmitters. If the aggregate excitatory input from other neurons reaches a certain threshold, the neuron receiving these signals fires, transferring the signal on to its neighbors. Through this process, signals travel from one neuron to the next along complex neural pathways that weave their way through the brain, producing all of our thoughts and behaviors. In the 1940s Donald Hebb (1949) proposed that neural connections are strengthened when groups of neurons are actively generating signals (i.e., firing) at the same time. This idea is the origin of the oft-heard phrase "neurons that fire together, wire together." The more often groups of neurons fire simultaneously, the more strongly and efficiently signals are transmitted among them, a process known as *long-term potentiation*. Repeated activation of neural circuits binds them together in patterns of connectivity that underlie the creation of memory traces or *engrams*. The more frequently these neural connections are used, the stronger they become, making memories longer-lasting and easier to retrieve.

> ◎ The typical neuron shares information by "firing" an electrical impulse down its axon, where this impulse causes the release of various neurotransmitter chemicals at tiny junctions between neurons called synapses.

Through studies of patients who have experienced brain damage, scientists have learned more about the biological basis of complex memory systems. Scientists have discovered that damage to the hippocampus, for example, disrupts the ability to form new long-term memories. Nobel Prize winner Eric Kandel (2006) explains that memory is a mental function distinct from perception, motor activity, or cognitive ability, and that temporary and long-term memory systems perform separate functions and involve different brain regions. Though damage to the hippocampus can affect the formation of long-term memories, this does not mean that long-term memory is located in the hippocampus, however. As is the case with many brain functions, the story is considerably more complex. Although the hippocampus has been shown to be crucial for memory formation, the patterns of activity related to long-term storage and retrieval of information spread across a variety of areas in the cerebral cortex.

> ◎ Memory is a mental function distinct from perception, motor activity, or cognitive ability, and temporary and long-term memory systems perform separate functions and involve different brain regions.

The question of how and why some pieces of information are remembered long-term and others are forgotten continues to be the subject of research in various disciplines. However, some important understandings have now been firmly established by neuroscience. For example, we now know that the brain needs time to solidify memories in long-term storage, a process called *consolidation.* Another significant finding is that for temporary memory, synapses use existing proteins inside the cell, whereas the conversion from temporary to long-term memory involves the synthesis of new regulatory proteins (Kandel, 2006).

> ◎ We now know that the brain needs time to solidify memories in long-term storage, a process called *consolidation.*

In summary, life-long learning requires that new information be specifically consolidated within long-term memory to produce permanent storage. As educators, it is important to understand that acquiring knowledge that can be subsequently retrieved and applied is not something that just happens. Learning is a neuro-physiological phenomenon that occurs through biochemical processes in the brain and the growth and reorganization of neural connections. In the next section, we will examine teaching practices that can facilitate learning and aid in the creation of long-term memories, thereby helping students master the content, skills, and concepts that are crucial for academic success.

ARTS INTEGRATION FOR MASTERY OF CONTENT, SKILLS, AND CONCEPTS

Though rote learning certainly has been overemphasized in the past, the fact that students need to remember basic information related to what they are learning cannot be ignored. There is no way around the need for students to have at their disposal content knowledge ("knowing that . . .") and procedural skills ("knowing how . . ."). Though conceptual understanding is what teachers are rightly striving for, facts and skills are often prerequisites to this deep understanding. It is impossible to understand subtraction, for instance, if you cannot count.

As previously noted, in order for information to be retained, it must make its way from short-term to long-term memory. In a review of research on factors known to improve long-term memory for information, Rinne, Gregory, Yarmolinskaya, and Hardiman (2011) argue that arts integration, the use of the arts as a pedagogical method for enhancing and reinforcing learning goals, represents a powerful strategy for helping to make sure that information "sticks" in children's memories. The argument is based on the notion that many forms of artistic practice naturally incorporate activities that have been shown in research from the neuro- and cognitive sciences to aid retention of information. Here we consider these research findings in some detail, as arts integration is at the core of the BTT Model and in particular of Brain-Target Four.

> ◎ Arts integration, the use of the arts as a pedagogical method for enhancing and reinforcing learning goals, represents a powerful strategy for helping to make sure that information "sticks" in children's memories.

Before a deeper consideration of the research, though, it is important to first distinguish between arts education and arts integration. Arts education, including instruction in instrumental music, vocal music, visual arts, theater, dance, and creative writing must be recognized as an important area of study for students of all ages. Although arts advocates (myself included) agree that engaging in the arts "for its own sake" is important for every child, a growing body of research is also demonstrating that the arts are positively related to academic performance and promote the development of cognitive skills and capacities that transfer to core academic disciplines (e.g., Fiske, 1999; Gazzaniga, 2008; Posner & Patoine, 2009). Even those who believe that transfer of the sort just alluded to is rare (e.g., Hetland, Winner, Veenema, & Sheridan, 2007) argue that engagement with artistic activity still serves to cultivate "habits of mind" important for academic success. These include dispositions such as persistence in working on tasks over a sustained period, expression of one's personal voice, and reflective self-evaluation of work. Though these dispositions are not associated with any particular content area, they certainly lead to more effective learning.

All three of the arguments offered previously in favor of arts instruction—the arts "for its own sake," as a means to enhancing academic and cognitive skills, and as a way of fostering useful dispositions—are good ones. Nonetheless, it needs to be recognized that there is yet another potential benefit of the arts that has to date been overlooked; that is, integrating artistic activities into instruction is likely to enhance long-term memory for content.

So how can the arts lead to better memory? Below, I review a variety of memory effects that have been the subject of considerable study over the last 30 years. Though conventional instruction could also be adapted to take advantage of these effects, I argue that arts-integrated instruction does the job *naturally*, guiding teachers' planning and implementation of instruction based on rigorous scientific research. Throughout the remainder of this chapter, you will hear from teachers who have experience in arts integration. The stories of these expert teachers further demonstrate the power of the arts in the classroom. They demonstrate activities that can be naturally incorporated into instruction without the need for specific training in arts instruction. Therefore, teachers who feel they are not "artistic" or are not highly trained in various forms of art need not worry; the process of using the arts in instruction does not require that one be a skilled artist. Rather, arts integration is about increasing learning through the promotion of artistic thinking and habits of working.

> ◎ Arts integration is about increasing learning through the promotion of artistic thinking and habits of working.

Repeated Rehearsal

One of the most important strategies for establishing long-term retention is rehearsal, the process of repeating information to oneself or others in an effort to commit it to memory. Just as muscles are built through their repeated use, memories can be built through repeated rehearsals. It has long been known that repeated rehearsal improves recall of information, especially when rehearsals are spaced over time (e.g., Rundus, 1971). Effective rehearsal strategies help to form more elaborate memory traces that tie pieces of information together or connect them to other content or concepts (Craik & Watkins, 1973).

Promoting rehearsal during instruction seems fairly intuitive. Teachers regularly give students multiple opportunities to rehearse information through classroom and independent assignments. Still, teachers often find it challenging to provide enough variety in activities within a compressed learning cycle to promote repeated rehearsal of information without constantly resorting to the same (sometimes tedious) methods and modalities. Grounding activities in various forms of art motivates students to rehearse information in new and creative ways with each iteration. This allows teachers to keep students interested while reinforcing learning on multiple occasions with appropriate space between repetitions. In addition, teaching with and through the arts helps to motivate student learning (Smithrim & Upitis, 2005) and promotes sustained attention to tasks (Posner & Patoine, 2009).

Elaboration

As noted above, repeated rehearsal can create more elaborate memory traces and increase retention. Research has also shown that the act of elaboration by itself is an effective way to make information more memorable (Anderson & Reder, 1979). This is particularly true when people relate information to themselves in some way (Klein & Loftus, 1988). The arts provide students with numerous ways to elaborate on subject matter and relate it to their own lives. For example, students can elaborate on what they learn in any content area through the visual arts (e.g., drawing a scene from history or literature in which students place themselves), the performing arts (e.g., writing and acting out a skit that depicts a concept as it applies to them), creative writing (e.g., poetry or rap that demonstrates understanding and includes important facts and details), or tableau (e.g., assuming a body posture to represent a scene from a story or historical event).

> ◎ The act of elaboration by itself is an effective way to make information more memorable.

From the Expert Teacher

Eye of the Beholder

The arts can provide a new context in which students can apply their newly mastered knowledge. I design relevancy and personal agency into all my learning units. Through projects that require students to find and make personal meaning and examine real social issues, they can see that art has a place in their lives—offering them a chance to actively participate in the world around them.

For example, my eighth-grade students took part in a unit I called "EYE OF THE BEHOLDER." Students examined social ills beginning with questioning their lives and the world at large. They address questions such as: What have you seen that you wish you had not seen? What injustices have you encountered in your own life, your community, your school, or the world? What things do you wish you could change in the world? What things are wrong with life as we live it?

Students selected social justice topics based on a real experience, or ones that evoked strong feelings; something that enraged them. Through the use of printmaking and collage, students were to open our eyes—peers, teachers, the community—to a problem in the world. This project was about building public

(Continued)

awareness and action around topics of social injustices and taking the class-room experience outside of the school. Students wrote to local organization and in the end donated their artwork to their organization of choice. Adam, for example, chose environmental degradation as his theme. He volunteered with various local organizations and was one of the founding members of the school's Environmental Club. His poster reflects the decay and destruction he experiences daily. Adam wrote a letter to the Chesapeake Bay Foundation to offer his artwork and his pledge to continue to work for the environment. Maggie chose homophobia as her theme. She researched the lives of various openly gay public figures and came across a Time *magazine article about Leonard P. Matlovich. She chose to use one of his quotes for her poster explaining that his words said it all. Her poster includes the quotation, "When I was in the military they gave me a medal for kill-ing two men and a discharge for loving one."*

Vanessa Lopez-Sparaco
Teacher, Middle School Art

Generation

Too often in traditional instructional programs, students are pas-sive recipients of information and ideas—they listen to lectures, read texts, and reproduce information they have already received by complet-ing worksheets, writing out short answers, or choosing responses from multiple-choice questions. There is strong evidence, however, that when people are not just provided information in written or oral form, but rather generate that information themselves in response to some kind of prompt, their recall of that information is significantly improved (Slamecka & Graf, 1978). Although the robustness of the generation effect is well estab-lished, its cause remains a matter of some debate. Some have argued that the generation effect arises from deeper processing of information (Kane & Anderson, 1978) or greater cognitive effort relative to simply receiving information (Tyler, Hertel, McCallum & Ellis, 1979). Another possibility is that against the background of information typically encountered in daily life—the vast majority of which is simply received—information that has been generated is unusual and is processed more and remem-bered better as a result (McDaniel & Bugg, 2008). In general, if teach-ers identify content that is important and seek out ways to get students to generate relevant information, this will make content "stick" better. Although it may seem daunting to try and find ways to coax students into generating information, the arts can be a very useful tool for doing just this. For example, if students are asked to depict ideas visually, they

◎ When people are not just provided information in written or oral form, but rather generate that information themselves in response to some kind of prompt, their recall of that information is significantly improved. Generating information through art also engages students in various forms of divergent thinking—thinking that leads to a variety of possible outputs or solutions.

will naturally generate details that they might otherwise simply be told to them, and these details will be retained better. Generating information through art also engages students in various forms of divergent thinking—thinking that leads to a variety of possible outputs or solutions. The topic of divergent thinking will be covered in greater depth when we consider creative problem-solving in conjunction with Brain-Target Five.

Enactment

Enactment involves physically acting out information or ideas and is naturally a part of activities such as role-playing or theatrical improvisation. Studies have demonstrated that retention of information is improved when participants actively perform an action phrase instead of merely reading that same information (Engelkamp, Zimmer, Mohr, & Sellen, 1994; Mohr, Engelkamp, and Zimmer, 1989). Acting usually involves some sort of motor activity, and Mohr and colleagues argue that this aids memory. However, it is also possible that the "unusualness" of enacted information—as with generated information—is what does the trick (McDaniel & Bugg, 2008). In addition to enhancing memory for information, enactment also has the benefit, like generation, of engaging students in divergent thinking.

Using dramatic enactment as a teaching tool—from simple role-playing to staging full-fledged theatrical productions—has been shown to have positive effects on learning (Catterall, 2002, 2009; Deasy, 2002). Catterall (2009) outlines a compendium of studies that demonstrate how dramatic enactment in academic settings has a positive influence on both scholastic performance (e.g., story comprehension, character analysis, writing proficiency) and social skills (e.g., peer interactions, conflict resolution skills, self-concept). The physical and mental processes involved in acting out material instead of simply reading or listening to it have the power to cement targeted content into long-term memory. And it should not be forgotten that dramatic enactment is just plain fun, and activities that students find fun are obvious assets for teachers.

◎ Using dramatic enactment as a teaching tool—from simple role-playing to staging full-fledged theatrical productions—has been shown to have positive effects on learning.

From the Expert Teacher

Physics and the Arts—A Natural Fit

I am a high school physics teacher. I am a dancer. While those two professions may seem like polar opposites, to me they come together in how I teach every day. In dance I use body motions to convey the desired emotions to an audience; in the physic laboratory I use explorations and mathematics to convey the desired learning objectives to my students. In my classroom these two practices naturally merge in amazing ways.

This started my first year when I asked my students to explain Newton's three laws of motion to me in some art form. I was expecting a few songs, cartoons, and an overwhelming display of posters. While I did get a few posters, I mostly got a vast array of art forms and my students blew me away with their creativity. There was everything from rap songs complete with back-up vocals and a dance, to a play titled "Three Laws: The Life and Physics of Sir Isaac Newton." Most of my students wanted to demonstrate to their peers how they were able to make physics fun, and in the end I videotaped a number of student performances. The next few years, I even used the video clips in my teaching to help explain the ideas of inertia, acceleration, and action-reaction forces—leading off with a folk song called "Think Science."

This project caused me to take my classes in whole new directions as often as I could. Previously I had been using the standard practice of lecture, lab, home-work format of physics, but now I was including prerecorded clips of dancers and figure skaters spinning in circles to explain angular momentum. I was asking musicians to play their portable instruments to demonstrate the properties of waves and sounds. I was using photography to explain refraction, or the bending of light, in optics. Whenever I can within the physics content, I get the students involved in viewing and creating art. And their skills often exceed mine in so many artistic ways.

Now as students come back to see me during alumni days, they are eager to tell me about physics in their daily lives and how topics we covered in class keep coming up in their experiences. Like why you bend your knees (pile) before or landing a jump—to store more elastic potential energy before the jump or to increase how long it takes to change your momentum thereby decreasing the force impacted to your body coming down. They may not remember the speed of light ($c = 2.99*10^8$ m/s), but they remember how a fish-eye camera lens bends the light to create the effect.

Stephanie Rafferty
Teacher, High School Physics

Production

The production effect describes improvements in memory that arise when words are produced aloud rather than silently read (MacLeod, Gopie, Hourihan, Neary, & Ozbuko, 2010). In a context in which surrounding material is read, orally producing key words or phrases makes them distinct, and Ozbuko and MacLeod (2010) argue that this is what causes them to be retained better. Teachers who emphasize multisensory learning, whether through materials based on multiple intelligences, formal programs for students with dyslexia, or simply through sheer instinct, have long recognized the value of using multiple modalities for expressive language tasks. The performing arts provide a natural way for students to orally produce key content in creative, elaborative ways. Art forms such as music, poetry, rap, and skits provide similarly powerful vehicles for oral production of content that teachers want students to remember over the long-term.

> ◎ The production effect describes improvements in memory that arise when words are produced aloud rather than silently read.

From the Expert Teacher

Shakespeare and Hip-Hop

Coming from the world of professional music into that of teaching in a school with mostly low-income minority students, I felt like an alien from another world, and it quickly became apparent that if I was going to have any success in reaching the students, I would need some communication skills not included in the standard teachers' "tool box." I knew that I needed to plant the seeds for creativity and build trust between myself as the teacher and each student in order to make the subject matter relevant.

The first time I witnessed the spark of learning being ignited was when I began to teach a class on Shakespeare's "Othello." The students had no interest in the outdated language that held no relevancy for them. I had planned a standard lesson that followed the usual guidelines; however, upon hearing a pre-class discussion about the previous night's episode of the "Sopranos," a television serial about a New Jersey mob family and its violent machinations, I decided to abandon the standard procedure and try something different in hopes of making a more profound connection.

We began by moving our chairs in a circle and talking about some very basic human instincts and emotions: jealousy, insecurity, greed, and infidelity. The students openly related how each of these played into their lives. From there, we moved on to a brief discussion of the television show, and how all these same

(Continued)

emotions are used to develop plot and to create an arc for the story. Once we had looked at the various characters in the show, I explained to them that this play-wright living several hundred years ago wrote a story in which his characters felt many of the same things and acted in much the same fashion as did the characters in their favorite show, and that he was just using the language of his day. I suggested that reading the play would be much more fun if we had volunteers for the various parts. So many hands went up that we had to limit the number of lines so that each student would have an opportunity to read. Their enthusiasm was infectious, and the more they read, the more they assumed the dramatic personae of the characters. Even when they took it "over the top," I encouraged them, since it showed me that their imaginations were at work. At the end of the reading, we compared how the emotions and actions portrayed in the "Sopranos," were similar to those in "Othello." The vocabulary of Shakespeare, which is archaic and can sometimes be an impediment, became less of an issue due to the overall spirit of the students, and we were able to examine the language when we paused to change parts. I asked them to think of corresponding words in today's hip-hop vocabulary. The teacher at this point became the student.

As part of their assignment, they were asked to examine the character whose lines they read, and using the language of their own time, suggest how they might voice today what Shakespeare had written in his own "lingo" several hundred years before. Some of the students took it one step further, and using their imaginations, combined elements of hip-hop poetry to give the characters in "Othello" a whole new life. Enacting the roles of this story not only resulted in greater engagement of the students in the lesson, but their newfound excitement for learning to spill over to other classes as well.

Joseph Izen
Professional Musician; Teacher, High School English

Effort After Meaning

The concept of "effort after meaning" was first described by one of the pioneers of modern psychology, Frederic Bartlett (1932). Effort after meaning refers to the thinking that one engages in to make sense of stimuli in the environment—for example, sentences, images, and events. Effort after meaning is an important factor for memory; research has shown that when people must puzzle over a stimulus a bit in order to understand it, they end up remembering that stimulus better than they would if its meaning were made more obvious (Auble & Franks, 1978). For example, Auble and Franks presented study participants with ambiguous sentences, such as, "The man was hungry because the pole broke." Participants naturally struggled for a short time to make sense of that

> ◎ Effort after meaning is an important factor for memory; research has shown that when people must puzzle over a stimulus a bit in order to understand it, they end up remembering that stimulus better than they would if its meaning were made more obvious.

sentence. If they had been told immediately that "the man was a fisherman," they would not have had to exert as much effort to understand the text, and therefore would have had weaker long-term retention of the sentence. Zaromb and Roediger (2009) argue that the act of exerting special effort to understand information is a relatively unusual occurrence, and, as with generation and enactment, this leads to greater processing and better memory for content.

The exertion of effort after meaning is something that occurs naturally when people interpret art. In order to make sense of a painting or poem, for instance, students often must grapple with ideas before being able to understand the meaning of what's in front of them. If teachers embed the content they teach within a piece of art, students will need to make an effort in order to get at the underlying idea, and this will likely lead to better memory of that idea. There are ample opportunities to place educational content in artistic contexts. For example, visual art is full of geometry, and many poems and songs reference historical figures and events. When this kind of information is presented to students through art rather than in isolation in a textbook or on a worksheet, students will naturally need to make an effort to understand the material they

> ◎ Exertion of effort after meaning is something that occurs naturally when people interpret art.

encounter. And this effort need not be an arduous one. With art, many students will make this effort joyfully, because they find art to be interesting and stimulating.

Pictorial Representation

The saying that "a picture is worth a thousand words" is not mere folklore. Studies have shown that people often remember information better when it is presented in the form of pictures rather than words, even when the memory is assessed through verbal measures (e.g., Shepard, 1967). This "picture superiority effect" may occur at least in part because pictures are encoded both through visual and verbal mental processes while encoding words requires only verbal processing (Paivio, 1971). Moreover, pictures may require a greater level of conceptual processing

> ◎ The saying that "a picture is worth a thousand words" is not mere folklore.

than words, potentially leading to better retention of pictorial representations (McBride & Dosher, 2002).

Programs such as Artful Thinking (www.pz.harvard.edu), which originated from Harvard's Project Zero, use visual images such as works of art to encourage students to develop thinking processes and dispositions—such as curiosity, observation, comparison, and connection of ideas—that are important for learning. For example, students might view a painting and make observations about technical details of the painting, its relation to other genres from the historical period, or the painter's purpose in producing the work. Using pictorial representations helps to make students' thinking visible and promotes deeper conceptual processing through thoughtful questioning, consideration of subject matter from historical and social viewpoints, and exploration of new points of view.

> ◎ Using pictorial representations helps to make students' thinking visible and promotes deeper conceptual processing through thoughtful questioning, consideration of subject matter from historical and social viewpoints, and exploration of new points of view.

Contrary to intuitions, recent research suggests that children younger than age 8 do not exhibit better memory for pictures than for words and that the picture superiority effect develops over time, possibly as children gain a capacity for self-directed recollection (Defeyter, Russo, & McPartlin, 2009). However, this does not mean that younger children cannot benefit from visual representations. They certainly can, especially when alternative verbal expressions would be more complex. This is made clear by the account of the expert teacher below.

From the Expert Teacher

A Picture Is Worth a Thousand Words

Teachers have struggled for years with teaching children how to keep their desks neat and organized. Based on what I have learned from Brain-Targeted Teaching, I see the value in using visual rather than merely verbal communications to reinforce skills and practices. In considering Brain-Target Two, I became more aware of the importance of classroom routine and organization. Brain-Target Three helped me to recognize how visual representations are important for understanding. In reviewing the memory effects of Brain-Target Four, I see every day the importance of visual representation in helping children learn.

For example, after telling my first graders where to place their books/supplies in an organized manner in their desks, I found that students' memory for that information lasted only about a day. Giving them visual reminders prompted the students to be more organized with the items stored in their desk. With the help of a graphic designer, we were able to have a poster-sized desk map displayed in the

(Continued)

room as well as individual maps on each student's desk. The desk map serves as a visual reminder and a focal point for the class when given the prompt to clean up. In this sense, a picture is truly worth a thousand words.

Kathy Rivetti
Teacher, Lower Elementary Grades

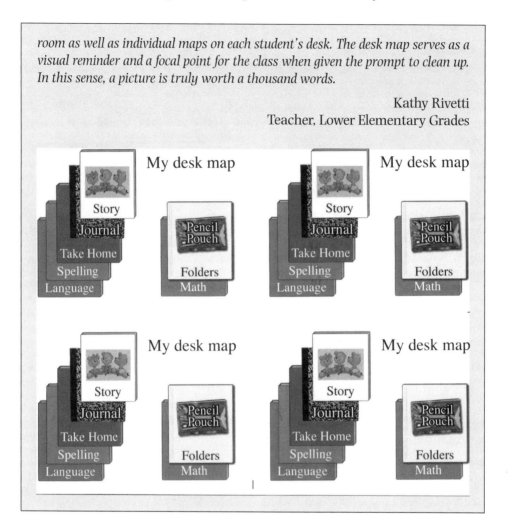

Emotion and Memory

Most of us remember vivid details when we recall catastrophic events such as the terrorist attacks of September 11, 2001. We may have keen recollection of visual images from newscasts and remember where we were, who we were with, the exact time of day when hearing the news, and even the weather. For catastrophic events or even pleasant ones such as a birth or a wedding, our brains are capable of creating "flashbulb memories" that last a lifetime.

Events producing flashbulb memories and ideas that carry emotional meaning can have lasting effects on learning. Research suggests that emotional arousal influences what we pay attention to (Talmi, Anderson, Riggs, Caplan, & Moscovitch, 2008), and this can affect immediate as well as long-term memory. Moreover, information that causes either positive or negative emotional arousal is remembered better over the long-term than that which is emotionally neutral (Cahill & McGaugh, 1995). As described in Chapter 4 on Brain-Target One, there is also evidence that positive emotions influence global understanding and promote better performance on cognition and creative thinking tasks (Frederickson & Branigan, 2005).

> ◎ Information that causes either positive or negative emotional arousal is remembered better over the long-term than that which is emotionally neutral.

Artistic activities provide the perfect way for students to explore what they are learning through emotional expression. Any form of artistic activity has the potential to forge emotional connections to content that are richer and more rewarding than those achieved using conventional teaching strategies. The arts encourage provocative questions, careful observations, exploration of multiple viewpoints, and new modes of interpretation.

PEDAGOGICAL STRATEGIES FOR FORMING STRONG MEMORIES

Mnemonics

Many of us have relied on mnemonics throughout our lives to remember information such as the order of notes on the treble clef (EGBDF— "Every Good Boy Does Fine"). For information that must be straightforwardly committed to memory, mnemonics clearly work. Mnemonics can take the form of acrostic sentences as in the example above. Acronyms are useful mnemonics too. Many of us learned, for example, "ROY G. BIV" to remember the order of the colors in the light spectrum (red, orange, yellow, green, blue, indigo, violet) and "Please Excuse My Dear Aunt Sally" for the order of operations in arithmetic (parenthesis, exponents, multiplication, division, addition, subtraction). Mnemonics can also take the form of rhymes and phrases such as "i before e except after c" or "In fourteen hundred ninety-two, Columbus sailed the ocean blue." Mnemonics may stick with us for life, remaining our primary means of recalling information. For instance, it may be difficult for many of us to recall which months have 30 days without reciting to ourselves "Thirty days hath September, April, June, and November."

> ◎ For information that must be straightforwardly committed to memory, mnemonics clearly work.

A meta-analysis of research on the use of mnemonic strategies was conducted by Scruggs and Mastropieri (2000). They collected studies on the use of letter strategies like those described previously, studies on the use of keywords, and studies of providing "pegwords" on which information can be "hung" (e.g., "a jury of elves" reminds a student that juries have 12 members). The results of the meta-analysis showed that mnemonic strategies are highly effective at aiding recall across age groups and for students both with and without special needs. Thus, it is clear that teachers should provide students with mnemonic devices to help them remember material. In addition, having students create mnemonic devices for themselves—while encouraging artistry and creativity— would surely make for a fun and effective class activity.

Desirable Difficulties

Teachers quite naturally spend a lot of time and effort to make learning easier for their students. In many cases, this is a good and useful instinct— if students are unable to understand or digest the material they're being taught, they're certainly not going to learn it to mastery. However, as was seen in the earlier section on how the arts engage students in "effort after meaning," sometimes making things just a bit more *difficult* can actually lead to better learning. This is certainly not true in all (or even most) cases, and any effort to introduce difficulty must, of course, be undertaken with caution. Nonetheless, it is important to consider recent research indicating that increasing difficulty can sometimes aid memory. For example, Diemand-Yauman, Oppenheimer, and Vaughan (2011) have shown that making written materials slightly more "disfluent"—that is, making it just a bit harder for our perceptual systems to deal with what we read— can lead to deeper processing and therefore better retention of material.

> ◎ Sometimes making things just a bit more *difficult* can actually lead to better learning. It is important to consider recent research indicating that increasing difficulty can sometimes aid memory.

Everyone has likely had the experience when reading a book or article of kind of glazing over a paragraph without really processing what's in it. When you get to the end of the paragraph, you inevitably ask yourself the question, "What did I just read?" This would seem to occur because one is perhaps reading a bit *too* fluently. That is, a good reader is likely capable of absent-mindedly reading text without really processing or understanding what that text is saying. Diemand-Yauman and colleagues (2011) showed—in a real-life high school setting—that simply changing printed materials to a slightly harder-to-read font led to substantial gains in course performance, likely due to an increase in processing of information (it is important to note that this increase in difficulty was not large enough to be noticeable to students). The lesson here is not that teachers should make learning tasks as hard as possible. Rather, as teachers are surely aware, sometimes students' level of attention and focus may slip, and therefore presenting information in formats that require students to process information more thoroughly can be a good idea. Of course, no one would want to make a task harder for a student who is already struggling. Research is showing, however, that teachers should perhaps think from time to time about how making tasks harder in certain ways, especially if the difference is not noticeable to students, can potentially lead to learning gains. Oftentimes, embedding information in the arts may do just this.

> ◎ Simply changing printed materials to a slightly harder-to-read font led to substantial gains in course performance.

Chunking

Chunking aids memory by grouping items in an organized way so that they can be retrieved more easily than items in an unstructured list. Phone numbers and social security numbers, for example, are made easier to remember by creating smaller groups of numbers that are separated with hyphens. One of the best known studies on the use of chunking was carried out by Chase and Ericsson (1981) with an undergraduate student, SF, who trained over a period of about 2 years to memorize long strings of digits. At first, SF had a digit span of about 7, which is comparable with that of the average person. Over the subsequent 2 years, however, SF was able to increase his digit span to around 80 digits. So how did he accomplish this feat? As it turns out, SF was an avid long-distance runner and began to chunk short strings of digits in such a way that they corresponded to running times for various distances. Over time, SF developed more interpretations that could be given to strings of numbers, such as ages or years, and eventually he could break extremely long strings into chunks that could be assigned distinct meanings and commit to memory the order of the chunks.

> ◎ Chunking aids memory by grouping items in an organized way so that they can be retrieved more easily than items in an unstructured list.

Chunking information for students as well as teaching them to chunk information on their own is something all teachers should do when they present a large number of individual items that need to be committed to memory. As was discussed earlier, there's no one-size-fits-all prescription for the size and number of chunks. What's important is simply that each chunk be manageable enough for students to keep a few chunks in mind at any given time. As seen with the example of SF above, giving chunks meanings or interpretations can be a big help. Students can divide information into categories to help organize what they learn. For example, students could use a Venn diagram to categorize items based on shared and unshared properties. Color coding in visual displays can also assist in chunking information. Students, for instance, could use different colored pens to group similar items or create collages that visually demonstrate how chunks of information are related. If students can remember that there's a "blue chunk," a "red chunk," and a "green chunk," and then can recall what each chunk is composed of, this will make it much easier for them to remember the entire set of information.

Interleaving

Interleaving refers to the process of intentionally ordering learning tasks so that the same task is not done several times in a row. In contrast to *blocked* structures (aaa, bbb, ccc), *interleaved* structures mix tasks together (abc, bca, cab). Interleaving practice sessions or presentations of material has been shown to increase task performance and retention over what is achieved using a blocked format. For example, Kornell and Bjork (2008) found that subjects could better identify the artists of particular paintings when they were presented in an interleaved or random order rather than being blocked by the artist. Rohrer and Taylor (2007) found similar results for learning mathematics content. Rohrer and Pashler (2010) posit that interleaving aids learning by helping the learner better discriminate differences in content. They point out that most mathematics textbooks rely heavily on blocked sets of practice problems, despite the fact that this may not be as productive as doing mixed sets of problems requiring the application of a variety of different skills, as is common in cumulative reviews.

> ◎ In contrast to *blocked* structures (aaa, bbb, ccc), *interleaved* structures mix tasks together (abc, bca, cab). Interleaving aids learning by helping the learner better discriminate differences in content.

Interleaving is not a difficult strategy to implement in the classroom, as it requires little more than a bit of forethought. Teachers can easily weave different kinds of tasks into a lesson if they plan, for example, to cover three topics over three days, rather than one topic each day. Alternatively, teachers could simply make a daily habit of reviewing selected material from previous lessons. Time on any given topic need not be lost—it just needs to be "spread around" a bit more. Although it may be simple and easy just to cover a section of the textbook each day, there is clear evidence that this is not the best way of delivering instruction. Instead, it's best to intersperse different forms of material and practice within each lesson. Here too, integration of the arts can be an asset. Students can be asked to create artistic products incorporating a variety of ideas that have been considered in conjunction with a given topic. The open-ended and generative nature of artistic activity allows for as many new and creative combinations of content as students can imagine. Thus, the visual and performing arts afford ample opportunity for students to revisit and think about material in an interleaved, as opposed to blocked, kind of way.

> ◎ Although it may be simple and easy just to cover a section of the textbook each day, there is clear evidence that this is not the best way of delivering instruction.

BRAIN-TARGETED TEACHING LEARNING UNITS

As this chapter illustrates, mastery of content, skills, and concepts requires that information be consolidated within long-term memory, and this happens when students actively produce or do something with what they are being taught. Though many educators talk about "active learning," this means little unless one can say what this looks like in practice and can suggest pedagogical methods for engaging students in this kind of learning. As has been shown in this chapter, the arts represent a natural way to get students involved in activities that will lead to long-term retention and promote the kind of engagement that is required for deep conceptual learning (Hardiman, 2010). Next, we will return to Clare and Suzanne's learning units to see how they have integrated the arts into the study of literature and science.

WHAT DOES A BRAIN-TARGETED TEACHING UNIT LOOK LIKE IN THE CLASSROOM?

Learning Unit: Surviving Alone in the Wilderness: A study of the novel *Hatchet* by Gary Paulsen

Grade/Content: Fifth-Grade/Language Arts

Author: Clare O'Malley Grizzard

Overarching Goal of Unit: Students will increase language arts skills of reading for understanding through analysis of character, plot, main idea, and symbolic language.

Brain-Target Four: Teaching for Mastery of Content, Skills, and Concepts

As we moved into Brain-Target Four and planning for instruction, we held onto the three essential questions or big ideas of our study: learning to use the natural environment; listening to your inner voice; and becoming a different kind of observer. Each aspect used multiple arts-based activities, including drawing, mural-making, role-play, and creative writing, which created a level of personal connection and added depth to our novel study.

Learning to Use the Natural Environment

It was important to relate to the physical setting of *Hatchet* to build the empathetic bond between reader and character. Investigating our school's campus environment led to a unique learning experience for the urban students of the fifth grade. With binoculars, sketchbooks, and collection buckets, they journeyed out, as if on an expedition, to discover the environment in a new way. We took nature walks with the mission of collecting natural objects to bring back to our classroom. We used them in creating nature centers and for drawing from observation. We used natural materials to create journal and handmade paper for sketchbook pages. Classroom discussions covered issues on environmentalism, conservation, and tales of survival. The related subjects made for very lively and engaged debate throughout the novel study.

One student shared how he enjoyed these activities: "I really liked going outside during class time. It made it easier for us to think about Brian and what he went through when his plane crashed. We could close our eyes, listen to the birds, feel the cool wind, and pretend we were there with him. When we opened our eyes, we saw the details of our environment in a new way."

Listening to Your Inner Voice

Drama provided many opportunities for evoking the lived-through experience. Using drama techniques seemed at first challenging for our teachers, but never for the students. Whether being prompted to put themselves in the shoes of young Brian the survivor, or to perform vocabulary in frozen tableau, or to act out the reaction of Brian's desperate parents at home, they reacted with enthusiasm and a natural ability to put themselves into new roles and explore their own responses. Beyond skills-based instruction, knowing just a few drama techniques was all we needed; role-play and tableau activities and variations on them gave students the chance to react to much more than just the immediate text at hand.

In addition to supporting traditional activities for reading and writing, our approach to writing took on a very personal voice when it was integrated with the arts. Assignments were approached as reflective statements, whether they were journal entries, diary posts, field notes, or letters to family. Students were introduced to the concept of an Artist's Statement. It reinforced classroom arts vocabulary and methodology and used students' writing to help them more effectively understand their own learning and the process of building of literacy skills. As my coteacher indicated, "The kind of writing that I want to encourage is that in which I hear the student's voice in their writing . . . their own voice."

◎ In addition to supporting traditional activities for reading and writing, our approach to writing took on a very personal voice when it was integrated with the arts.

Becoming a Different Kind of Observer

Developing keen focus and becoming aware of detail are the tools that Brian used to finally find his food source in the novel—a key learning experience. We translated that experience to the students by introducing observational drawing. This is not drawing from memory or from imagination. In this approach to drawing, students are taught to draw only what they observe. Students emerged from the task not only having read about someone who is a keen observer, but also having gained new vision themselves.

Compared with teaching this unit through traditional methods, students were more engaged, assessments demonstrated deeper understanding, and the sense of investigation and discovery made the classroom come alive.

Learning Unit: Genetics and Heredity—Thinking Outside the Punnett Square

Unit designed by: Suzanne P. McNamara

Overarching Goal: Students will apply their understanding of genetics and heredity in discussions centered on current medical and social issues as well as on the appreciation of human diversity.

Brain-Target Four: Teaching for Mastery of Content, Skills, and Concepts

As educators, it is our goal to help students acquire skills and knowledge that can be used meaningfully throughout their lives. Simply exposing students to new information in creative ways is not enough. Students need to be given the opportunity to allow their brains to process, store, and retrieve information. Teachers could be viewed as "brain developers," and all classroom doors could hold signs: "Construction Zone: Brains in Progress." A well-planned and executed lesson does not necessarily translate to student learning.

> ◎ Teachers could be viewed as "brain developers," and all classroom doors could hold signs: "Construction Zone: Brains in Progress."

Just because a child can memorize a chant "2 + 2 = 4," this does not mean that he or she actually understands the concept of addition. The material covered in a high school genetics class can be very conceptual, requiring students to visualize processes that they cannot actually see. Therefore, it can be difficult for some students to truly understand the information and not just memorize it. Teachers must use instructional practices that best target the brain's ability to acquire and store information.

A major concept in a high school genetics class for students to learn is the structure and function of deoxyribonucleic acid (DNA). Students were exposed to this information in a variety of ways so that they had time to reorganize, modify, and consolidate these new memories from the material covered during class. At the beginning of the genetics

unit, students were asked to draw a sketch of a DNA molecule and describe its importance in the study of life. This short activity helped to determine and assess prior knowledge of the material. The students were first shown a BioFlix animation, created by a graphic-design artist, of a three-dimensional DNA molecule. This interpretation walked students through a visual representation of the molecule, specifically noting its structure, function, and location. After students were introduced to this molecule from the animation, they were given the opportunity to work in groups to make a model using candy. Binding together Twizzlers with toothpicks and marshmallows, the students identified the major molecules that make up DNA.

In the lab, students extracted DNA from strawberries. Although they could not see the individual molecules, they were able to distinguish a small sample of wound-up DNA. By following the various steps of this procedure, they were given a "hands-on" inquiry-based approach to figuring out where the DNA is located in the cells. Outside of the classroom, students were given an assignment to create a cartoon about DNA's structure and function. Many students came up with clever ways to remember the various molecules that make up DNA and used other characters to help convey their message. Students were given the opportunity to read and view their classmates' cartoons in a "gallery walk" around the classroom, providing feedback on sticky notes.

As the exploration of the DNA molecule continued, students were placed into small groups and given the task of putting on a play about DNA replication, a major function of the molecule. Not only did this activity help foster creativity, but it also helped to reinforce and consolidate this newly learned information. Finally, as an extension to this instruction, students watched a short video clip, read articles, and participated in a discussion about the Human Genome Project. By providing real-world references to this information, students could make connections between what they learn in their biology class and what they experience in the world around them.

Together, these instructional strategies fostered personal connections with the material, engaged students to keep their attention, assessed their prior knowledge, and provided a variety of ways for students to "rehearse" this new information. All of these influence how well students retain and store information.

Brain-Target Five

*Teaching for the Extension and
Application of Knowledge*

Creativity and Innovation in Education

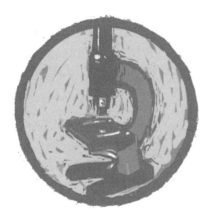

*The principle goal of education in the schools should be creating
men and women who are capable of doing new things, not simply
repeating what other generations have done; men and women who
are creative, inventive and discoverers, who can be critical and
verify, and not accept, everything they are offered.*

—Jean Piaget

W e begin our study of Brain-Target Five with the words of Cory, a
seventh-grade student from an urban school district. He states,
"School is boring for me and I mostly think it's a waste of time. It's usually the same thing all day long, like teachers talking at us and giving

us lots of things to read from our textbooks and handouts, and then finding answers to questions and writing them on workbook sheets. The only time I think I really learn is when I get to do something real. Like last week we did something really cool. We made a survey to find out how people in the neighborhood felt about safety and community services. We then interviewed neighbors in stores and bus stops. We took all the answers and created charts and graphs. Then we wrote letters to city officials to explain improvements that could make the neighborhood better. I learned a lot and I wish school was always this much fun."

Cory's frequent disinterest in school is common for many students in our schools today. Challenged by issues such as class size, lack of resources, classroom management, a dense array of topics to cover, administrative paperwork, test preparation requirements, and lack of time for collaborative and innovative lesson planning, teachers are forced to rely on teaching methods that not only fail to motivate students to learn but also make little attempt to promote creative thinking. With a steady diet of this kind of instruction, Cory may be poised to be one of the 6,000 students who drop of high school every day and one of the 1.2 million who drop out every year across our nation's schools (Zhao, 2009).

Luckily, although the many challenges teachers face seem insurmountable, teaching children to be creative thinkers is not. Brain-Targeted Teaching (BTT) offers a framework for establishing creative strategies for all children. Recall that in the last chapter, we focused on teaching selected learning objectives to mastery—a notion that assumes that students retain information in long-term memory. Our *expert teachers* demonstrated how to design arts-integrated activities to give students multiple, yet novel and creative ways to enhance retention of content. In most traditional teaching methods, when students have mastered the lesson objectives, teachers typically test students using an end-of-unit assessment and then move on to the next book chapter or unit of study. In the BTT Model, however, once students have acquired knowledge, an important next step must occur to foster deep understanding and true learning.

Brain-Target Five, the stage of the model described in the current chapter, focuses on this next step: expanding instruction so that students are given the opportunity to think creatively by applying skills and content in meaningful, active, real-world problem-solving tasks. As Cory describes above, this type of instruction allows students to see how instructional goals relate to their own lives in real-world problem-solving; this connection helps make the learning experience more meaningful and fun. The research presented in this chapter explores how creative thinking takes shape in the mind and brain and how it might be different from conventional thinking. In addition, the discussion considers how theoretical notions and empirical findings from the brain sciences can inform the design of instructional practices in order to promote creative thinking in the classroom.

TWENTY-FIRST CENTURY SKILLS

The aims of Brain-Target Five are closely aligned with the goals of the 21st-century skills movement. As Daniel Pink (2006) argues, skills requiring sequential, literal, textual, and analytic modes of thinking are necessary for students but are not sufficient. Rather, for students to receive instruction consistent with the goals of the 21st-century skills movement, they must be given ample opportunities to be inventive and to apply knowledge in ways that contribute to developing and fostering the creative mind. Moreover, the ability to think critically and the capacity to solve problems creatively are vital skills extending far beyond the classroom in that they have driven great discoveries and important changes in industry, health care, technology, environmental practices, and public policy.

> ◎ For students to receive instruction consistent with the goals of the 21st-century skills movement, they must be given ample opportunities to be inventive and to apply knowledge in ways that contribute to developing and fostering the creative mind.

Unfortunately, as described above, teachers are faced with a number of factors that prevent them from being able to provide students with enough (or any) opportunities to develop such skills. With some exceptions, teaching that promotes creative thinking as the foundation of instruction is often hit or miss and is rarely institutionalized in curricular or instructional practices in school systems (Rotherham & Willingham, 2009). Along these lines, Rotherham and Willingham (2009) warn that "we cannot afford a system in which receiving a high quality education is akin to a game of bingo" (p. 16). So, as this chapter unfolds, we consider ways that all students at any age can receive rigorous and meaningful instruction to engage the creative mind and foster the thinking skills advocated by both Brain-Target Five and the 21st-century skills movement.

From the Expert Professor

BTT Meets Higher Education

I recently attended a conference on undergraduate biology education and found that some of the most successful professors are using techniques that fit in well with Brain-Targeted Teaching Model. One award-winning instructor stressed activity and movement. She devised a game to help teach her students the nitrogen cycle. Her students enjoyed it and showed a dramatic increase in meeting higher-level learning outcomes.

I have been teaching university-level bioinformatics and molecular biology for quite some time and I am realizing that some of my more successful teaching techniques are grounded in the tenets of Brain-Targeted Teaching. I have used a belt and telephone wire to explain higher-order supercoiling of DNA, and how specific enzymes relieve that supercoiling. The visuals and the students' use of those manipulatives really help them to conceptualize the problem. Moving forward in that course, my students have been able to recognize supercoiling as a crucial issue when they studied DNA replication, gene expression, and cell division.

After many stimulating discussions with peer instructors who are really pushing to improve science education, I can really see how I can apply the Brain-Targeted Teaching Model even more extensively. After attending the workshop on BTT, I was inspired to replace the standard cookbook laboratory exercises with lab projects where the students are given materials and a goal to design the experiments themselves. It occurred to me that while lab exercises are hands-on activities, students are really just following a recipe. If they design the experiments, they are developing creativity and understanding the process on a higher level, much like the chef who knows how to improvise.

I am finding that it works in the computer lab. I teach a hands-on bioinformatics course, where students use computers to analyze DNA and protein sequences. I have always found that the best way to learn bioinformatics is to do it and students have usually appreciated the grueling exercises that I design for them. I am finding that a slight redesign of some of those structured activities to allow for students to "help write the recipe" seems to improve conceptual understanding of some difficult issues. I really see students who now seem more willing to engage other students in discussing the problems and how to approach them and their thinking definitely becomes more creative.

Bob Lessick, PhD
Undergraduate and Graduate Bioinformatics

Creativity and Innovation in the Classroom

Brain-Target Five endorses the extension and application of knowledge through the promotion of creativity and innovative thinking (see also Hardiman, 2010). Fostering creativity and similar skills presupposes that creativity is in fact an unfixed and impressionable quality; fortunately, many educators and scientists as well as a growing body of research support this assumption (e.g., Bruner, 1965; Bull, Montgomery & Baloche, 1995; Cropley, 2001; DeHaan, 2009; Dugosh, Paulus, Roland, & Yang, 2000). For example, Dugosh and colleagues (2000) found that an individual's ability to brainstorm ideas was positively affected by exposure to other ideas, consistent with the argument that creativity processing can be influenced. Other findings demonstrate that individuals asked to find solutions to a problem can think of more ideas and more creative ideas when they consider the implications of the ideas as well as a plan for how to implement the idea (Byrne, Shipman, & Mumford, 2010).

Despite the evidence, a common misconception in our culture is that creativity, innovative thinking, and problem-solving skills are traits bestowed only upon gifted individuals who demonstrate great intelligence or unusual talents. What is more, instructional practices and even educational systems more broadly are constrained by this notion. A striking example of how this misconception takes shape is the sharp differences one often finds in classes for gifted students compared to remedial classes. That is, most curricula and instruction provided in any "Gifted and Talented" program across the country include activities that tap into creative problem-solving such as complex science projects or interdisciplinary research assignments. These creativity-promoting activities may be rare in more conventional classrooms, especially in instructional programs offered for students with learning differences or those designed to prepare students for standardized testing. In these more conventional classrooms, students are instead often offered a limited menu of instructional strategies designed to promote skills and content necessary to succeed on tests.

> ◎ A common misconception in our culture is that creativity, innovative thinking, and problem-solving skills are traits bestowed only upon gifted individuals who demonstrate great intelligence or unusual talents.

Such instruction relies on *convergent thinking,* which encourages students to find the single, right solution to a problem. Most educators would agree that convergent-thinking tasks dominate educational practice and are the hallmark of accountability measures (Runco, 2004). In contrast, an activity that promotes *divergent thinking* leads students to generate multiple and varied solutions and approaches to finding solutions thereby enhancing creative problem-solving. The kind of teaching endorsed in Brain-Target Five (and in the BTT Model in general) supports both convergent and divergent thinking for students of all ability levels.

> ◎ An activity that promotes *divergent thinking* leads students to generate multiple and varied solutions and approaches to finding solutions thereby enhancing creative problem-solving.

Before delving into theoretical frameworks and research involving creativity, it is important to make clear in what way—if any—creativity is related to intelligence. A high level of creativity capacity likely requires a strong knowledge base in a given area. This store of knowledge, often referred to as adaptive expertise, goes beyond a mere list of facts and incorporates the ability to process and understand patterns of information and to be able to flexibly apply the information in novel situations (e.g., Hatano & Ouro, 2003; Schwartz, Bransford, & Sears, 2005). Crawford and Brophy (2006) describe adaptive expertise as engaging "reasoning and problem-solving processes that enable experts to continue to learn and adapt to new situations" (p. 4). Although it is possible (and even likely) that one's level of adaptive expertise is related in some way to one's level of *intelligence*, many if not most educators and scientists agree that *creativity* encompasses more than just intelligence (e.g., MacKinnon, 1966) and that creativity and intelligence are separate entities (e.g., Runco, 2004). For example, work by Runco and Albert (1986) demonstrated that some creativity measures require only a minimum level of intelligence for creative performance. Also, in a study using structural equation modeling, Plucker (1999) examined the relationship between adult creative achievement and scores on divergent thinking tasks and intelligence tests. Although scores for both types of tests contributed to the creative achievement, the divergent thinking test score contributed three times that of the intelligence test score. These findings among others have helped switch the focus of research on creativity from separating creativity and intelligence to understanding "the correlates, benefits, and conditions of creativity" (Runco, 2004, p. 679). Moreover, the evidence supports the idea that fostering creativity should not be associated solely with gifted education, and, because creativity is not essentially innate, it can and should be taught in our schools. As we shall see in the next section, engagement in creative activities can lead to measurable changes in brain volume, structure and function as well as increased performance on cognitive tests (Andreasen, 2005).

◎ Creativity and intelligence are separate entities. Creativity is not essentially innate, it can and should be taught in our schools.

From the Expert Teacher

Collections of Your Science Teacher

One of the most challenging yet rewarding parts of my Brain-Targeted Teaching units are activities that require students to use their knowledge meaningfully. I try to promote divergent thinking, which is often jarring for the students. They are so

(Continued)

accustomed to getting the "right answer" that they would be frustrated at first by the fact that the process of generating ideas, not finding a single solution, was the point of the lesson.

My first unit of the year requires students to discern between factual and inferential knowledge and to make observations and draw conclusions. I designed a lesson that required them to write a creative paragraph about me based on arti-facts from my life that I displayed around the classroom. They observed items such as pictures, old toys, school yearbooks, collections, CDs, movies, and articles of clothing and accessories. Their assignment was to write a piece that would be used in a real context, such as a biosketch that appears in a journal, a Facebook profile, or an obituary (yes, some of the students share my sense of humor).

This activity brought the lesson to life and also tapped into Brain-Target One, as the students became more connected to me as both their teacher and as a "real person" with some of the same interests they have. In reading their creative writing assignments, I was struck by how insightful the students were as they combined ideas from observing the objects to create a personal story of my life. Some students created a fictional representation and others stayed with facts. Some of them included sketches and cartoons. One of the most important outcomes of this activity was that most students applied that kind of thinking in other, more traditional assignments. They began to combine sometimes disparate content topics in our science unit to think about creative questions and solutions to the scientific principles they were learning. This was a simple task, yet it dem-onstrated to students the importance of careful observations, that their conclu-sions must be supported by data, and that multiple conclusions can be reached from observations.

I have found that students remember this type of creative activity at the end of the school year and beyond. I am always amazed when former students come back to my classroom to discuss some of the activities that required them to apply the material. They have stronger memories of the content than if I had just had them read the text and answer questions in the end of chapter review.

Georgia Woerner
Teacher, Middle School Science

What Do the Brain Sciences Tell Us About Higher-Order Thinking and Creativity?

As applying information in novel, original and useful ways relies on cre-ative thinking, here we consider whether the ability to think creatively can be reflected in neural processes and whether training or teaching through certain methods leads to observable changes in neural activi-ty. The brain regions involved in creative thinking—and in particular divergent thinking—largely include the prefrontal regions of the cerebral cortex (see Dietrich & Kanso, 2010, for a review) that are often associated with higher-order cognitive or executive function processes. Those processes are characterized by the ability to use working memory to plan and organize activities and to engage in problem-solving and abstract thinking (Denckla, 1996).

> ◎ The brain regions involved in creative thinking—and in particular divergent thinking—largely include the prefrontal regions of the cerebral cortex.

Extensive research on brain plasticity during the past two decades demonstrates that significant changes occur in the brain as the result of repeated sensory experience (see Fu & Zuo, 2011, for a review). For example, studies have shown that the brain strengthens existing networks when an individual is involved in multiple exposures to sensory stimuli (Karmarkar & Dan, 2006). Another well-documented example of brain plasticity is demonstrated in a study of London taxicab drivers. Chosen as subjects for the study because of extensive training on navigational skills and the need to remember numerous street locations, Maguire and colleagues (2000) found that taxi drivers showed a significant increase in the size of the hippocampus, a brain structure associated with memory, relative to a control group, and that within the taxi driver group the volume of the hippocampus was correlated with the number of years of experience the individual had in driving the taxi. These findings suggest that the daily activities requiring one to recall thousands of locations resulted in increased brain volume in this specific brain region.

Changes in brain structure have also been found in individuals who take part in activities, such as a playing musical instrument, that require creative thinking. That is, a growing body of research shows differences in brain volume and structure in musicians who spent years training and performing relative to nonmusicians (e.g., Schlaug, Jäncke, Huang, Staiger, & Steinmetz, 1995). Hyde and colleagues (2009) took this research one step further and sought to determine if those with musical training had anatomical changes as a result of this training or if they had been attracted to studying music because they already possessed pre-existing brain structures that would make them more likely to continue to practice music. The researchers examined the effect of musical training in 6-year-olds with no prior musical training. One group of children, the "instrumental" group, received an average of 15 months of instrumental musical training in the form of weekly keyboarding lessons and the remainder of the children, the "control" group, received 15 months of weekly group music class in which they sang and played with drums and bells. The results demonstrated that compared with the control group, the instrumental group exhibited increased brain size in multiple areas of the brain, including the frontal lobe that controls higher-order thinking. The children in the instrumental group also showed increased motor control skills and auditory process-ing. These findings suggest that teaching children creative tasks results in changes not only in cognitive functions but also in brain structure.

> ◎ Teaching children creative tasks results in changes not only in cognitive functions but also in brain structure.

In addition to considering how training or experience changes the brain, research has explored the differences in various modes of thought—for example creative thinking versus more conventional think-ing. In terms of cognitive processing, highly creative thinking is often differentiated from more conventional thought because it relies in part on divergent thinking, which, given the same input or content, generates multiple acceptable solutions. Harvard Professor David Perkins (2001) asserts that creativity is the break-through or out-of-the box kind of thinking that involves patterns of thought different from ordinary problem-solving. And a growing body of research is demonstrating that our brains appear to work differently when we are engaged in tasks that require this kind of thinking. For instance, Fink and colleagues (2007) used the electroencephalogram (EEG) to record brain activity during tasks that required subjects to generate responses regarded as highly creative, as measured by fluency (i.e., number of ideas) and originality of ideas. They found a stronger increase in EEG activity when subjects displayed more original ideas compared to less original ones, suggesting that creative thinking can be reflected in patterns of brain activation. In another study, Chávez-Eakle and colleagues (2007) examined cognitive patterns as well as neural activity of individuals regarded as highly creative relative to control subjects. Using the Torrance Tests of Creative Thinking (TTCT), a well-known test of creative performance, the researchers assessed sub-jects' ability to produce multiple, original, and flexible ideas. As subjects completed test items, the researchers measured differences in brain cere-bral blood flow in both the individuals who had been identified as highly creative and in average control subjects. Subjects who scored in the highly creative range on the TTCT showed significantly greater activity in brain areas thought to be involved in emotion, working memory, and novelty response.

> ◎ In terms of cognitive processing, highly creative thinking is often differentiated from more conventional thought because it relies in part on divergent thinking.

Bowden and Jung-Beeman (2007) propose that because the left and right hemispheres are associated to some extent with different cognitive processes, creative thinking can be measured by studying hemispheric differences during the production of a particular kind of creative thought. Using both EEG and functional magnetic resonance imaging (fMRI) technology, Bowden and Jung-Beeman studied the neural components of insight, which they define as a deep and sudden understanding of a complex situation and which is often described as the "AHA!" moment. Moments of insight are associated with breaking free of conventional assumptions and common associations between pieces of information in order to discover novel solutions to problems. The results of Bowden and Jung-Beeman's study revealed greater right hemispheric activation when subjects report solving problems through insight. The authors suggest that findings like these that tell us about when and how the brain engages in problem-solving might "improve methods of education by allowing teachers to design lessons so that students are more likely to have insights" (p. 98).

> ◎ Moments of insight are associated with breaking free of conventional assumptions and common associations between pieces of information in order to discover novel solutions to problems.

Johns Hopkins University researcher Charles Limb has also contributed to our understanding of differentiated neural processing during a creative act (Limb & Braun, 2008). Using fMRI, Limb and Allen Braun, his colleague at the National Institutes of Health, observed brain activity of professional jazz pianists during the spontaneous playing of improvisational jazz. They compared this spontaneous playing condition with one in which the musicians played a previously memorized jazz score. The results indicated significant differences in brain activity between the two conditions. During improvisation, functional brain scans indicated a widespread deactivation of the dorsolateral prefrontal cortex, typically associated with self-regulation, self-monitoring, focused attention, and inhibition. Turning off this brain area may be associated with a type of "defocused, free-floating attention that permits spontaneous unplanned associations, and sudden insights or realizations" (p. e1679). The researchers also found increased activity in the medial prefrontal cortex, a brain region that has been linked with actions of self-expression and individuality.

Studies such as Limb and Braun's explore brain processes underlying creativity by considering the particular case of improvisation. The relationship between improvisation and creativity has also been noted by others including Keith Sawyer (2006), who makes a strong case for the use of improvisation to promote innovation and creative problem-solving. While studying both jazz and theater groups, Sawyer observed that the collaborative and improvisational nature of group work inspires the successful production of novel products. With regard to the field of education, Sawyer (2006) argues that our economy is becoming one built on innovation and the creation of knowledge, and, if students are to be successful in the future, education needs to follow the practice of other industries. That is, as innovation or creative problem-solving occurs in collaborative settings such as improvisational conversation or musical performance, instructional methods in our schools need to provide students with opportunities to participate in such collaborative activities with their teacher and peers.

> ◎ Our economy is becoming one built on innovation and the creation of knowledge, and, if students are to be successful in the future, education needs to follow the practice of other industries.

It is important to note that working in groups does not always lead to more and better ideas compared with when people work as individuals (see Mullen, Johnson, & Salas, 1991, for a review). Brophy (2006) found that groups brainstormed more solutions and more original solutions for multi-part tasks and individuals were more successful for single-part tasks. These results highlight the need for recognizing the type of problem before a teacher asks students to work in groups.

CONTENT VERSUS PROCESS IN THE 21ST-CENTURY SKILLS MOVEMENT

Most scientists agree that creative thinking does not occur without having first mastered a body of content knowledge (e.g., Csikszentmihalyi, 1996; Heilman, Nadeau, & Beversdorf, 2003); this notion is consistent with the idea of adaptive expertise discussed earlier in the chapter. As Ulrich Kraft (2007) states, "Fresh solutions result from disassembling and reassembling the building blocks in an infinite number of ways. That means the problem solver must thoroughly understand the blocks" (p.17). In other words, after having mastered a domain of knowledge, individuals are able to find solutions to novel problems by associating pieces of learned information in different ways. Such creative problem-solving raises acquired knowledge to a level far beyond basic mastery.

> ◎ After having mastered a domain of knowledge, individuals are able to find solutions to novel problems by associating pieces of learned information in different ways.

Currently educators and education policymakers debate whether curricula should focus on facts and content or on teaching critical thinking skills. But, given the perspectives described above, this dichotomy oversimplifies the teaching and learning process because teachers must address *both* parts. Along these lines, Rotherham and Willingham (2009) argue that knowledge and thinking skills should be interwoven within the school curriculum in all content areas. Without a strong body of content and skills, students will not have knowledge to apply creatively in real-world situations, and without creative-thinking skills, students will not be able to take learned concepts to new, untaught levels. Moreover, students need to have content knowledge and thinking skills applicable in multiple subject areas so that students can generate solutions to problems spanning disciplines.

◎ Without a strong body of content and skills, students will not have knowledge to apply creatively in real-world situations.

One of the sharpest debates regarding teaching content versus process is in the area of mathematics. Although most state accountability tests focus on mathematics content that can be measured on multiple-choice tests, many advocacy groups hold that students must not only master math skills but must also be able to apply that knowledge in real-world contexts. For example, a new publication from the National Council of Teachers of Mathematics (NCTM), *Focus in High School Mathematics: Reasoning and Sense Making,* provides teachers with a framework to design activities that lead students to the deep application of mathematics skills (www.nctm.org). As the U.S. Department of Education seeks to create national standards in reading and mathematics, it must consider the point made by Yong Zhao (2009) that to remain competitive in a global economy, our students will need to display global competence, which includes not only knowledge but also the ability to integrate information across disciplinary domains through creative and innovative problem-solving.

From the Expert Teachers

From the Ancient World to Your World

In teaching the sixth-grade course in Ancient Civilizations, it is challenging to see how the content can be connected to the students' own lives in tasks that apply learning to real-world contexts. One of the learning goals for this course is to have students see how geographical features in the environment led to various aspects of the culture of a civilization. After students learned some of the major features of geography and studied aspects of early civilizations of Mesopotamia, they then worked in groups to apply this knowledge to create their own version of a primitive culture. For their imaginary "tribe," students built shelters, determined food supply, and crafted religious beliefs, and relevant artifacts.

This lesson gives them a better understanding of the content than they could get merely through reading the textbook chapter. The students had fun imagining how a culture would develop considering features such as terrain, water supply,

(Continued)

and weather. They enjoyed working in groups and learned processes of building consensus within the group and assuming various roles and responsibilities in the group task.

This activity also led them to a deeper connection to their own cultural experiences. In the final activity that connected to real-world application, students examined how the geography of our city has shaped their neighborhoods, family traditions, and lives. For example, a student who lives near the inner harbor area of Baltimore was fascinated with how that community grew from a need for workers in the shipbuilding industry. He traced the immigrant groups who moved into the area because of availability of jobs in building and sailing merchant ships. He learned why the housing is so varied in his neighborhood, from large three-story homes of wealthy merchants who settled in the area to oversee building projects to small "pint-sized" homes to accommodate the transient sailors. This activity helped students understand why they were studying the influence of geography in the development of all cultures from ancient civilizations to modern day.

Dan Hellerback and Alexandra Fleming
Teachers, Middle School Social Studies

What Does This Mean for Teachers?

In most classrooms today, instruction is focused squarely on convergent thinking and at least some scientists believe this kind of instruction is squeezing the creativity out of children. Kraft (2007), for example, argues that as we reinforce neural pathways through continuous repetition of the same type of convergent thinking activities, we may be diminishing the pathways that promote the creative mind. In order to develop the creative mind, as creativity expert Sir Ken Robinson (2001) asserts, creativity can and should be explicitly taught in our schools. The hope is that incorporating particular explicit instruction into the classroom can create new modes of thinking that children will implicitly employ not only in school but also in life.

Promoting creative thinking and more generally teaching for 21st-century skills will require teachers not only to impart content but also to provide students with frequent opportunities to engage in activities that make possible and encourage divergent thinking, thus allowing for new and distinct free-flowing thoughts. Educators are likely in the habit of probing students for a solution to a problem; the challenge for educators, then, is to change the potential overreliance on seeking the one "right answer" to questions in class, on worksheets, and on curriculum assessments. Although this may come naturally for some teachers, others will feel uneasy moving

◎ Promoting creative thinking and more generally teaching for 21st-century skills will require teachers not only to impart content but also to provide students with frequent opportunities to engage in activities that make possible and encourage divergent thinking, thus allowing for new and distinct free-flowing thoughts.

away from the primary use of conventional teaching methods. And teachers' practices as well as their attitudes toward their practices are critical: Teachers' theories and concepts of how students should perform in class have been shown to either dampen or enhance creativity in the classroom (Beghetto, 2006) and few teachers feel that they are fully trained to design creative teaching activities (Kampylis, Berki, & Saariluoma, 2009).

Overhauling traditional instructional methods is made more difficult because of what the students have come to know and expect. That is, from the time students enter school, they are rewarded for thinking logically and for providing the right answers on a multitude of standardized tests, from accountability assessments to college entry examinations. As a result, teachers not only have to adjust their practices but also have to teach students how to learn in new ways as they will ultimately face a world in which more than a single solution exists.

As we reflect on Cory's story at the beginning of this chapter, there is no question that our students deserve better than most receive in our classrooms today. Public policy, teacher training, and school practices must support teachers in designing and implementing instruction that fosters creative and engaging learning. And teacher preparation programs should explicitly show teachers how to facilitate creative behavior in their students.

From the Expert Teacher

Using Technology for a Virtual Trip to Madrid

Whenever I ask my high school Spanish students what they want to accomplish by taking the course, the inevitable answer is to be able to communicate with Spanish speakers in real-life situations. Students want to use language during foreign travel experiences, during encounters with native speakers of Spanish in our own country, and for future careers as members of the global environment.

When parents come to meet the teacher at the start of a school year, I ask how many of them had studied a second language in high school. All hands are raised. Yet, when I ask how many are proficient communicators in that language, there is almost never a raised hand. I want to make sure that my students never respond in that way.

(Continued)

Although pure language acquisition certainly occurs in childhood, neurolinguistic studies indicate that even adult learners can progress from second language learning to a proficient degree of language acquisition. The key is to teach for the purpose of communication for which language was designed. The Brain-Targeted Teaching Model provides me with a concrete, educational framework based on neuroscience to design units and lessons that foster communicative proficiency compatible with the brain's natural learning systems.

One example of a communicative, task-based lesson that I have used to encourage creativity and purposeful use of the target language is a virtual trip on Google Earth. Through technology, improvisation, and imagination, my students find themselves transported to the streets of Madrid. Their performance goal is to demonstrate the ability to navigate the city, in order to reach The Prado Museum on foot. Culture is infused into the lesson, as a virtual tour of the masterpieces awaits the students when they are all able to reach El Museo del Prado. The students move beyond the input and content of Brain-Target Four by engaging in conversations to ask and tell distances, request and follow directions, and describe the location of places in relation to other places. Lessons planned with Brain-Target Five in mind, foster the opportunity for creative and purposeful use of the target language. The faces of my students when they reach the museum let me know that they feel accomplished. They have communicated to get to their destination, without realizing that they learned prepositions of place, vocabulary, and the imperative mood.

Elayne Melanson
Teacher, High School Spanish

Brain-Target Five Activities

As explained in the previous chapter, on Brain-Target Four, acquiring a body of knowledge and demonstrating mastery in traditional and nontraditional ways are important components of education. A teacher focuses on teaching content and skills to mastery through multiple exposures to key content, and the arts become a particularly useful vehicle for providing engaging learning activities to achieve that mastery. Here in Brain-Target Five, teachers encourage students to extend learning and move beyond the content through activities that require creative and critical thinking.

The following are examples of the types of activities associated with Brain-Target Five:

- Conducting investigations and surveys

- Engaging in problem-based learning by designing a task that requires thinking across disciplines

- Generating multiple solutions to a problem

- Designing experiments to test hypotheses in project-based learning models

- Analyzing perspective of historical figures or literary characters

- Building projects that tap into multiple domains of artistic tasks

- Asking novel questions that have multiple responses

- Connecting unusual elements of a question to produce an innovative answer

- Creating metaphors and analogies to explain a concept

- Discussing open-ended questions to probe for assumptions, clarifications, and consequences

- Allowing regular time for reflection of students' own learning goals

- Restating a problem in multiple ways

- Diagramming a solution in visual representations

- Creating stories and narratives to explain concepts

- Collaborating in group learning activities within the classroom and within the broader learning environment

Brain-Target Five Summary

As our expert teachers explained and our two sample units included below demonstrate, high quality classroom instruction requires students to be innovative and creative thinkers. Research from the brain sciences demonstrates that this kind of thinking engages neural processes that are distinct from those that support other sorts of thinking; studies in plasticity tell us that repeated experiences sculpt the brain. Thus, developing students' cognitive and academic skills and preparing them for work and life in the 21st-century demands that classroom instruction include activities that encourage and support creative and innovative thinking, which are just the types of activities that Brain-Target Five promotes.

We now return to Clare's description of *Surviving Alone in the Wilderness* and Suzanne's unit *Thinking Outside the Punnett Square* to find out how they encourage their students to apply their learning creatively.

WHAT DOES A BRAIN-TARGETED TEACHING UNIT LOOK LIKE IN THE CLASSROOM?

Learning Unit: Surviving Alone in the Wilderness: A study of the novel *Hatchet* by Gary Paulsen

Grade/Content: Fifth-Grade/Language Arts

Author: Clare O'Malley Grizzard

Overarching Goal of Unit: Students will increase language arts skills of reading for understanding through analysis of character, plot, main idea, and symbolic language.

Brain-Target Five: Teaching for the Extension and Application of Knowledge:

In Brain-Target Four, we saw a nontraditional journey through the novel *Hatchet.* The students' understanding of the story's plot, characters, and themes were enhanced through various art experiences. Students engaged in role-playing, explored drawing from observation, and used sensory, descriptive words from the story to create a tone poem. Other activities included investigating nature through walks during different times of the day to observe the changes of sounds and light in the environment.

Our next goal was to deepen students' engagement with the novel through Brain-Target Five activities that would encourage creative thinking and application of the learning unit themes. Students were charged with designing an original product structured on the three main story themes: *Learning how to use the natural environment, listening to one's inner voice,* and *becoming a different kind of observer.* The product was to be a guidebook of survival tips. Students were told that they were to imagine they had survived a similar experience as the main character and were to leave behind a "how-to" guide for the next person who might be in the same circumstance—stranded in an unfamiliar space.

We led the students through guided visualization of being stranded in the wilderness. Students were then given the option of choosing the Canadian wilderness, which is the setting of the book, or creating their own space to display survival skills and develop a guidebook.

One student, for example, chose his inner city neighborhood as the subject of the survival guidebook. He explored the theme of *becoming a different kind of observer* by looking through the lens of a camera for the first time and creating a photo essay of his neighborhood. He used his "real-world" environment by interviewing neighbors to learn about what resources existed in the community and how those changed over time. He learned where the daycare centers were in the neighborhood, found a church-based youth group, and met the city employees such as sanitation workers, firefighters, and police who tended to the community. He created for his city block a "survival booklet" that included available services and contact information for those who could help in an emergency.

In the guidebook's reflective writing, he addressed the theme *listening to one's inner voice* by answering questions such as: How can I feel safer at home? Who can I turn to in an emergency? What will make me feel stronger when I experience peer pressure from older boys in the neighborhood?

Teaching the novel in this way became an emotionally rich experience for the children. The active participation with the characters was much

deeper for them than when it was taught through traditional methods such as choral reading, vocabulary development, and essay writing. They demonstrated heightened attention during all of the tasks throughout the learning unit. Moreover, the children's retention of the details of the novel was impressive. Their writing became alive with description and feeling in a way we had not seen before. Students clearly enjoyed the learning experience—they simply rediscovered the pure joy of reading.

Learning Unit: Genetics and Heredity—Thinking Outside the Punnett Square

Grade/Content: 10th-Grade/Biology

Author: Suzanne P. McNamara

Overarching Goal of Unit: Students will apply their understanding of genetics and heredity in discussions centered on current medical and social issues as well as an appreciation for human diversity.

Brain-Target Five: Teaching for the Extension and Application of Knowledge:

Project Description: Students will prepare a medical history chart including proper diagnosis, a treatment plan, and prognosis of various human genetic disorders. They will use information that they have gathered from their research to diagnosis their "patient" and present their medical opinion to their classmates.

Genetics is one of my favorite units to explore with high school students. Engaged in the content, students often ask many questions concerning their genetic makeup. They want to know, for example, why they look more like one parent, why broad shoulders "run in the family," or why their biological sister has green eyes when the rest of their family has shades of brown. These relevant and higher order thinking questions are often suppressed, however, by vocabulary-dense lessons about pea plants, monohybrid crosses, and Punnett squares. Students quickly realize that their genetic family tree is far too complex to discuss in class, and the majority of their time will be spent studying monogenetic traits like peapod shape and color.

When teaching for 21st-century skills, students need to be given opportunities to think critically and apply these fundamental concepts of genetics to the world around them. Throughout this unit, students were challenged to hypothesize the answers to their complex questions by generating ideas concerning the role that DNA plays in their uniqueness. Challenged by applying genetic concepts to their own lives, students were required to make sense of this content. Working in teams, students were asked to assume the role of doctors assigned to a genetic disorder patient case. In order to solve the case, students needed to work together to properly diagnosis their assigned patient with an appropriate genetic disorder and provide an adequate treatment plan including an accurate prognosis. Students were provided with the basic medical history of their patient and were given resources rich in research about human genetic disorders.

At first, putting together the pieces of the puzzle was challenging for students. They would have felt much more comfortable if assigned a certain genetic disorder to research and present. Not only did this activity challenge them to solve a problem, but it also required them to work together and think critically about the impact that DNA can play on gene expression. In teams, students collaborated to share their research and ideas with each other in order to solve the medical case of their patient.

I launched this activity with a video segment from the NOVA program titled "Cracking the Code of Life." Students watched parents Allison and Tim Lord interact with their oldest son, Hayden, who was diagnosed with the genetic disorder Tay-Sachs, an incurable degenerative brain disease. My students were shocked to learn that this one-letter mutation in Hayden's genome could result in creating a protein that is unable to dissolve fat in his brain. The video unfolds relevant genetic information that parallels other recessive traits discussed previously in class, which made the content more meaningful and allowed students to develop a personal connection with the content through Hayden. They could see, firsthand, the impact that a genetic mutation could have on a person. Students were then instructed to use Hayden's medical case as a model for their own patient.

Their task was to use the provided basic medical history of their patient to make an accurate diagnosis, develop a treatment plan, determine a prognosis, and present their medical opinion to their peers. Wearing white lab coats, teams prepared a presentation highlighting relevant information about their patient and the diagnosed genetic disorder. This project gave students an opportunity to engage in activities that promoted creativity, innovation, critical thinking, and problem-solving. In addition, students gained a deeper appreciation of human diversity and continued to ask challenging genetics questions.

This problem-based activity encouraged students to use their knowledge and skills learned from this unit and apply them in a real-world creative thinking exercise. After all, this is what medical professionals do every day!

Brain-Target Six

Evaluating Learning

Creativity becomes more visible when adults try to be more attentive to the cognitive processes of children than to the results they achieve in various fields of doing and understanding.

—Loris Malaguzzi, Founder of the Reggio Emilia Approach

Brain-Target Six, which focuses on evaluating student learning, is the final element of the Brain-Targeted Teaching (BTT) Model. However, it is important to keep in mind that all six Brain-Targets apply to all stages of the teaching and learning process and that evaluation does not occur only at the completion of a unit. Rather, evaluation in various forms should be happening during every phase of the teaching and learning process in order to provide guideposts for both teachers and students to help assess progress and continually improve instruction. In addition to offering formative feedback for documenting the attainment of learning goals, the impact of assessment on memory is equally important to Brain-Target Six. In this chapter, we consider research that demonstrates how feedback can be a powerful tool for enhancing learning and memory. We then look at how traditional types of assessment such as tests, quizzes, mid-chapter reviews, and benchmark assessments can be supplemented or supplanted by alternatives such as arts-integrated activities, portfolio assessments, and performance assessments. Ideal evaluation reaps benefits for retention and understanding while also engaging students in critical and creative thinking.

◎ Evaluation in various forms should be happening during every phase of the teaching and learning process.

RESEARCH TO PRACTICE

EVALUATION TO ENHANCE LEARNING

In recent years, a relatively large body of research from education, psychology, and cognitive science has shown that tests and other assessments do much more than simply tell the teacher how much learning has occurred. Assessments provide feedback that informs and motivates students while enhancing their memory for material in specific ways. First, assessments provide students with useful feedback that increases learning (e.g., Pashler, Cepeda, Wixted, & Rohrer, 2005). Second, assessments cause students to retrieve information actively, which by itself has been shown to improve retention (e.g., Karpicke & Roediger, 2008). Third, intentionally "spacing" multiple assessments of the same material over specified time intervals can prompt students to engage in patterns of study and active retrieval that further increase retention (e.g., Kornell, Castel, Eich, & Bjork, 2010).

◎ Assessments provide feedback that informs and motivates students while enhancing their memory for material in specific ways.

Frequent and Timely Feedback

In a meta-analysis of educational research reviewing the most effective strategies for improving student achievement, Marzano, Pickering, and Pollock (2001) identified timely corrective feedback as one of the best ways to improve student achievement. Specifically, their analysis found that simply giving feedback about whether an answer was right or wrong had a negative effect, whereas providing the correct answer following incorrect responses had a positive effect. The effects of corrective feedback appear to be strongest when teachers explain why responses are accurate or inaccurate and/or ask students to continue working on tasks until they have attained success.

> ◎ Effects of corrective feedback appear to be strongest when teachers explain why responses are accurate or inaccurate and/or ask students to continue working on tasks until they have attained success.

Consistent with the findings of the meta-analysis cited above, Pashler and colleagues (2005) found in a study of memory for native/foreign language word pairs that giving participants only right/wrong feedback produced the same results on subsequent tests as giving no feedback at all. In contrast, participants who were provided the correct response after they had produced an incorrect answer exhibited the greatest improvement on the final free-recall assessment—retention of the material increased by 494%. Fazio, Huesler, Johnson, and Marsh (2010) also found that when responses are incorrect, giving only right/wrong feedback conveys little helpful information to the learner. They did find, however, that right/wrong feedback enhanced memory for *correct* responses if participants had low levels of confidence in those responses. Fazio et al. (2010) argue that if participants thought their answer would probably be incorrect, the surprise of learning that it actually was correct caused them to pay more attention to their response, leading to better retention of the material. Further, Finn and Metcalfe (2010) have shown that feedback can be effectively "scaffolded" by providing hints incrementally rather than just giving students the correct answer. This way, students receive helpful feedback but arrive at the correct responses themselves. In the study by Finn and Metcalfe, scaffolded feedback produced better long-term retention than did other types of feedback (traditional corrective feedback, minimal feedback, or answer-until-correct multiple-choice feedback).

> ◎ Feedback can be effectively "scaffolded" by providing hints incrementally rather than just giving students the correct answer.

Effective feedback depends not only on the *kind* of feedback but also on its *timing*—and students' awareness of the timing—which may be particularly important for student motivation. When students know that they won't receive feedback for awhile, they (perhaps unconsciously) make less of an effort to perform well. Kettle and Häubl (2010) conducted an experiment to investigate the effects of timing on performance feedback in an academic setting. Students knew ahead of time when they would receive grades on a presentation they were giving. The proximity of feedback ranged between zero (same day) and 17 days after the presentation. The results of the study revealed that performance increased linearly in direct relation to the proximity of feedback. In other words, students who knew they would receive feedback sooner tended to perform better than students who knew they would receive grades after a greater delay. The researchers concluded that the anticipation of timely feedback likely motivated participants' performance.

> ◎ Students who knew they would receive feedback sooner tended to perform better than students who knew they would receive grades after a greater delay.

The above findings have important implications for the busy teacher who might be tempted simply to mark incorrect responses on a test or quiz without providing students with prompt feedback. With regard to the former the type of feedback, students will likely fail to benefit from practice tests or benchmark assessments that tell them only the percentage of responses they got correct. In addition to drawing attention to incorrect responses, we should be sure that students learn the correct answers when they are wrong and also attend to what they got *right*. A good way to get students to attend to correct responses is to have them correct their own work using an answer key (knowing the score will be checked by the teacher). This strategy also allows students to get prompt feedback soon after completing an assessment, taking advantage of the link between the timing of feedback and student motivation. To summarize, useful and important evaluation strategies for teachers include the following: (a) ensuring that students receive timely feedback; (b) communicating to students beforehand that they will receive such feedback; (c) scaffolding feedback by incrementally providing hints that allow students to arrive at correct answers themselves; and (d) allowing students to continue to work on learning tasks until they demonstrate full understanding of the material.

> ◎ Students will likely fail to benefit from practice tests or benchmark assessments that tell them only the percentage of responses they got correct.

Although direct feedback from the teacher is powerful, this is not the only approach. A plethora of computer-assisted programs exist to provide students with immediate feedback and scaffold learning based on the type and frequency of errors. Another simple strategy for getting students feedback quickly is peer review. This can be done by assigning students to partners with whom they have developed a trusting and supportive relationship, by instituting more formal classwide peer tutoring programs, or by implementing team-guided student performance reviews.

From the Expert Teacher

Fun With Spelling

As a special educator and reading specialist, I have encountered many students with language-based learning differences and dyslexia who continue to have great difficulties with spelling long after their reading skills have improved. Traditional spelling programs rely on memorizing a list of related words. Testing comes after a number of days of drills. Some students who consistently have poor spelling when writing perform quite well on this kind of spelling test because they are able to memorize the list for the test. They do not, however, transfer their knowledge, and their spelling may continue to be undecipherable even to themselves.

An alternative to the traditional spelling test is the spelling recognition test. Students are able to think about how a word is spelled and apply skills they have learned. Students spend time learning letter combinations for a particular sound (i.e., "o" sound spelled ow [snow], o-e [note], oa [boat], or o [most]). They practice spelling by building words sound by sound, paying attention to the spelling of the target sound. They also read the words with the various spellings in isolation and in stories throughout the week. For the test, students recall the various spellings of the target sound and write them across the top of their paper, as shown below. They are told that for this test they are going to spell lots of words wrong. In fact, the more wrong words the better. Students think, "Yeah, I can do that." Students are told that one of the words is the accepted spelling and they should circle that one.

oa	ow	o	o-e
boat	bowt	bot	bote
snoa	snow	sno	snoe
moast	mowst	most	moste

Students take ownership of the process because they have produced and recognized what they have done right. If a student makes an error, the teacher does not put an "X" by the incorrect spelling but a circle around the correctly spelled word, which they had written themselves.

Paula Mainolfi
Teacher, Special Education and Reading Specialist

Active Retrieval of Information

Prior research has demonstrated that actively retrieving information from memory appears to benefit long-term retention much more than does simply studying. Karpicke and Roediger (2008), for example, compared the effect of repeated testing with that of repeated studying for long-term retention of foreign language vocabulary. They found that repeated testing of English/foreign language word-pairs produced significantly greater retention than did repeated studying. This has commonly been referred to as the "testing effect," though in theory any activity that would cause students to retrieve information (not just tests) would yield the effect. When students have to retrieve information actively, as occurs when they are tested, this appears to play a role in reinforcing memory for that information. Standard studying relies on the more passive receipt of information and does not seem to have the same effect. Although studying is surely better than nothing, it does not recruit memory systems in the same way as retrieval of information. Since time for schoolwork is always limited, students will often be better served by retrieval practice (e.g., self-quizzing) than by studying alone (e.g., re-reading). It is important to model retrieval practice for students so that they understand what this means (e.g., "no looking at the answers") and to encourage students to engage in retrieval practice as a strategy for committing information to memory. Students tend to believe (incorrectly) that studying is more effective than retrieval practice (Kornell & Son, 2009). The old standard practice of flashcards can help students understand what retrieval entails (and effects of active retrieval explain why flashcards are so effective).

◎ Actively retrieving information from memory appears to benefit long-term retention much more than does simply studying. Students will often be better served by retrieval practice (e.g., self-quizzing) than by studying alone (e.g., re-reading).

Karpicke and Blunt (2011) argue that educators intuitively provide students with activities that focus too heavily on acquiring and studying information and not enough on having them practice retrieval of information to reconstruct what they know. But how might retrieval practice stack up against a more elaborative form of studying, such as concept mapping? In a pair of experiments, Karpicke and Blunt investigated the relative benefits of retrieval practice versus elaborative studying (creating concept maps) for learning of science content. Learning was measured both by verbatim recall of concepts and by the ability of students to draw inferences involving multiple concepts—a measure of "deeper" understanding. The results indicated that active retrieval of information consolidates learning in a more powerful way than even elaborative forms of studying. Karpicke and Blunt posit that, because the act of retrieval itself strengthens memories in a unique and specific way, retrieval practice should be recognized as critical to the learning process.

Educators would be remiss if they view testing only as a way to *measure* learning; as the research discussed above shows, testing also has the power to *cause* learning. It is important to note that testing as understood here should not be equated with the kind of standardized testing commonly associated with accountability measures. Rather, the idea is that students should frequently test their knowledge on their own, or in response to teacher prompts, with the goal of consolidating learning. As will be seen later in this chapter, knowledge can be tested in creative ways through arts-integrated activities that eliminate all of the negative connotations accompanying the word "test."

> ◎ Testing also has the power to *cause* learning.

From the Expert Teacher

Tic-Tac-Toe Assessment

As part of my Native Americans unit, I use projects to assess the students' mastery of the content and give them a choice of how they want to display learning. Each student receives a Tic-Tac-Toe board that describes nine different small projects. Students then choose three assessment methods in a row, going any direction. The students enjoy the challenge of picking their desired projects and feel empowered by having choices in how to assess learning. I designed the game board to assure variety in the methods of assessment. Some projects involved writing and researching while others included more hands-on activities.

For example, one row requires students to write two paragraphs explaining why cultures of Native Americans developed differently, then follow a recipe containing some of the main ingredients that Native Americans often used, and finally build a model of one type of Native American home along with a paragraph describing it. Each row included projects that would help me to assess what they had learned while also letting them have fun and use their different strengths and interests. I was amazed at the effort and excitement that they put into their projects. One student became so engaged that she built a life-size tepee!

Kristen McGinness
Teacher, Elementary School

Spacing Effects

We have discussed in previous chapters the growing practice in our schools of trying to teach too much subject matter in too little time in order to cover all required material. This practice leads to a "teach, test, and move on" approach that is not amenable to deeper, more protracted interactions with content. It also discourages review and retesting of previously mastered material at later points in time. Researchers have long recognized the efficacy of introducing delays between learning events; this is commonly called the "spacing effect" (e.g., Kornell et al., 2010). Recent research has found the neurological mechanism that explains why the spacing effect is important for the consolidation of memory. In animal studies, Okamoto, Endo, Shirao, and Nagao (2011) observed specific protein synthesis occurring in the cerebellum when learning was spaced but not when it was massed (learning occurred all at once). The researchers suggest that this study adds a biological explanation to the well-known advantages of spacing over time exposures to learning particular tasks.

◎ Researchers have long recognized the efficacy of introducing delays between learning events.

Behavioral research demonstrating the benefits of spacing learning has considered the particular effects of spacing intervals lasting minutes or hours (see Cepeda, Pashler, Vul, Wixted, & Rohrer, 2006, for a meta-analysis). However, in a recent study, Cepeda, Vul, Rohrer, Wixted, and Pashler (2008) examined the effects of delaying review of previously learned material (study/retest) over intervals ranging from short (e.g., 1 day) to very long (e.g., approximately 1 year). The result was a set of spacing recommendations that differ depending on how long information needs to be retained. At one extreme, Cepeda and colleagues (2006, 2008) found that when final testing takes place about a week after initial learning, the optimal lag before reviewing material is about a day or two. At the other extreme, for tests taking place in a year or so, the optimal spacing is 1 to 2 months.

What does this mean for classroom instruction? If the goal is for students to remember information for an upcoming unit test 4 to 6 weeks after content is initially taught, then content should be revisited with a follow-up study/test session after about a week. Conversely, if teachers need students to retain information longer (e.g., up to a full school year for final exams or standardized tests), then content should be revisited only after a month or more has passed. Though Cepeda and colleagues (2008) did not investigate intervals longer than a year, if the goal is retention for many years or a lifetime, it is likely that content will need to be revisited multiple times over several years with large gaps in between. It is very important to note, as Cepeda and colleagues do, that the downside of having too *short* of a gap between learning events is much worse than the downside of overshooting what's optimal. Retention increases sharply as the space between learning events approaches optimality, but retention declines only very slowly as one exceeds the optimal spacing. The biggest take-away from this research for teachers is this: *Make it a priority to revisit previously taught content after a significant delay and have students study/test their knowledge.*

Research on the effects of feedback, active retrieval of information, and spacing of learning events has strong implications for many aspects of education. This research can inform the work of individuals who make important educational decisions, from policymakers, who set standards and testing policies, to textbook publishers, who sequence content and curriculum reviews, to classroom teachers, who must ultimately make the day-to-day decisions regarding what their students will do in class.

MULTIPLE KINDS OF ASSESSMENTS

As was discussed in previous chapters, quality teaching involves the interplay of a variety of pedagogical methods, from conventional direct instruction to highly student-centered instruction that fosters creative, divergent thinking through student-generated products. Similarly, the challenge of effective evaluation is to balance the use of assessments that require selection of the correct answer with those that call for students to construct open-ended responses, solve problems, and apply knowledge.

> ◎ The challenge of effective evaluation is to balance the use of assessments that require selection of the correct answer with those that call for students to construct open-ended responses, solve problems, and apply knowledge.

Few educators would deny that testing drives teaching—that is, the way we test and what we test largely affects the way we teach and what we teach. In my interactions with teachers across the country, it has become clear to me that the strictures of high-stakes testing and accountability measures have influenced the way teachers craft lessons and measure results. The federal government's Government Accountability Office indicated that out of 48 states studied, 38 administered yearly tests made up of mostly multiple-choice questions (Ashby, 2009). No wonder teachers complain that these sorts of narrow assessments compel them to teach in ways they don't believe maximize student learning. Teachers must match teaching techniques and student assessments to the current format of achievement tests so that students are prepared to be savvy test-takers. If teachers never have students practice and prepare to take standardized tests, they are doing them a great disservice; for the foreseeable future, at least, students cannot avoid these kinds of assessments. Fortunately, however, with the reauthorization of the Elementary and Secondary Education Act, policymakers and the general public are calling for assessments that provide broader measures of educational attainment (including better multiple-choice tests), addressing areas such as thinking skills and problem-solving abilities (Toppo, 2010).

As we look to educate students to think creatively, our teaching as well as our testing must reflect this challenge. Several states have moved toward the use of performance measures in the past (e.g., Maryland and Kentucky). Although the experiences of these states indicate that such assessments are more challenging to administer and score than "bubble tests," Toch (2011) suggests that countries using alternatives like portfolio or performance assessments—such as Singapore, Australia, and England—have increased their scores on the Programme for International Student Assessment (PISA) test, which, despite being mainly a multiple-choice test, taps into students' abilities to think critically and solve problems.

> ◎ As we look to educate students to think creatively, our teaching as well as our testing must reflect this challenge.

In contrast to current standardized achievement tests that too often measure low-level recall of factual information rather than higher-order thinking (Brookhart, 2010), I will describe some forms of alternative assessment that change what teachers focus on and what children learn in response. These assessments make it possible to gauge important critical thinking skills: investigation, synthesis of disparate ideas, exploration of multiple points of view, problem-solving, metacognition, and demonstration of global understanding through metaphorical thinking.

Portfolio Assessments

Portfolio assessments are collections of student work that track progress over time. Portfolios often combine both student-selected and teacher-selected work, and include not merely traditional assessments (worksheets, quizzes, and tests) but also samples of audio-visual work, poster displays, and arts-integrated content projects. For some students, a collection of this kind of work may present a more full and accurate picture of progress and understanding than do tests that focus almost solely on memorized information. Portfolios are a powerful tool to demonstrate progress in attaining learning objectives, and such visible progress can be a strong motivator for students and teachers alike.

> ◎ Portfolios are a powerful tool to demonstrate progress in attaining learning objectives, and such visible progress can be a strong motivator for students and teachers alike.

From the Expert Teacher

The Power of Student Portfolios

Feedback through portfolios is an especially informative way to teach my students. I select items that students will include in the portfolio and allow the students to choose the work they want to show me, peers, and parents. I ask that they include some writing that analyzes how they are learning. I scaffold their writing by giving students sentence threads that they complete such as, "This math unit was hard because . . ." or "The part I liked the most about this science unit was . . ." or "Something new that I learned was . . ." or "The problems I'm still not sure of are. . . ." During the unit, I ask students to meet with me individually and with peers to demonstrate what they have learned and which activities helped them learn best.

Students not only like being able to analyze their own learning but also to evaluate my creative thinking in crafting activities for them. We all acknowledge that teaching basic skills can be rote and dry, but I feel challenged everyday to make learning exciting and relevant to their lives.

Robin Melanson
Teacher, Middle School Science and Mathematics

Portfolio assessment can also encourage metacognition (awareness of one's own thought processes) that permits students to set their own learning goals and then track their progress. Even for traditional forms of assessment like tests and quizzes, students can use the process of building a portfolio to gain a deeper understanding as they review and write about what questions they got wrong on a test, why they came up with the wrong response, how they would correct the response, and how they might prepare differently for the next assessment.

Student Journals

Student journals are another powerful tool for evaluating and enhancing student learning. Though journal writing may take a number of different forms, two seem particularly useful in educational settings: *reflective journals* and *learning logs*. When students create reflective journal entries, their aim is to contemplate what they have learned and explore in a relatively freeform fashion potential connections to other ideas and applications to their own lives or those of others around them. Reflective journal writing has been shown to encourage more metacognition and the use of more sophisticated cognitive strategies during learning tasks (McCrindle & Christensen, 1995). As Dyment and O'Connell (2010) point out, however, it is important that reflective journal writing engage students in critical thinking and does not lead them to offer mere descriptive accounts of events. Without sufficient guidance, students are prone to slipping into this purely descriptive form of writing, the benefits of which for learning are probably minimal. Thus, teachers should be sure to model for students the practice of critical reflection through journal writing so that the benefits for students are maximized.

◎ Reflective journal writing has been shown to encourage more metacognition and the use of more sophisticated cognitive strategies during learning tasks.

Learning logs represent a somewhat more constrained and objective kind of writing task (Carr, 2002). When students create learning logs, they work to explicitly recount the important ideas they have come to understand as a result of instruction. For example, students might be prompted to respond to questions like "What are three important ideas I learned today" or "Are there any ideas that I would like to understand better." This more constrained style of journal writing may be more efficient and easier to engage in for many students (especially younger ones), as students are provided with a more specific focus and a clear starting point. Learning logs may also be especially useful for teachers who are trying to keep track of progress for each of the individual students in the class. Students may oftentimes be more willing to candidly describe what they do and don't understand if they can avoid doing so in front of the class. Teachers should consider the benefits of both learning logs and reflective journals for their students and utilize whatever combination seems most appropriate for the particular population of students they serve.

◎ Learning logs may also be especially useful for teachers who are trying to keep track of progress for each of the individual students in the class.

Performance Assessments

Performance assessment measures a student's ability to apply knowledge through the performance of activities such as experimenting, weighing evidence, evaluating sources, designing a plan of action to solve a real-world problem, developing multiple points of view, and demonstrating through artistic expression an understanding and interpretation of content.

Performance assessments are often graded through the use of a rubric, which makes it possible to assess performance on several different criteria. A rubric should be given to students at the start of a project or (better still) at the beginning of the learning unit to give students the "big picture" of what they will be expected to do to demonstrate understanding (see Chapter 6 on Brain-Target Three). Rubrics can be holistic, providing students with an overall score derived from a subjective combination of multiple criteria, or they can be analytic, specifying precisely how points should be assigned for each criterion and how different criteria are weighted (see the following for a sample analytic rubric).

Example Performance Assessment Activity and Rubrics

Learning objective: Understand how the geographical features in the environment influence the cultural beliefs, government, religion, and education of a civilization.

Content: Students are presented major features of geography and culture of early civilizations. Next, using Mesopotamia as an example, the students are shown how particular features might constrain the culture—the knowledge, beliefs, and behaviors—as well as the government, religion, and education of a Mesopotamian culture.

Activity: Students will be directed to apply the knowledge they have learned about the workings of a civilization to create their own primitive culture. They will identify the geography of the region in which the civilization can be found and various features of the civilization: the cultural or belief system, government, religion, and education. They will then describe *why* the geography supports each of the particular features you describe.

Grading Criteria Given to Students (Holistic Rubric):

1. Content: Recognize and specify all of the major parts of a civilization
   a. Have you identified a geography as well as the four features (government, religion, education, culture) of your civilization?
2. Critical Thinking: Plausible explanations for why the geography supports each feature
   a. Are your explanations comprehensible and logically sound? That is, is each identified feature possible given the geography you describe? For example, a nomadic community would likely not have a goddess of agriculture.
3. Originality: How do your identified geography and features compare to the example given by the teacher and to the other groups
   a. How different is your set of features relative to those in the example described by the teacher?
4. Extension: Are you including new information beyond what was presented by the teacher?
   a. Does your civilization reflect additional experiences or knowledge that was not taught in this lesson but that you have, from your own culture or from other lessons taught in school?

(continued)

Grading Criteria (Analytic Rubric):

	Content Knowledge	Critical Thinking	Originality of Features	Extension of Information
Weight:	**X 1**	**X 1**	**X 2**	**X 2**
Total Score:				
3 Points	Precisely identifies the geography and each feature of the civilization: government, religion, education, and culture.	Provides reasonable and thorough explanation for why each feature could be found in a civilization with a particular geography.	Identified geography and features are unique: they are all different from those used in the Mesopotamia example and mostly different from those described by other groups.	Most of your civilization reflects your knowledge from other disciplines or personal experiences that are unrelated to what was taught.
2 Points	Partly or vaguely identifies (some or all) geography and features of the civilization.	Provides reasonable, but possibly vague explanation for why some or all of the features could be found in a civilization with a particular geography.	Identified geography and features are somewhat original: some are different than those used in the Mesopotamia example and some differ from those described by other groups.	Some of your civilization reflects your knowledge from other disciplines or personal experiences that are unrelated to what was taught.
1 Point	Incompletely identifies elements for some features of the civilization. Some features may be left unspecified.	Provides unlikely and/or possibly vague explanation for why some of the features could be found in a civilization with a particular geography.	Identified geography and features are mostly the same as those used in the Mesopotamia example and most features overlap with those described by the teacher in class.	Very little of your civilization reflects your knowledge from other disciplines or personal experiences that are unrelated to what was taught.

Assessing creative thinking and problem-solving through rubrics represents a helpful way for teachers to evaluate student learning by using dimensions that are not accessible to more traditional measures. Debates continue, however, about how (or whether it's even possible) to "grade" creativity. Moreover, Brookhart (2010) points out that it is common in educational practice for teachers to reduce assessments of creativity in student work to mere judgments of aesthetic or artistic appeal (e.g., a neat design drawn on the cover of a report). Effective assessment of creative thinking must involve a deeper understanding of the creative process. Rubrics intended to guide teachers and students with respect to what counts as creative thinking should assess the student's ability to combine disparate elements of learned content to formulate unique and original ideas.

> ◎ Rubrics intended to guide teachers and students with respect to what counts as creative thinking should assess the student's ability to combine disparate elements of learned content to formulate unique and original ideas.

From the Expert Teacher

Creativity in Mathematics

As a second-grade teacher who enjoys teaching through the arts, evaluating learning in alternative ways speaks to my natural way of teaching. I use the principles of the arts to teach and measure students' divergent thinking and their ability to solve open-ended mathematics problems. I also encourage students to include an expression of a personal connection to the real-world application of the math unit.

While I still use traditional methods of assessment, much of the evaluation is based on projects that allow students to be creative, such as making a product to demonstrate a mathematics concept. For example, when studying measurement, I administered the typical mid-chapter review. Then I decided that a more creative way to assess student learning would be to ask them to draw a map of a farm. They had the choices of which animals and physical features they would include. They then had to determine the area and perimeter of the pens for each group of animals based on the size and number of animals they chose. I gave the students a scoring key to determine what elements will be graded and allowed them to self-assess before I scored their work. Students had this rubric at the start of the unit so there were no surprises for them. The only surprise came to me when I saw the amazing work they had done and how proud they were of their learning.

Rebecca Singer
Teacher, Elementary Mathematics
(Continued)

Name _Kevin_

14/14 Good!

Midchapter Review

Do your best!

Estimate. Then measure.

	Estimate	Measure
1 ————	about 2 inches	about 2 inches
2 ———	about 1 inches	about 1 inches
3 ————	about 5 cm	about 5 cm
4 ———	about 3 cm	about 4 cm

Measure each path.

5 about 2 inches

6 2 2 2 about 6 cm

Measure. Add to find the perimeter.

7) [4] | 10 cm

8 2 [2] 2 8 cm

Draw a diagram to solve.

9 A map shows a square garden. There is a big tree in each corner. There are 2 small trees between each big tree. How many trees are in the garden?

Use your own paper.

12 trees

10 How did you solve problem 9? _Draw a diagram_

How do you estimate the length of an object? _Do a good gess_

CHAPTER 10 Midchapter Review

three hundred sixty-three • 363

P=26
A=26 squnits

Barn

P=16
A=16 sq. units
pigs

P=25
A=26 sq. units
farm house

A=6 sq. units
P=10
chickens

A=26 sq. units
P=20 sq. units
horses

cows
A=45 sq. units
P=28

Lake

(Continued)

Area and Perimeter on a Farm Rubric

Give yourself one ☺ for each item you included in your drawing.

_____I drew pens for at least 4 animals.

_____I found the perimeter of each pen.

_____I found the area of each pen.

_____I remembered to record the perimeter and area for each pen on my map.

_____I added details to my map.

I gave myself_____ ☺'s.

Your teacher will check your work and give you one ☺ for each item you included.

_____You drew pens for at least 4 animals.

_____You found the perimeter of each pen.

_____You found the area of each pen.

_____You remembered to record the perimeter and area for each pen on your map.

_____You added details to your map.

Your teacher gave you _____ ☺'s.

As we have reviewed in this chapter, effective teaching and effective testing are two sides of the same coin. Evaluation of learning is an ongoing process that begins as soon as one starts teaching and continues indefinitely in order to sustain what has been learned. Evaluation and feedback are essential to making learning efficient, and assessments—insofar as they prompt students to test their knowledge—can be a powerful catalyst for lifelong retention. We now return one last time to the BTT units of Clare and Suzanne to see the creative ways they have evaluated their unit's learning goals.

> ◎ Evaluation and feedback are essential to making learning efficient, and assessments—insofar as they prompt students to test their knowledge—can be a powerful catalyst for lifelong retention.

WHAT DOES A BRAIN-TARGETED TEACHING UNIT LOOK LIKE IN THE CLASSROOM?

Learning Unit: Surviving Alone in the Wilderness: A study of the novel *Hatchet* by Gary Paulsen

Grade/Content: Fifth-Grade/Language Arts

Author: Clare O'Malley Grizzard

Overarching Goal of Unit: Students will increase language arts skills of reading for understanding through analysis of character, plot, main idea, and symbolic language.

Brain-Target Six: Evaluating Learning

As an arts specialist working with classroom teachers, evaluating learning in the BTT Model speaks to my way of teaching: promoting divergent thinking, open-ended problem-solving, and expression of a personal connection to the curriculum.

In collaborating with Linda Bluth in the design of the *Hatchet* unit, we used portfolios extensively to exhibit the students' efforts and progress. The portfolio contents were chosen by the students and the teacher, and included reflective writing and self-assessment relative to the content students are learning. During the unit, students were able to review their portfolios, which provided them with continual feedback, enabled them to recognize growth, and allowed them to reset their own goals.

Although some traditional methods such as quizzes and tests were still part of our units, most of the evaluation of student learning was based on performance of real tasks, such as the creation of a guidebook/box, which documented performance as well as students' writing.

Performance assessments included rubrics, checklists, and observational charts to assess students' achievement in perceptual, language, and motor skills. We used rubrics that measure individual growth and customized them for learning differences among students. Students were given the rubric at the start of the task so they knew the goals and outcomes for learning.

We expanded the rubrics, checklists, and observational charts to demonstrate students' mastery of specific objectives using drama, which included collaborative work, understanding of vocabulary though drama, tableau, and role-playing.

Visual art assessments included the following:

- Reflective writings, including artist's statement

- Landscape criteria—background, middle ground, foreground

- Expressive portraits criteria

- Printing with natural materials checklist

- Handmade paper checklist

- Sketchbook checklist

- Natural materials survival kit checklist

Our goal was to encourage students to become more thoughtful judges of their own work and others' work through critical dialogues and critiques and artists' statements.

Prompts for Artist Statement:

- In this artwork I became a different kind of observer by _____.

- I found it challenging when_____.

- I found it easier when I _____.

- I surprised myself when I _____.

- I think that this artwork helped me understand Brian better because _____.

- I can see that using materials from the environment has improved my art making because_____.

- Some of the details of my environment I see in a new way are _____.

- I was able to write about my feelings better because _____.

- My thoughts about art making were changed because _____.

- I like this artwork because _____.

Analytic Rubric for Guidebook and Survival Box

Analytic Rubric for Guidebook/ Survival Box	Observational Drawing	Construction of the Survival Box	Field Sketches	Journal Construction
3 Points	At least three drawings of natural with a strong realistic style, relative size agreement.	Completed box that is sized for books. Used natural-themed materials. Shows careful craftsmanship.	At least three sketches out of doors of natural objects or settings.	Journal construction shows excellent craftsmanship, using natural materials for cover, and four handmade papers for inside pages.
2 Points	At least two drawings of natural objects with some realism	Somewhat completed box that is sized for books. Used natural-themed materials. Shows some-what careful craftsmanship.	At least two sketches of natural objects or settings.	Journal construction shows good craftsmanship, using some natural materials for cover. At least three handmade papers for inside pages.
1 Point	At least one drawing of natural objects with some real-ism.	Unfinished, sized poorly, not carefully done, little nature-themed materials.	One sketch done out of doors of natural objects or settings.	Journal construction shows poor to basic craftsmanship, using some natural materials for cover. At least one to two handmade papers for inside pages.

Learning Unit: Genetics and Heredity—Thinking Outside the Punnett Square

Unit designed by Suzanne P. McNamara

Overarching Goal: Students will apply their understanding of genetics and heredity in discussions centered around current medical and social issues as well as the appreciation of human diversity.

Brain Target Six: Authentic Assessment of Learning

In order to truly help students in the learning process, they must be given immediate, frequent, and relevant feedback about their performance. This type of constant evaluation supports the brain's natural learning systems. Too often, however, feedback is limited to the grades received on tests and quizzes, and maybe an occasional project or paper. Although more manageable for teachers, this traditional approach to assessment does little to inform instruction or enhance learning. Traditional forms of assessment provide students with information about how well they could answer questions about this new material, but do not provide them detailed information about the progress of their learning. For many forms of traditional assessment, a "70%" does not necessarily mean that the student really understands 70% of the information covered on the assessment. Furthermore, these numbers provide little guidance for students in understanding what they know and don't know.

In this unit, students were given several nontraditional assessments. Toward the middle of the unit, after learning about pedigrees, they were assigned a family pedigree project, which would continue throughout the remainder of the unit. Students were asked to pick a genetic trait that runs in their own biological family or in a famous biological family (i.e., Jacksons, Obamas, the British Royal Family, etc.). Then they were to construct a pedigree for this genetic trait, including at least three generations of family members, using accurate symbols and notations.

The students were to bring in a draft of this assignment so that their peers and the instructor could review it and provide helpful feedback. The final draft of the assignment was turned in 1 week later, and was graded and returned so that students could use the feedback to continue with the second part of the assignment. The next part required students to use the information they learned about Mendelian inheritance to show the cross between two mating individuals of their family and report the possible outcomes; they did this for three sets of mating individuals. In addition to the feedback that they received about this portion of the project, each student was given a hypothetical statement about his or her family, "What would happen if . . . ?" This final portion of the project allowed the instructor to further differentiate the project to address the needs of each student and encouraged all students to think critically about the information covered in the assignment.

Another authentic assessment used in this unit was a lab practical in which students were required to work in their groups, applying the information they learned about inheritance, to figure out the lab scenario. Each lab group received information about a crime scene, where samples of human urine were found as evidence. Students had to work together to determine which individuals had the black urine disease, alkaptonuria, to

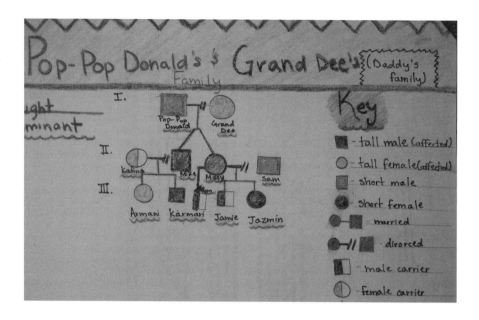

solve the case. Using Punnett squares and lab testing techniques, the students were required to apply the information they learned throughout the unit. This assessment gave them the opportunity to think critically about genetics and solve complex problems.

The final authentic assessment required students to create a board game that addressed all of the standards covered throughout the unit. Students worked individually to create question cards to challenge their peers in class. After the games were designed, the students played them in groups and provided feedback to the designer. All students could revise their game before handing it in on the day of the unit test. Students had to write their own questions and answers to their game and were encouraged to make it challenging for their classmates to help them better prepare for the end-of-unit test.

Evaluating student learning should happen consistently throughout every unit. It can provide helpful insight as to the effectiveness of the instruction. If the goal for each student is learning the content, then there must be constant assessments for understanding and frequent (and relevant!) feedback about their performance in order to ensure that students have truly mastered the material.

10

Implementing Brain-Targeted Teaching in a School and Classroom

The Emotional
Climate

Evaluation and
Assessment

The Physical
Environment

Application of
Knowledge

Big Picture
Learning Design

Mastery of Content,
Skills, and Concepts

The Brain-Targeted Teaching Model

It is the supreme art of the teacher to awaken joy in creative expression and knowledge.

—Albert Einstein

I believe that many educators presently use strategies consistent with some or even all of the components of the Brain-Targeted Teaching (BTT) Model as a regular part of their teaching repertoire. Beyond recognition of their use of good strategies, these teachers may find that the model offers a deep research base and a rationale for these best practices. The model can also provide support to teachers new to the profession or those who continually seek out new ways to enhance their practice; the model provides guidance and direction in the form of a unified framework for understanding how learning occurs and for identifying additional teaching strategies that are most effective. In thinking about applying the model not only in the classroom but also in whole schools, the model speaks to school leaders by supporting a vision of learning focused on the acquisition of deep content knowledge as well as creative thinking and problem-solving. This vision leads to deep and rigorous learning in a joyful and engaging school environment. Finally and possibly most important, the model provides a common language of instruction that helps to unify a school faculty and community around evidence-based best practices.

While sharing the model with educators in schools and conferences locally and nationally and learning of their experiences in implementing Brain-Targeted Teaching, I have been enlightened as to how the model influences teaching practices from early childhood through higher education; it has been exciting for me to be the learner! As the words of *expert teachers* have demonstrated throughout this book, the model can take on many shapes and forms. Clare and Suzanne have demonstrated how traditional teaching can be transformed when teachers approach a learning unit through a new lens. In short, I have learned the power that teachers gain when they understand the ways in which research from the neuro- and cognitive sciences can inform and guide effective instruction.

BRAIN-TARGETED TEACHING IN THE SCHOOL

GETTING STARTED

Although there is no single approach to implementing the BTT Model, I will offer strategies that have been successful, emphasizing the importance of supportive leadership and collaborative planning.

Instructional Leadership and Support

The school leader—principal, head of school, CEO—must have deep knowledge of any instructional program or process and must not only support but also guide its implementation. This entails communicating to all stakeholders how this (or any program) furthers the school's vision and mission. An effective way to implement the BTT model from a school leadership perspective is to embed its principles in broad-based expectations for school climate, instructional planning, teaching practices, and evaluation. The targets set forth in the model can become part of a school's yearly or long-range plan for creating a successful school that meets achievement benchmarks in tested areas while simultaneously offering students a well-rounded and challenging, yet joyful educational experience.

Curricular Decisions and Instructional Planning

Much of what and how teachers teach is dependent on school leaders who give teachers responsibilities that dictate how they must spend their planning time. In light of the BTT Model, then, a strong recommendation for school leaders is to facilitate regular opportunities for teachers to engage in collaborative planning. As teachers in elementary grades design learning units, those who teach the same grade in self-contained classrooms benefit from sharing ideas and materials. In addition, collaborating with teachers from other grades helps in coordinating content and scaffolding activities to help students progress to ever-increasing levels of complexity in concept and skill acquisition. Likewise, teachers at the secondary level benefit from collaborative planning, whether through content departments or in interdisciplinary planning teams with teachers representing various content areas. Also, as arts integration is a central component of the model, engaging school-based arts educators as well as practicing artists from the community is valuable at all levels.

As the chapter on Brain-Target Three explains, the approach to writing a learning unit is holistic as well as analytical. That is, learning unit design begins by choosing the standards, content, skills, and concepts to be taught and mapping connections among the unit's elements through visual representations. Only then does one specify learning objectives and activities that will provide multiple exposures to the content (especially through arts integration), promote creative problem-solving, and provide multiple approaches for measuring achievement.

Although writing the entire unit "up front" takes more time in the beginning than planning day-by-day, ultimately the benefits of having a well-thought-out learning unit reap rewards for the teacher and students alike. In addition to benefiting the teacher and students in the classroom where the unit is taught, the upfront writing and planning leads to a heightened spirit of collaboration among faculty as they brainstorm activities and share outcomes. In addition, teachers who are often viewed as "special subject" teachers (visual and performing arts, physical education, technology, and foreign language) take on new roles in the school; their expertise in active learning helps content teachers design creative learning tasks.

From the Expert Teacher

Using BTT to Support New Teachers

As an experienced teacher, I enjoy using the Brain-Targeted Teaching model to design interdisciplinary units. Usually I put together pieces that I've taught before into a unified whole that creates more effective teaching and learning. Now that I am in a teacher support position, I have wondered how effective my units would be when implemented by another teacher. I found the answer when two colleagues implemented a social studies/language arts unit that I wrote titled "Dream Keeper." Both teachers are in their first year teaching first grade, using traditional curricula. I introduced the unit to them using the six targets to communicate the cohesiveness of a BTT unit.

*We discussed the importance of making the **emotional connection** using the Langston Hughes poem "The Dream Keeper" and supporting the students in their journey learning about slavery through great children's literature. The teachers had already created comfortable **classroom environments** with read-aloud rug areas, book displays, art centers, and a sense of security to be able to explore the heartfelt theme of dreaming, which includes learning about "too-rough fingers of the world" (dream spoilers) and "dream keepers."*

*Soon the classrooms and hallways were filled with the children's artwork portraying characters from the books and ideas about their own dreams. The **concept map** (based on the poem) allowed the teachers to quickly understand the framework of looking at each piece of literature with the same analytic lens and build scaffolding for the students to grasp higher level concepts, such as freedom, taking risks, repentance, and empathy, that many experienced teachers would not attempt with youngsters of any age. As the unit progressed into teaching **skills, content, and concepts**, I began to see each teacher create new activities to build understanding. This section of the unit has a "menu" of read-aloud books and related activities. This format provides teacher choice and stimulates creativity to expand upon individual interests. For instance, after reading Henry's Freedom Box, one teacher had his students create two-paneled drawings showing how Henry escaped and how they would escape. The breadth of answers ranged from very concrete ideas such as climbing out a window to abstract ones such as climbing a ladder to catch Aunt Harriet's Underground Railroad in the sky! While*

(Continued)

extending and applying knowledge culminated in a group poster advertising the Underground Railroad, there were opportunities linked to each read-aloud for students to apply what they were learning about slavery to dreams for their own lives and the world.

These first-year teachers were amazed to see the depth of understanding their first graders exhibited in discussions, written work, and artwork. They wished every unit could provide the level of engagement they observed. I saw teachers energized and connected to their students in ways that had not previously existed. Doing this BTT unit also allowed the teachers to get to know their students on a personal level that traditional curricula rarely provide. It was enlightening for me to use the model as a way to support new teachers to become experts in engaging children for creative and rigorous learning.

Catherine Gearhart
Instructional Support Specialist

All at Once or Little by Little?

School leaders must decide whether to implement the model schoolwide initially, or rather to develop and support a smaller group of faculty who write and demonstrate units to peers, with the eventual goal of having the model adopted by all teachers. Both approaches are useful depending on the school's readiness and need. The latter is the approach I took as a school principal when the model was first being developed. After training faculty in the background and components of the model, I facilitated collaborative planning time for several groups of teachers to plan and "field test" interdisciplinary units. These teachers made observations related to the effectiveness of the model and its overall success in achieving learning goals. They then prepared a PowerPoint presentation to demonstrate the units at professional development sessions and faculty meetings. Throughout the school year, more and more teachers participated in the process. I found that teachers enjoyed learning from each other; many wanted to participate after hearing their students enthusiastically sharing activities from other classes where teachers were implementing the model.

As the faculty became more familiar with the BTT Model, I engaged them in reflection on their teaching practices pertaining to each target. The chart, "Rate Your Brain Targets" (shown following) provided a simple way for teachers to determine areas of focus for enhancing their practice. For example, a teacher who indicated a need to improve on Brain-Target Two (physical environment) might be paired with a colleague particularly adept in that area.

Rate Your Brain Targets

I "own" these targets:

....because I:

I do OK with these targets:

...but would like to get better at:

I would like some coaching with these targets:

...because I want to enhance my practice by:

WHAT DOES A SCHOOL IMPLEMENTING BRAIN-TARGETED TEACHING LOOK LIKE?

Schoolwide implementation of the model should garner observable rewards. Below, I list several indicators of successful implementation through the lens of each brain target:

Brain-Target One—Emotional Climate for Learning

- Conversations between adults—including teachers, support staff, and leadership—and children demonstrate mutual respect

- Behavior-specific praise for effort is freely given

- Teachers greet students at the door as they enter the classroom. Teachers use each student's name and offer pleasant conversation

- Classroom routines are rules that are clearly evident and fairly applied; they focus on respect and the elimination of any form of bullying

- Rituals provide quick and enjoyable ways to motivate and engage students

- Celebrations are evident throughout the school and in every classroom

- Every child is able to identify caring adults within the school and classroom

- Multicultural themes are evident throughout the school and in every classroom

- Every learning unit includes activities that foster personal connection to the content

- Students are given choices in learning and evaluation activities

- Humor is used frequently and appropriately to provide a relaxed environment

Brain-Target Two—Physical Environment

- The school's halls, meeting spaces, and classrooms reflect a clean and orderly environment

- Classroom displays reflect the current unit of study and exhibit students' work rather than only commercially made products

- Lighting and sound are optimal in classrooms and throughout the school

- Seating arrangements are flexible as space allows for movement

- Soft music and suitable scents are evident in classrooms when appropriate

- Time is available for quiet reflection

Brain-Target Three—Learning Design

- Content standards are used in curriculum planning; the scope is multidisciplinary and the curriculum spirals through important content, skills, and concepts in each grade

- Learning goals are clearly displayed for students

- Concept maps and other visual representations are evident

- Collaborative planning within and across grade levels are part of the weekly schedule

- Ongoing professional development, mentoring, and coaching support curricular and instructional decisions

- Learning goals and activities are readily accessible to parents and the community though multiple means, including concept maps

- Teachers share learning units in a professional library

Brain-Target Four—Teaching for Mastery of Content, Skills, and Concepts

- Observable activities provide a range of experiences to reinforce learning

- The visual and performing arts are evident in instructional activities

- Activities reflect the needs of remedial as well as accomplished achievers

- Student work shown in the classroom and halls displays arts-based projects that show acquisition of content

- Benchmark assessments and other testing programs document student mastery of content, skills, and concepts

- Learning activities build on prior knowledge

- Homework and out-of-school activities reinforce learning goals

Brain-Target Five—Teaching for the Extension and Application of Knowledge: Creativity and Innovation in Education

- Students are provided with opportunities for divergent thinking within classroom discussions, class activities, and projects

- Critical thinking and problem-solving activities are visible in lesson activities and work projects

- Real-world application of content is incorporated into each learning unit

- Students are given multiple opportunities to extend knowledge beyond presented material and to display creative thinking through novel projects, assignments, and performance tasks

Brain-Target Six—Evaluating Learning

- Assessments of learning goals are provided throughout the lesson

- Students are given regular opportunities for active retrieval of information

- Feedback on performance is timely and students are told in advance when to anticipate feedback

- "Scaffolded feedback" is provided to allow students to arrive at correct responses

- Student portfolios are used to demonstrate student learning

- Performance assessments are used to demonstrate student learning

- Assessments are spaced to provide regular review of content

- Holistic and analytic scoring rubrics are used liberally to assess learning

BRAIN-TARGETED TEACHING IN TEACHER PREPARATION PROGRAMS: A STORY FROM A TEACHER EDUCATOR

Throughout this book, I have focused on implementing the BTT Model mostly in elementary and secondary schools. Knowing that the model also could be incorporated into higher education teacher preparation programs, I became intrigued with a story that a colleague at Johns Hopkins

University School of Education, Gordon Porterfield, shared with me about using the model with his class. And I will now share it with you:

Gordon was there at the inception of the BTT Model when he taught theater to middle school students. As a faculty associate now at Johns Hopkins, Gordon developed an innovative graduate-level course for first- and second-year teachers, all of whom teach in the Baltimore City Public Schools. The course, *Teacher as Thinker and Writer*, applies a variety of BTT approaches to promote creative teaching and learning. He uses his own classroom to model arts-based activities and application of knowledge so teachers can see relevance of these techniques at every grade level and in any subject area. Gordon is an especially strong advocate for the use of theater in urban classrooms. He believes that theater is accessible to *all* students and can be used by *any* teacher, whether experienced in theater or not, to engage students in meaningful learning. According to Gordon, teachers often know their content but beg for concrete suggestions to motivate their students, many of whom seem impervious to conventional instructional techniques and strategies. He contends that theater, much like play, can be a powerful motivational tool to foster student engagement. In thinking about ways to use the tenets of BTT in his graduate level class, he had a dream one night about a new class activity and implemented it for the first time this past semester:

"Boys and girls," he said, addressing his class of early career teachers as if they were middle schoolers, I'm giving you a choice of assignments for this week. You may either write a summary of an article from an educational journal (assigned by me) or memorize and verbatim recite to the class an eight-line poem (also assigned by me). Which do you prefer?"

His graduate students, having done more than their share of journal article reviews, opted unanimously to memorize and recite the poem. Gordon then gave each student a different eight-line poem, all by the notoriously dense and difficult Emily Dickinson, and directed them to memorize the poem and be prepared to recite it for the next class.

Gordon was amazed when, having had 7 days to learn the poem, many of the students were unprepared for the recitation. He knew, had he given the journal article assignment, every member of the class— without exception—would have turned it in. The students who claimed to be prepared to recite were clearly ill at ease and struggled just to get the words out, giving scant attention to the meaning of the poem. Those not ready to recite offered myriad excuses: "It was too hard"; "I couldn't figure out what some of the words meant"; "I was exhausted"; and "I had too much else to do." Gordon was shocked by their excuses as he knew that they would have spent hours on the journal article and turned it in on time but found themselves paralyzed by having to memorize and recite an eight-line poem.

The activity occasioned a lively, productive discussion as to the workings of the brain while memorizing, the value of memorization in itself, the value of spacing study times, the deep thinking that the poems required, and the challenge of performing in front of their peers a poem that stretched their minds and imaginations. At the end of the next class, when everyone had finally done the recitation, Gordon asked each student to evaluate the activity (anonymously) in terms of its value and application in a teacher education class. Gordon expected the worst, and was surprised and delighted by the positive response. Every teacher felt the experience was a unique and valuable way to move them beyond traditional teaching methods and to better understand the needs of the learners in their own classrooms. Many said that being pushed beyond their comfort zone gave them perspective of how some of their own students felt in the learning environment. They gave examples of how they might be able to use the arts, especially theater, to promote their own students' deeper engagement with the content.

When Gordon and I discussed the significance of this activity in relation to the tenets of the BTT Model, his closing comment was, "Well, the students certainly learned much about pedagogy with this assignment, and Emily would've been pleased." I was pleased too. That simple activity and the students' responses to it reinforced my conviction that applying relevant research from neuro- and cognitive sciences can have an enormous impact on how educators **at any level** should approach the teaching and learning process. Successful schools of the 21st century must reflect the growing evidence from the learning sciences about how students think and learn.

It is my hope that the research and practical applications presented throughout this book and through the framework of the BTT Model will enlighten educators to consider *how* learning best occurs so that all instructional activities—from those offered to young children to adults—result in deep, engaging, joyful, and lasting learning.

Let's give the last word to Ms. Dickinson:

The brain is wider than the sky,
For, put them side by side,
The one the other will include
With ease, and you beside.

The brain is deeper than the sea,
For, hold them, blue to blue,
The one the other will absorb,
As sponges, buckets do.

The brain is just the weight of God,
For, lift them, pound for pound,
And they will differ, if they do,
As syllable from sound.

Appendix I

Alignment of Brain-Targeted Teaching With Cognitive Taxonomies, Teaching Standards, and Learning Frameworks

N ow that our journey through the Brain-Targeted Teaching (BTT) Model is complete, some teachers may recognize components of the model that are already part of their daily teaching practice. They may also recognize the alignment of the model with similar educational programs and practices adopted by their school or local and state districts. Indeed, the BTT Model aligns with common thinking skills and teaching frameworks such as Dimensions of Learning (Marzano, 1992) that teachers have studied in teacher preparation or professional development programs. In addition, the instructional framework of the model is compatible with many (if not most) programs that schools may have adopted, from schoolwide behavioral intervention models to organizational frameworks such as Universal Design for Learning (Rose & Meyer, 2002). In the section that follows, we examine three thinking skills hierarchies, or cognitive taxonomies, and three sets of teaching standards or frameworks for learning. I also demonstrate how the tenets of these hierarchies and frameworks align with principles and components of BTT.

COGNITIVE TAXONOMIES

Cognitive taxonomies are frameworks that provide a hierarchy of thinking processes from basic forms of knowledge acquisition to more complex higher-order thinking. Here, we review three common frameworks—Bloom's Taxonomy, Dimensions of Learning, and Depth of Knowledge.

Bloom's Taxonomy

More than 50 years ago, Benjamin Bloom and David Krathwohl (1956) identified levels of cognitive performance that progress from simple to more complex forms of thinking. The six levels and their descriptions are as follows:

- *Knowledge* refers to recalling, labeling, or defining information

- *Comprehension* entails understanding, restating, and summarizing

- *Application* involves using facts and details to solve problems

- *Analysis* requires making sense of information by examining its parts

- *Synthesis* necessitates putting together components or ideas in a new way

- *Evaluation* concerns exercising judgments and re-examining biases and points of view

More recently, Anderson and Krathwohl (2001) offered a revised version of Bloom's Taxonomy in which the framework is organized around two dimensions, *Knowledge* and *Cognitive Processes*. *Knowledge* refers to the information students must be familiar with such as facts, content, and concepts. *Cognitive Processes* are a hierarchy of thinking skills similar to the original taxonomy, with creativity recognized as the highest level.

Dimensions of Learning

Similar to Bloom's Taxonomy, the Dimensions of Learning (Marzano, 1992) defines the learning process through "loose metaphors for how the mind works during learning" (p. 2). They are as follows:

- *Attitudes and Perceptions* related to optimal classroom climates

- *Acquiring and Integrating Knowledge* involving the acquisition of declarative and procedural knowledge

- *Extending and Refining Knowledge* involving thinking skills such as classifications, inductive and deductive reasoning, analysis of errors, and perspectives

- *Using Knowledge Meaningfully* involving skills such as problem-solving, decision-making, and investigation

- *Habits of Mind* encouraging metacognitive strategies for the learner

Depth of Knowledge

Finally, the pedagogy associated with Depth of Knowledge (Webb, 2002) identifies four levels of thinking, including the following:

- *Recall* and *reproduction* of content, skills, and concepts

- *Skill* and *Concept* acquisition for constructing meaning

- *Strategic Thinking* to use acquired information in problem-solving

- *Extended Thinking* to apply knowledge beyond acquired information

ALIGNMENT WITH BRAIN-TARGETED TEACHING

We can certainly see similarities among the three models described above and their alignment with BTT. Like BTT, these cognitive taxonomies focus first on the acquisition of knowledge then turn to its application through creative problem-solving. Building on these taxonomies, BTT provides a heuristic approach to provide a readily accessible model for effective instruction. In other words, the BTT model incorporates research from neuro- and cognitive sciences, taxonomies of thinking, and research-based best practices in ways that transport theoretical notions about thinking into classroom teaching and learning.

TEACHING STANDARDS AND TEACHING AND LEARNING FRAMEWORKS

In addition to cognitive taxonomies, the BTT model relates to common teaching standards and teaching frameworks. Below I briefly review teaching standards commonly used in teacher preparation programs: the Interstate Teacher Assessment and Support Consortium Standards as well as two other common frameworks for teaching and learning. I then consider how each might align with BTT.

Interstate Teacher Assessment and Support Consortium (InTASC) Standards

The Interstate Teacher Assessment and Support Consortium (InTASC) is a program of the Council of Chief State School Officers (CCSSO, 2010) developed to provide guidelines for effective teaching. In 1992, CCSSO developed 10 Model Standards for Beginning Teacher Licensing and Development. In 2010, these standards were updated to reflect modern teaching and learning contexts and now apply to teachers at any stage in their career. The new Model Core Teaching Standards address the knowledge, dispositions, and performance aspects of teaching and are built around four themes: learner and learning, content, instructional practice, and professional responsibility. The first category of standards, *Learner and Learning*, emphasizes the importance of understanding human development and learning as well as individual learner differences, and of creating a positive learning environment that fosters active engagement, collaboration, and self-motivation. *Content* standards underscore teachers' competence in the subject matter and their ability to show connections among concepts, and their application of these connections and concepts to real-life issues. *Instructional Practice* standards focus on using diverse instructional and assessment practices. Finally, the standards in the *Professional Responsibility* category highlight the importance of collaboration and the continuous pursuit of professional growth.

Framework for Teaching

The Framework for Teaching (Danielson, 1996) is a set of instructional components based on a constructivist view of teaching and learning. This view posits that learning takes places as an interaction between the learners' experiences and ideas and that, as a result, learning builds on the learners' prior knowledge. Aligned with InTASC standards, the components of Framework for Teaching are grouped in similar domains of Planning and Preparation, Classroom Environment, Instruction, and Professional Responsibilities. The Planning and Preparation domain encompasses such aspects as knowledge of content, resources, and pedagogy, as well as knowledge of learners. It emphasizes the ability to set clear instructional goals, design coherent instruction, and administer appropriate assessments. The Classroom Environment domain is concerned with both comfortable physical space and a positive emotional atmosphere of respect that provides a culture for learning. The domain of Instruction focuses on clarity and flexibility of content presentation, engagement of students in learning, and appropriate feedback. Finally, the domain of Professional Responsibilities stresses the importance of continual professional growth, contribution to school community, and reflection on teaching and student learning.

Universal Design for Learning (UDL)

Emphasizing individual differences of learners and the need to reach every student, Universal Design for Learning (Rose & Meyer, 2002) offers a framework that helps teachers adapt instruction to unique learner needs through carefully articulated goals and individualized methods, materials, and assessments. Based on the idea of Universal Design in architecture, UDL stresses the importance of usability and access for all by applying the idea of built-in flexibility and improved access to information and learning. UDL is based on the idea that there are three principles or learning networks which are each supported by multiple and flexible methods. The first, *recognition*, or the "what" of learning, is supported by multiple and flexible methods of representation. The second principle involves the *strategic* learning network, or the "how" of learning, and is supported through multiple and flexible methods of expression and apprenticeship. Finally, the third principle builds on the *affective* learning network, or the "why" of learning, and is supported by multiple and flexible methods of engagement. According to the authors, the selection of these multiple methods for each learning network is guided by neuroscience research.

All three principles of Universal Design for Learning are contained within the components of the Brain-Targeted Teaching Model. For example, as UDL promotes using multiple methods of engagement, Brain Target Four notes that it is necessary to present content in different ways while Brain Target One recognizes the importance of appreciating the emotional climate of individual students in the classroom if they are to be ready to learn. The table that follows breaks out the potentially less transparent alignment of Brain-Targeted Teaching with InTASC Principles and the Framework for Teaching:

INTASC PRINCIPLES	*FRAMEWORK FOR TEACHING*	*BRAIN-TARGETED TEACHING*
Making content meaningful Innovative application of content	Demonstrating knowledge of content and pedagogy	BT Three: Learning design with concept map and connections BT Five: Apply knowledge
Child development and learning theory Learner development	Knowledge of students	BT One: Establish welcoming emotional climate BT Two: Create a learning supportive physical environment

Learning styles/diversity Learner differences	Establishing a culture for learning Engaging students in learning Demonstrating flexibility and responsiveness	BT One: Establish welcoming emotional climate BT Two: Create a learning supportive physical environment
Instructional strategies/ problem solving	Instruction Designing coherent instruction	BT Three: Learning design with concept map and connections BT Four: Repetition; in addition to work sheets use arts to make content come alive BT Five: Apply knowledge
Motivation and behavior Learning environment	Managing classroom procedures Managing student behavior	BT One: Establish welcoming emotional climate BT Two: Create a learning supportive physical environment
Communication/knowledge	Communicating with students Using questioning and discussion techniques	BT Four: Repetition; use arts to make content come alive
Planning for instruction	Planning and preparation Setting instructional outcomes Demonstrating knowledge of resources The classroom environment Organizing physical space	BT Two: Create a learning supportive physical environment BT Three: Learning design with concept map and connections
Assessment	Designing student assessments Maintaining accurate records Using assessment in instruction	BT Five: Apply knowledge in real-world settings BT Six: Creative assessment through art forms, drama

(Continued)

(Continued)

Reflection and professional growth	Professional responsibilities	BT One–Six: Teaching practices informed by a deep body of research from educational and neuro- and cognitive sciences
	Reflecting on teaching	
	Participating in a professional community	
	Growing and developing professionally	BT Three and Four: Design of learning units that foster interdisciplinary collaboration among content teachers and with arts educators
	Showing professionalism	
Interpersonal relationships, collaboration	Creating an environment of respect and rapport	BT One: Establish the emotional climate for learning
	Communicating with families	

BT, Brain Target.

Appendix II

Brain-Targeted Teaching Implementation Checklist

The Brain-Targeted Teaching Implementation Checklist is a tool designed to help educators successfully put into practice the Brain-Targeted Teaching Model. It is intended to serve as a guidepost for self-assessment and coaching rather than a rigid system of evaluation. The checklist provides a snapshot of each of the six brain targets by offering indicators that should be included in effective instruction. Naturally, not every indicator will be observed during every lesson, and some indicators are relevant to more than one brain target. The checklist should be viewed as a communication tool for peer-to-peer and peer-to-administrator guidance and support.

Brain-Target One: *Setting the Emotional Climate for Learning*

Positive Language

Strategy	Observed
Teacher praises students for positive behaviors	
Teacher uses behavior-specific praise	
Teacher uses direct communications rather than veiled language	
Notes:	

Predictability

Strategy	Observed
Classroom routines are evident	
Special events, goals, and/or successes are celebrated	
Notes:	

Emotion and Connectedness in School

Strategy	Observed
Student(s) emotions were gauged and acknowledged	
Positive teacher-student connection is evident	
Consistent classroom expectations are evident	
All students are involved in the lesson	
Instructional activities are content-based, rigorous, engaging, differentiated, and meaningful	
Opportunities are available for cooperative work with peers	
Positive messages are sent home about students	
Teacher provides a supportive environment for learning	
Teacher demonstrates warmth and kindness	
Humor is evident in classroom interactions	
Notes:	

Student Control and Choice	
Strategy	**Observed**
Activity centers are used in the classroom	
Students are given a choice from selected reading materials	
Students can choose the method in which to demonstrate their understanding of content	
Traditional, standardized assessment methods are supplemented with authentic assessments, engagement in the arts, and/or critical thinking	
Activities relate to curriculum objectives	
Notes:	

Reflection and Mindfulness	
Strategy	**Observed**
Teacher focuses on positive interactions	
Students are given opportunities for quiet reflection	
Notes:	

Brain-Target Two: *Creating the Physical Learning Environment*	
Attention and Novelty	
Strategy	**Observed**
Room is free of clutter	
Posters and class work reflect current content	
Desks are appropriately arranged (e.g., small clusters, large circle, theater style, etc.) depending on lesson	
Window blinds are open to optimize natural light	
Lamps are used to increase lighting if necessary	
Notes:	
Sound / Scent	
Strategy	**Observed**
A relaxing atmosphere is created using background sounds (e.g., classical music, wind chimes, or nature sounds)	
Time for quiet reflection is built into the lesson	
Classroom smells fresh and inviting: Orange, vanilla, and lavender help reduce anxiety	
Notes:	
The Effects of Movement	
Strategy	**Observed**
Children are able to move about freely as appropriate	
Various workstations (e.g., reading center, math center) are set up throughout the classroom	
Yoga, stretching, and/or creative movement breaks are taken	
Notes:	

Brain-Target Three: *Designing the Learning Experience—Creating the "Big Picture"*	
Strategy	**Observed**
Visual representations such as graphic organizers are used to give students the "big-picture" framework for the unit	
Essential concepts, content, and skills are evident in lesson or unit and communicated to students in accessible ways	
Learning goals are identified and communicated to students in accessible ways	
Student activities involve multiple sensory modalities, promoting long-term retention	
Learning activities are purposeful and relate to learning goals; students are able to identify how activities relate to learning goals	
Required evaluations (benchmarks, end-of chapter test, etc.) are identified	
Rubrics are included for how assignments will be graded	
Notes:	

Brain-Target Four: *Teaching for Mastery of Content, Skills, and Concepts*	
Strategy	**Observed**
Emotional connections are incorporated into lessons	
Activities call upon prior knowledge	
Teacher begins lesson with "big-picture" concept	
Teacher engages students in repeated rehearsals of information	
Teacher allows time between rehearsals for information to promote long-term retention	
Learning tasks are varied in order to provide novelty and sustain students' attention	
Information is "chunked" to break it down into smaller cohesive segments	
Teacher presents mnemonics that can help students remember patterns, rules, or word lists	
Teacher summarizes information that is presented through text or lecture	
Creativity is fostered through the use of visual arts, music, and movement	
Teacher empowers students to make choices	
Technology is integrated into the curriculum	
Notes:	

Brain-Target Five: *Teaching for the Extension and Application of Knowledge—Creativity and Innovation*	
Strategy	**Observed**
Students acquire knowledge and demonstrate mastery in traditional and nontraditional ways*	
Teacher encourages students to extend learning through activities that require application of information in new and creative ways that go beyond what was presented in text or by the teacher	
Real-life activities are used for learning	
Open-ended questions are used, allowing for multiple and innovative responses	
Teacher provides students opportunities to explain concepts in creative ways	
Divergent thinking is encouraged, thus facilitating creative behavior in their students	
Notes:	
*The following are examples of activities associated with Brain-Target Five	
Conducting investigations and surveys	
Engaging in problem-based learning by designing a task that requires thinking across disciplines	
Generating multiple solutions to a problem	
Designing experiments to test hypotheses in project-based learning models	
Analyzing perspectives of historical figures or literary characters	
Building projects that tap into multiple artistic domains	
Connecting unusual elements of a question to produce an innovative answer	
Creating metaphors and analogies to explain a concept	
Discussing open-ended questions to probe for assumptions, clarifications, or consequences	
Restating a problem in multiple ways	
Diagramming a solution in visual representations	
Creating stories and narratives to explain concepts	
Collaborating in group learning activities within the classroom and within the broader learning environment	

Brain-Target Six: *Evaluating Learning*	
Feedback	
Strategy	**Observed**
Teacher provides students with immediate, frequent, and relevant feedback about their performance	
Teacher provides corrective feedback explaining why responses are accurate or inaccurate	
Feedback is scaffolded (e.g., teacher provides hints so that students arrive at answer on their own)	
Students continue on tasks until they achieve success	
Teacher continually offers students information about their performance	
Notes:	
Active-Retrieval of Content	
Strategy	**Observed**
Teacher provides opportunities to practice retrieving information	
Students "test" themselves	
Content is studied, revisited, and assessed at appropriate intervals	
Notes:	
Assessment	
Strategy	**Observed**
Multiple types of assessments are used	
Teacher integrates authentic performance assessments	
Rubrics are given to students prior to completing activities	
Evaluation includes both oral and written responses	
Student and teacher portfolios are used	
Evaluations involve multiple sensory modalities	
Notes:	

References

Alexander, C., Ishikawa, S., Silverstein, M., Jacobson, M., Fiksdahl-King, I., & Angel, S. (1977). *A pattern language*. New York, NY: Oxford Press.

Amsterlaw, J., Lagattuta, K. H., & Meltzoff, A. N. (2009). Young children's reasoning about the effects of emotional and physiological states on academic performance. *Child Development, 80*(1), 115–133.

Anderson, J., & Reder, L. (1979). An elaborative processing explanation of depth of processing. In S. A. Cermak (Ed.), *Level of processing in human memory* (pp. 385–403). Hillsdale, NJ: Lawrence Erlbaum.

Anderson, L. W., & Krathwohl, D. R. (2001). *A taxonomy of learning, teaching, and assessing: A revision of Bloom's taxonomy of educational objectives*. New York, NY: Longman.

Andreasen, N. (2005). *The creating brain: The neuroscience of genius*. New York, NY: Dana Press.

Ariga, A., & Lleras, A. (2011). Brief and rare mental "breaks" keep you focused: Deactivation and reactivation of task goals preempt vigilance decrements. *Cognition, 118*(3), 439–443.

Ashby, C. M. (2009). *No child left behind act: Enhancements in the department of education's review process could improve state academic assessments. Report to the chairman, committee on health, education, labor, and pensions, U.S. senate. GAO-09-911*. Washington, DC: US Government Accountability Office.

Auble, P., & Franks, J. (1978). The effects of effort toward comprehension on recall. *Memory & Cognition, 6*(1), 20–25.

Ausubel, D. P. (1960). The use of advance organizers in the learning and retention of meaningful verbal material. *Journal of Educational Psychology, 51*(5), 267–272.

Baddeley, A., & Hitch, G. (1974). Working memory. *The psychology of learning and motivation* (pp. 47–89). New York, NY: Academic Press.

Barker, S., Grayhem, P., Koon, J., Perkins, J., Whalen, A., & Raudenbush, B. (2003). Improved performance on clerical tasks associated with administration of peppermint odor. *Percept Motor Skill, 97*(3), 1007–1010.

Bartlett, F. C. (1932). *Remembering: A study in experimental and social psychology*. New York, NY: Cambridge University Press.

Beghetto, R. A. (2006). Creative justice? The relationship between prospective teachers' prior schooling experiences and perceived importance of promoting student creativity. *Journal of Creative Behavior, 40*(3), 149–162.

Berkowitz, A. L., & Ansari, D. (2010). Expertise-related deactivation of the right temporoparietal junction during musical improvisation. *NeuroImage, 49*(1), 712–719.

Bertucci, P. (2006). *A mixed-method study of a brain-compatible education program of grades K–5 in a Mid-Atlantic inner-city public elementary/middle school.* Unpublished doctoral dissertation, Johnson & Wales University, Providence, RI.

Biegel, G. M., Brown, K. W., Shapiro, S. L., & Schubert, C. M. (2009). Mindfulness-based stress reduction for the treatment of adolescent psychiatric outpatients: A randomized clinical trial. *Journal of Consulting and Clinical Psychology, 77*(5), 855–866.

Bloom, B. S., & Krathwohl, D. R. (Eds.). (1956). *Taxonomy of educational objectives: The classification of educational goals. Handbook I: Cognitive domain.* New York, NY: Longman.

Bookheimer, S. (2002). Functional MRI of language: New approaches to understanding the cortical organization of semantic processing. *Annual Review of Neuroscience, 25*(1), 151.

Boon, R., Burke, M., Fore, C., & Spencer, V. (2006). The impact of cognitive organizers and technology-based practices on student success in secondary social studies classrooms. *Journal of Special Education Technology, 21*(1), 5–15.

Bowden, E. M., & Jung-Beeman, M. (2007). Methods for investigating the neural components of insight. *Methods, 42*(1), 87–99.

Bradley, R. H., Corwyn, R. F., Pipes McAdoo, H., & García Coll, C. (2001). The home environments of children in the United States part I: Variations by age, ethnicity, and poverty status. *Child Development, 72*(6), 1844–1867.

Bransford, J. B. (2000). *How people learn: Brain, mind, experience and school.* Washington, DC: National Academy Press.

Bronson, P., & Merryman, A. (2010, July 19). The creativity crisis. *Newsweek,* 44–50.

Brophy, D. R. (2006). A comparison of individual and group efforts to creatively solve contrasting types of problems. *Creativity Research Journal, 18*(3), 293–315.

Brookhart, S. M. (2010). *How to assess higher-order thinking skills in your classroom.* Alexandria, VA: Association for Supervision and Curriculum Development.

Brown, P. (2007). *In the classroom, a new focus on quieting the mind.* Retrieved from http://www.nytimes.com/2007/06/16/us/16mindful.html.

Bruner, J. S. (1965). The growth of mind. *American Psychologist, 20*(12), 1007–1017.

Bull, K. S., Montgomery, D., & Baloche, L. (1995). Teaching creativity at the college level: A synthesis of curricular components perceived as important by instructors. *Creativity Research Journal, 8*(1), 83.

Burke, C. (2010). Mindfulness-based approaches with children and adolescents: A preliminary review of current research in an emergent field. *Journal of Children Families and Students, 19,* 133–144.

Byrne, C. L., Shipman, A. S., & Mumford, M. D. (2010). The effects of forecasting on creative problem-solving: An experimental study. *Creativity Research Journal, 22*(2), 119–138.

Byrnes, J. P. (2008). *Cognitive development and learning in instructional contexts.* Boston, MA: Pearson.

Cahill, L., & McGaugh, J. L. (1995). A novel demonstration of enhanced memory associated with emotional arousal. *Consciousness and Cognition, 4*(4), 410–421.

Cadwell, L. (1997). *Bringing Reggio Emilia home: An innovative approach to early childhood education.* New York, NY: Teachers College Press.

Cadwell, L.B. (2003). Bringing learning to life: The Reggio approach to early childhood education. New York, NY: Teachers College Press.

Campbell, D. (1997). *The Mozart effect: Tapping the power of music to heal the body, strengthen the mind, and unlock the creative spirit.* New York, NY: Avon books.

Carr, S. C. (2002). Assessing learning processes: Useful information for teachers and students. *Intervention in School and Clinic, 37*(3), 156–162.

Castellanos, F. X., Lee, P. P., Sharp, W., Jeffries, N. O., Greenstein, D. K., Clasen, L. S., ... Rapoport, J.L. (2002). Developmental trajectories of brain volume abnormalities in children and adolescents with Attention-Deficit/Hyperactivity Disorder. *JAMA: The Journal of the American Medical Association, 288*(14), 1740–1748.

Catterall, J. (2002). The arts and the transfer of learning. In R. Deasy (Ed.), *Critical links: Learning in the arts and student academic and social development* (pp. 151–157). Washington, DC: Arts Education Partnership.

Catterall, J. S. (2009). *Doing well and doing good by doing art.* Los Angeles, CA: Imagination Group.

CCSSO's Interstate Teacher Assessment and Support Consortium (InTASC). (2010). Model Core Teaching Standards: A resource for state dialogue (Draft for Public Comment). Retrieved from http://www.ccsso.org/resources/programs/interstate_teacher_assessment_consortium_(intasc).html.

Cepeda, N. J., Pashler, H., Vul, E., Wixted, J. T., & Rohrer, D. (2006). Distributed practice in verbal recall tasks: A review and quantitative synthesis. *Psychological Bulletin, 132*(3), 354–380.

Cepeda, N. J., Vul, E., Rohrer, D., Wixted, J. T., & Pashler, H. (2008). Spacing effects in learning: A temporal ridgeline of optimal retention. *Psychological Science, 19*(11), 1095–1102.

Champagne, D. L., Bagot, R. C., van Hasselt, F., Ramakers, G., Meaney, M. J., de Kloet, E. R., et al. (2008). Maternal care and hippocampal plasticity: Evidence for experience-dependent structural plasticity, altered synaptic functioning, and differential responsiveness to glucocorticoids and stress. *The Journal of Neuroscience, 28*(23), 6037–6045.

Chase, W., & Ericsson, K. (1981). Skilled memory. In J. R. Anderson (Ed.), *Cognitive skills and their acquisition* (pp. 277–293). Hillsdale, NJ: Lawrence Erlbaum.

Chávez-Eakle, R. A., Graff-Guerrero, A., García-Reyna, J., Vaugier, V., & Cruz-Fuentes, C. (2007). Cerebral blood flow associated with creative performance: A comparative study. *NeuroImage, 38*(3), 519–528.

Chiesi, H. L., Spilich, G. J., & Voss, J. F. (1979). Acquisition of domain-related information in relation to high and low domain knowledge. *Journal of Verbal Learning and Verbal Behavior, 18*(3), 257–273.

Chiou, C. (2008). The effect of concept mapping on students' learning achievements and interests. *Innovations in Education & Teaching International, 45*(4), 375–387.

Chudler, E. *Myths about the brain: 10% and counting.* Retrieved from http://brainconnection.positscience.com/topics/?main=fa/brain-myth.

Connell, J. P., Halpem-Felsher, B. L., Clifford, E., Crichlow, W., & Usinger, P. (1995). Hanging in there: Behavioral, psychological, and contextual factors affecting whether African American adolescents stay in high school. *Journal of Adolescent Research, 10*(1), 41–63.

Cowan, N. (2001). The magical number 4 in short-term memory: A reconsideration of mental storage capacity. *Behavioral and Brain Sciences, 24*(01), 87.

Craik, F. I. M., & Watkins, M. J. (1973). The role of rehearsal in short-term memory. *Journal of Verbal Learning and Verbal Behavior, 12*(6), 599–607.

Crawford, V. M., & Brophy, S. (2006). *Adaptive expertise: Theory, methods, findings, and emerging issues.* Retrieved from http://ctl.sri.com/publications/downloads/AESymposiumReportOct06.pdf.

Croninger, R. G., & Lee, V. E. (2001). Social capital and dropping out of high school: Benefits to at-risk students of teachers' support and guidance. *Teachers College Record, 103*(4), 548–581.

Cropley, A. J. (2001). *Creativity in education & learning: A guide for teachers and educators.* London, UK: Kogan Page.

Csikszentmihalyi, M. (1996). *Creativity: Flow and the psychology of discovery and invention.* New York, NY: HarperCollins.

Dahl, R. E. (2004). Adolescent brain development: A period of vulnerabilities and opportunities. keynote address. *Annals of the New York Academy of Sciences, 1021*(1), 1–22.

Danielson, C. (1996). *Enhancing professional practice: A framework of teaching.* Alexandria, VA: Association for Supervision and Curriculum Development.

Dyment, J. E., & O'Connell T. S. (2010). The quality of reflection in student journals: A review of limiting and enabling factors. *Innovations in Higher Education, 35,* 233–244.

Deasy, R. J. (2002). *Critical links: Learning in the arts and student academic and social development* Washington, DC: Arts Education Partnership.

Defeyter, M. A., Russo, R., & McPartlin, P. L. (2009). The picture superiority effect in recognition memory: A developmental study using the response signal procedure. *Cognitive Development, 24*(3), 265–273.

DeHaan, R. L. (2009). Teaching creativity and inventive problem solving in science. *CBELife Sciences Education, 8*(3), 172–181.

Delpit, L. (1988). The silenced dialog: Power and pedagogy in educating other people's children. *Harvard Educational Review, 58,* 280–298.

Denckla, M. B. (1996). Biological correlates of learning and attention: What is relevant to learning disability and attention-deficit hyperactivity disorder? *Journal of Developmental and Behavioral Pediatrics, 17*(2), 114–119.

Diemand-Yauman, C., Oppenheimer, D. M., & Vaughan, E. B. (2011). Fortune favors the bold (and the italicized): Effects of disfluency on educational outcomes. *Cognition, 118*(1), 111–115.

Dietrich, A., & Kanso, R. (2010). A review of EEG, ERP, and neuroimaging studies of creativity and insight. *Psychological Bulletin, 136*(5), 822–848.

Droz, M., & Ellis, L. (1996). *Laughing while learning: Using humor in the classroom.* Longmont, CO: Sopris West.

Dubinsky, J. M. (2010). Neuroscience education for Prekindergarten–12 teachers. *The Journal of Neuroscience, 30*(24), 8057–8060.

Dugosh, K. L., Paulus, P. B., Roland, E. J., & Yang, H. (2000). Cognitive stimulation in brainstorming. *Journal of Personality and Social Psychology, 79*(5), 722–735.

Dweck, C. S. (2008). The perils and promises of praise. *Educational Leadership, 65*(2), 34.

Edwards, L., & Torcellini, P. (2002). *A literature review of the effects of natural light on building occupants.* Golden, CO: National Renewable Energy Laboratory.

Engelkamp, J., Zimmer, H., Mohr, G., & Sellen, O. (1994). Memory of self-performed tasks: Self-performing during recognition. *Memory & Cognition, 22*(1), 34–39.

Epple, G., & Herz, R. S. (1999). Ambient odors associated to failure influence cognitive performance in children. *Developmental Psychobiology, 35*(2), 103–107.

Farah, M. J., Betancourt, L., Shera, D. M., Savage, J. H., Giannetta, J. M., Brodsky, N. L., ... Hurt, H. (2008). Environmental stimulation, parental nurturance and cognitive development in humans. *Developmental Science, 11*(5), 793–801.

Fazio, L. K., Huelser, B. J., Johnson, A., & Marsh, E. J. (2010). Receiving right/wrong feedback: Consequences of learning. *Memory, 18*(3), 335–350.

Ferry, B., Roozendaal, B., & McGaugh, J. L. (1999). Role of norepinephrine in mediating stress hormone regulation of long-term memory storage: A critical involvement of the amygdala. *Biological Psychiatry, 46*(9), 1140–1152.

Field, T., Martinez, A., Nawrocki, T., Pickens, J., Fox, N. A., & Schanberg, S. (1998). Music shifts frontal EEG in depressed adolescents. *Adolescence, 33,* 109–116.

Field, T., Hernandez-Reif, M., Diego, M., Feijo, L., Vera, Y., & Gil, K. (2004). Massage therapy by parents improves early growth and development. *Infant Behavior and Development, 27*(4), 435–442.

Fink, A., Benedek, M., Grabner, R. H., Staudt, B., & Neubauer, A. C. (2007). Creativity meets neuroscience: Experimental tasks for the neuroscientific study of creative thinking. *Methods, 42*(1), 68–76.

Finn, B., & Metcalfe, J. (2010). Scaffolding feedback to maximize long-term error correction. *Memory & Cognition, 38*(7), 951–961.

Finn, J. D., & Rock, D. A. (1997). Academic success among students at risk for school failure. *Journal of Applied Psychology, 82*(2), 221–234.

Fischer, K. W., Goswami, U., Geake, J., & the Task Force on the Future of Educational Neuroscience. (2010). The future of educational neuroscience. *Mind, Brain, and Education, 4*(2), 68–80.

Fischer, K., Daniel, D., Immordino-Yang, H., Stern, E., Battro, A., & Koizumi, H. (2007). Why mind, brain, and education? Why now? *Mind, Brain, and Education, 1,* 1–2.

Fiske, E. B. (1999). *Champions of change: The impact of arts on learning.* Washington, DC: Council of Chief State School Officers.

Fredrickson, B. L. (1998). What good are positive emotions? *Review of General Psychology, 2*(3), 300–319.

Fredrickson, B. L., & Branigan, C. (2005). Positive emotions broaden the scope of attention and thought-action repertoires. *Cognition & Emotion, 19*(3), 313–332.

Fu, M., & Zuo, Y. (2011). Experience-dependent structural plasticity in the cortex. *Trends in Neurosciences, 34*(4), 177–187.

Gabriel, A. E. (1999). Brain-based learning: The scent of the trail. *The Clearing House, 72*(5), 288–290.

Gardner, H. (1983). *Frames of mind: The theory of multiple intelligences.* New York, NY: BasicBooks.

Gardner, H. (1993). *Multiple intelligences: The theory in practice.* New York, NY: BasicBooks.

Gazzaniga, M. (1998). *The mind's past.* Berkeley, CA: University of California Press.

Gazzaniga, M. (2008). *Learning, arts, and the brain: The Dana consortium report on arts and cognition.* New York; Washington, DC: Dana Press.

Gazzaniga, M. S., Ivry, R. B., & Mangun, G. R. (2009). *Cognitive neuroscience: The biology of the mind* (3rd ed.). New York, NY: Norton.

Giedd, J. N. (2009). Linking adolescent sleep, brain maturation, and behavior. *Journal of Adolescent Health, 45*(4), 319–320.

Giedd, J. (2010). The teen brain: Primed to learn, primed to take risks. *Cerebrum* (pp. 62–70). New York, NY: Dana Press.

Giles, M. (1990). Music and stress reduction in school children at risk for conduct disorders. *Applications of Research in Music Education, 8*(2), 11–13.

Goodenow, C. (1993). Classroom belonging among early adolescent students. *The Journal of Early Adolescence, 13*(1), 21–43.

Goswami, U. (2006). Neuroscience and education: From research to practice? *Nature Reviews. Neuroscience, 7*(5), 406–413.

Gould, E., Reeves, A. J., Fallah, M., Tanapat, P., Gross, C. G., & Fuchs, E. (1999). Hippocampal neurogenesis in adult old world primates. *Proceedings of the National Academy of Sciences, 96*(9), 5263–5267.

Grimshaw, G. M., Adelstein, A., Bryden, M. P., & MacKinnon, G. E. (1998). First-language acquisition in adolescence: Evidence for a critical period for verbal language development, *Brain and Language, 63*(2), 237–255.

Guerra, N. G., & Bradshaw, C. P. (2008). Linking the prevention of problem behaviors and positive youth development: Core competencies for positive youth development and risk prevention. In N. G. Guerra & C. P. Bradshaw (Eds.), *Core competencies to prevent problem behaviors and promote positive youth development: New directions for child and adolescent development.*

Guggino, P. C., & Brint, S. (2010). Does the no child left behind act help or hinder K–12 education? *Policy Matters, 3*(3), 1–8.

Hamre, B. K., & Pianta, R. C. (2001). Early teacher–child relationships and the trajectory of children's school outcomes through eighth grade. *Child Development, 72*(2), 625.

Hardiman, M., & Denckla, M. (2010). The science of education: Informing teaching and learning through the brain sciences. In D. Gordon (Ed.) *Cerebrum* (pp. 3–11). New York, NY: Dana Press.

Hardiman, M. M. (2003). *Connecting brain research with effective teaching: The brain-targeted teaching model.* Lanham, MD: Rowman & Littlefield Education.

Hardiman, M. M. (2010). The creative-artistic brain. In D. Sousa (Ed.), *Mind, brain, and education: Neuroscience implications for the classroom* (pp. 226–246). Bloomington, IN: Solution Tree Press.

Hart, W., & Albarracín, D. (2009). The effects of chronic achievement motivation and achievement primes on the activation of achievement and fun goals. *Journal of Personality and Social Psychology, 97*(6), 1129–1141.

Hatano, G., & Ouro, Y. (2003). Commentary: Reconceptualizing school learning using insight from expertise research. *Educational Researcher, 32*(8), 26–29.

Hathaway, W. E. (1995). Effects of school lighting on physical development and school performance. *Journal of Educational Research, 88*(4), 228.

Hebb, D. (1949). *The organization of behavior: A neuropsychological theory.* New York, NY: Wiley.

Heilman, K. M., Nadeau, S. E., & Beversdorf, D. O. (2003). Creative innovation: Possible brain mechanisms.*Neurocase, 9*(5), 369–379.

Herz, R. S., Eliassen, J., Beland, S., & Souza, T. (2004). Neuroimaging evidence for the emotional potency of odor-evoked memory. *Neuropsychologia, 42*(3), 371–378.

Herz, R. S., Schankler, C., & Beland, S. (2004). Olfaction, emotion and associative learning: Effects on motivated behavior. *Motivation & Emotion, 28*(4), 363–383.

Heschong, L. (1999). *Daylighting in schools: An investigation into the relationship between daylighting and human performance.* San Francisco, CA: Pacific Gas and Electric Company.

Hetland, L., Winner, E., Veenema, S., & Sheridan, K. (2007). *Studio thinking: The real benefits of arts education.* New York, NY: Teachers College Press.

Higbee, K. L., & Clay, S. L. (1998). College students' beliefs in the ten-percent myth. *Journal of Psychology, 132*(5), 469.

Hillman, C. H., Buck, S. M., Themanson, J. R., Pontifex, M. B., & Castelli, D. M. (2009). Aerobic fitness and cognitive development: Event-related brain potential and task performance indices of executive control in preadolescent children. *Developmental Psychology, 45*(1), 114–129.

Hölzel, B. K., Carmody, J., Vangel, M., Congleton, C., Yerramsetti, S. M., Gard, T., & Lazar, S. W. (2011). Mindfulness practice leads to increases in regional brain gray matter density. *Psychiatry Research, 191*(1), 36–43.

Howard, P. (2000). *Owner's manual for the brain: Everyday applications from mind-brain research.* Atlanta, GA: Bard Press.

Howard-Jones, P. P., Pickering, S., & Diack, A. (2007). Perceptions of the role of neuroscience in education. Bristol, UK: The Innovation Unit.

Hubel, D. H., & Wiesel, T. N. (1970). The period of susceptibility to the physiological effects of unilateral eye closure in kittens. *The Journal of Physiology, 206*(2), 419–436.

Hyde, K. L., Lerch, J., Norton, A., Forgeard, M., Winner, E., Evans, A. C., & Schlaug, G. (2009). Musical training shapes structural brain development. *The Journal of Neuroscience, 29*(10), 3019–3025.

Hyerle, D. N. (2011). *Student successes with thinking maps.* Thousand Oaks, CA: Corwin.

Hygge, S. (2003). Classroom experiments on the effects of different noise sources and sound levels on long-term recall and recognition in children. *Applied Cognitive Psychology, 17*(8), 895–914.

Immordino-Yang, M. H., & Damasio, A. (2007). We feel, therefore we learn: The relevance of affective and social neuroscience to education. *Mind, Brain, and Education, 1*, 3–10(8).

Ivry, R. B., & Fiez, J. A. (2000). Cerebellar contributions to cognition and imagery. In M. S. Gazzaniga (Ed.), *The new cognitive neurosciences* (pp. 999–1011). Cambridge, MA: MIT Press.

Izard, C., Fine, S., Schultz, D., Mostow, A., Ackerman, B., & Youngstrom, E. (2001). Emotion knowledge as a predictor of social behavior and academic competence in children at risk. *Psychological Science, 12*(1), 18–23.

James, W. (1890). *Principles of psychology.* New York, NY: Holt.

Jenkins, J. (2001). The Mozart effect. *Journal of the Royal Society of Medicine, 94*(4), 170–172.

Joëls, M., Karst, H., Alfarez, D., Heine, V. M., Qin, Y., van Riel, E., … Krugers, H. J., (2004). Effects of chronic stress on structure and cell function in rat hippocampus and hypothalamus. *Stress, 7*(4), 221–231.

Joëls, M., Pu, Z., Wiegert, O., Oitzl, M. S., & Krugers, H. J. (2006). Learning under stress: How does it work? *Trends in Cognitive Sciences, 10*(4), 152–158.

Kampylis, P., Berki, E., & Saariluoma, P. (2009). In-service and prospective teachers' conceptions of creativity. *Thinking Skills and Creativity, 4*(1), 15–29.

Kandel, E. (2006). *In search of memory: The emergence of a new science of mind.* New York, NY: W.W. Norton & Company.

Kane, J. H., & Anderson, R. C. (1978). Depth of processing and interference effects in the learning and remembering of sentences. *Journal of Educational Psychology, 70*(4), 626–635.

Karmarkar, U. R., & Dan, Y. (2006). Experience-dependent plasticity in adult visual cortex. *Neuron, 52*(4), 577–585.

Karpicke, J. D., & Blunt, J. R. (2011). Retrieval practice produces more learning than elaborative studying with concept mapping. *Science,* doi:10.1126/science.1199327.

Karpicke, J. D., & Roediger, H. L., III. (2008). The critical importance of retrieval for learning. *Science, 319*(5865), 966–968.

Kempermann, G., Wiskott, L., & Gage, F. H. (2004). Functional significance of adult neurogenesis. *Current Opinion in Neurobiology, 14*(2), 186–191.

Kettle, K. L., & Häubl, G. (2010). Motivation by anticipation: Expecting rapid feedback enhances performance. *Psychological Science, 21*(4), 545–547.

Klein, S. B., & Loftus, J. (1988). The nature of self-referent encoding: The contributions of elaborative and organizational processes. *Journal of Personality and Social Psychology, 55*(1), 5–11.

Kornell, N., & Bjork, R. A. (2008). Optimising self-regulated study: The benefits— and costs—of dropping flashcards. *Memory, 16*(2), 125–136.

Kornell, N., Castel, A. D., Eich, T. S., & Bjork, R. A. (2010). Spacing as the friend of both memory and induction in young and older adults. *Psychology and Aging, 25*(2), 498–503.

Kornell, N., & Son, L. (2009). Learners' choices and beliefs about self-testing. *Memory, 17*(5), 493–501.

Kraft, U. (2007). Unleashing creativity. In F. Bloom (Ed.), *Best of the brain from Scientific American: Mind, matter, and tomorrow's brain* (pp. 9–19). New York, NY: Dana Press.

LeDoux, J. E. (1996). *The emotional brain: The mysterious underpinnings of emotional life.* New York, NY: Simon & Schuster.

Lehrner, J., Marwinski, G., Lehr, S., Johren, P., & Deecke, L. (2005). Ambient odors of orange and lavender reduce anxiety and improve mood in a dental office. *Physiology & Behavior, 86*(1–2), 92–95.

Lillard, A. S. (2005). *Montessori: The science behind the genius.* New York, NY: Oxford University Press.

Limb, C. J., & Braun, A. R. (2008). Neural substrates of spontaneous musical performance: An fMRI study of jazz improvisation. *PLoS ONE, 3*(2), 1–9.

Lonczak, H. S., Abbott, R. D., Hawkins, J. D., Kosterman, R., & Catalano, R. F. (2002). Effects of the Seattle social development project on sexual behavior, pregnancy, birth, and sexually transmitted disease outcomes by age 21 years. *Archives of Pediatrics Adolescent Medicine, 156*(5), 438–447.

Luiten, J., Ames, W., & Ackerson, G. (1980). A meta-analysis of the effects of advance organizers on learning and retention. *American Educational Research Journal, 17*(2), 211–218.

Lyons, J. (2001). *Do school facilities really impact a child's education?* Scottsdale, AZ: Council of Educational Facility Planners.

MacKinnon, D. W. (1966). What makes a person creative? *Theory into Practice, 5*(4, Creativity), 152–156.

MacLeod, C. M., Gopie, N., Hourihan, K. L., Neary, K. R., & Ozubko, J. D. (2010). The production effect: Delineation of a phenomenon. *Journal of Experimental Psychology: Learning, Memory, and Cognition, 36*(3), 671–685.

Maguire, E. A., Gadian, D. G., Johnsrude, I. S., Good, C. D., Ashburner, J., Frackowiak, R. S. J., & Frith, C.D. (2000). Navigation-related structural change in the hippocampi of taxi drivers. *Proceedings of the National Academy of Sciences, 97*(8), 4398–4403.

Marzano, R. (1992). *A different kind of classroom: Teaching with dimensions of learning.* Alexandria, VA: Association for Supervision and Curriculum Development.

Marzano, R., Pickering, D., & Pollock, J. (2001). *Classroom instruction that works: Research-based strategies for increasing student achievement.* Alexandria, VA: Association for Supervision and Curriculum Development.

Masten, A. S. (1986). Humor and competence in school-aged children. *Child Development, 57*(2), 461–473.

Mayberry, R. I., & Eichen, E. B. (1991). The long-lasting advantage of learning sign language in childhood: Another look at the critical period for language acquisition. *Journal of Memory and Language, 30*(4), 486–512.

Mayer, R. E. (1979). Twenty years of research on advance organizers: Assimilation theory is still the best predictor of results. *Instructional Science, 8*(2), 133–167.

McAleese, R., Grabinger, S., & Fisher, K. (1999). The knowledge arena: A learning environment that underpins concept mapping. *American Educational Research Association*, Montreal, Canada.

McBride, D. M., & Dosher, A.B. (2002). A comparison of conscious and automatic memory processes for picture and word stimuli: A process dissociation analysis. *Consciousness and Cognition, 11*(3), 423–460.

McCrindle, A. R., & Christensen, C. A. The impact of learning journals on metacognitive and cognitive processes and learning performance. *Learning and Instruction, 5*, 167–185.

McDaniel, M., & Bugg, J. (2008). Instability in memory phenomena: A common puzzle and a unifying explanation. *Psychonomic Bulletin & Review, 15*(2), 237–255.

McEwen, B. S., & Sapolsky, R. M. (1995). Stress and cognitive function. *Current Opinion in Neurobiology, 5*(2), 205–216.

Meltzoff, A. N., Kuhl, P. K., Movellan, J., & Sejnowski, T. J. (2009). Foundations for a new science of learning. *Science, 325*(5938), 284–288.

Mendelson, T., Greenberg, M. T., Dariotis, J. K., Gould, L. F., Rhoades, B. L., & Leaf, P. J. (2010). Feasibility and preliminary outcomes of a school-based mindfulness intervention for urban youth. *Journal of Abnormal Child Psychology: An Official Publication of the International Society for Research in Child and Adolescent Psychopathology, 38*(7), 985–994.

Miller, G. A. (1956). The magical number seven, plus or minus two: Some limits on our capacity for processing information. *Psychological Review, 63*(2), 81–97.

Mohr, G., Engelkamp, J., & Zimmer, H. D. (1989). Recall and recognition of self-performed acts. *Psychological Research, 51*(4), 181–187.

Montessori, M. (1967). *The absorbant mind.* New York, NY: Henry Holt.

Morrison, M. K. (2008). *Using humor to maximize learning: The links between positive emotions and education.* Lanham, MD: Rowman & Littlefield Education.

Mueller, C. M., & Dweck, C. S. (1998). Praise for intelligence can undermine children's motivation and performance. *Journal of Personality & Social Psychology, 75*(1), 33–53.

Mullen, B., Johnson, C., & Salas, E. (1991). Productivity loss in brainstorming groups: A meta-analytic integration. *Basic & Applied Social Psychology, 12*(1), 3–23

Nachimas, M., Gunnar, M. R., Mangelsdorf, S., Parritz, R. H., & Buss, K. (1996). Behavioral inhibition and stress reactivity: The moderating role of attachment security. *Child Development, 67,* 508–522.

Nadel, L., & Hardt, O. (2011). Update on memory systems and processes. *Neuropsychopharmacology, 36*(1), 251–273.

Nelson, P. B., & Soli, S. (2000). Acoustical barriers to learning: Children at risk in every classroom. *Language, Speech & Hearing Services in Schools, 31*(4), 356–361.

Okamoto, T., Endo, S., Shirao, T., & Nagao, S. (2011). Role of cerebellar cortical protein synthesis in transfer of memory trace of cerebellum-dependent motor learning. *The Journal of Neuroscience, 31*(24), 8958–8966.

Osmundson, E., Chung, G. K., Herl, H. E., & Klein, D. C. (1999). *Knowledge mapping in the classroom: A tool for examining the development of students' conceptual understandings* [Tech.Rep. no. 507]. Los Angeles, CA: CRESST/ University of California.

Ott, J. (1973). *Health and light.* New York, NY: Simon Schuster.

Ozubko, J. D., & MacLeod, C. M. (2010). The production effect in memory: Evidence that distinctiveness underlies the benefit. *Journal of Experimental Psychology: Learning, Memory, and Cognition, 36*(6), 1543–1547.

Paivio, A. (1971). *Imagery and verbal processes.* New York, NY: Holt, Rinehart, & Winston.

Pashler, H., Cepeda, N. J., Wixted, J. T., & Rohrer, D. (2005). When does feedback facilitate learning of words? *Journal of Experimental Psychology, Learning, Memory & Cognition, 31*(1), 3–8.

Pashler, H., McDaniel, M., Rohrer, D., & Bjork, R. (2008). Learning styles: Concepts and evidence. *Psychological Science in the Public Interest, 9*(3), 109–115.

Payton, J. W., Weissberg, R. P., Durlak, J. A., Dymnicki, A. B., Taylor, R. D., Schellinger, K. B., & Pachan, M.. (2008). *The positive impact of social and emotional learning for kindergarten to eighth-grade students: Findings from three scientific reviews.* Chicago, IL: Collaborative for Academic, Social, and Emotional Learning.

Pekrun, R., Goetz, T., Titz, W., & Perry, R. P. (2002). Academic emotions in students' self-regulated learning and achievement: A program of qualitative and quantitative research. *Educational Psychologist, 37*(2), 91–105.

Perkins, D. (2001). *The eureka effect: The art and logic of breakthrough thinking.* New York, NY: W.W. Norton & Co.

Phelps, E. A. (2006). Emotion and cognition: Insights from studies of the human amygdala. *Annual Review of Psychology, 57,* 27–53.

Phelps, E. A., & LeDoux, J. E. (2005). Contributions of the amygdala to emotion processing: From animal models to human behavior. *Neuron, 48*(2), 175–187.

Pink, D. (2006). *A whole new mind: Why right-brainers will rule the future.* New York, NY: Penguin Group.

Pinel, J. P. J. (2000). *Biopsychology* (4th ed.). Boston, MD: Allyn and Bacon.

Plucker, J. A. (1999). Is the proof in the pudding? Reanalyses of Torrance's (1958 to present) longitudinal data. *Creativity Research Journal, 12*(2), 103.

Poirel, N., Mellet, E., Houdé, O., & Pineau, A. (2008). First came the trees, then the forest: Developmental changes during childhood in the processing of visual local–global patterns according to the meaningfulness of the stimuli. *Developmental Psychology, 44*(1), 245–253.

Posner, M., & Patoine, B. (2009). How arts training improves attention and cognition. *Cerebrum.* Retrieved from http://dana.org/news/cerebrum/detail.aspx?id=23206.

Posner, M. R., Rothbart, M. K., & DiGirolamo, G. J. (1999). Development of brain networks for orienting to novelty. *Pavlov Journal of Higher Nervous Activity, 12,* 715–722.

Posner, M. R., & Rothbart, M. K. (2007). *Educating the human brain.* Washington, DC: American Psychological Association.

Psilos, P. (2002). *The impact of arts education on workforce preparation: Issue brief.* Washington, DC: National Governors' Association, Center for Best Practices.

Raizada, R. D. S., & Kishiyama, M. M. (2010). Effects of socioeconomic status on brain development, and how cognitive neuroscience may contribute to levelling the playing field. *Frontiers in Human Neuroscience, 4,* 1–11.

Ramsden, S., Richardson, F. L., Josse, G., Thomas, M. S. C., Ellis, C., Shakeshaft, C., Seghier, M. L., & Price, C. J. (2011). Verbal and non-verbal intelligence changes in the teenage brain. *Nature* (in press).

Rao, H., Betancourt, L., Giannetta, J. M., Brodsky, N. L., Korczykowski, M., Avants, B. B., ... Farah, M.J. (2010). Early parental care is important for hippocampal maturation: Evidence from brain morphology in humans.*NeuroImage, 49*(1), 1144–1150.

Ratey, J. J. (2008). *Spark: The revolutionary new science of exercise and the brain.* New York, NY: Little, Brown and Co.

Rauscher, F. H., Shaw, G. L., & Ky, K. N. (1993). Music and spatial task performance. *Nature, 365,* 611.

Recht, D. R., & Leslie, L. (1988). Effect of prior knowledge on good and poor readers' memory of text. *Journal of Educational Psychology, 80*(1), 16–20.

Resnick, M. D., Bearman, P. S., Blum, R. W., Bauman, K. E., Harris, K. M., Jones, J., Tabor, J., ... Udry, J. R.(1997). Protecting adolescents from harm. *JAMA: The Journal of the American Medical Association, 278*(10), 823–832.

Rice, J., Levine, L., & Pizarro, D. (2007). "Just stop thinking about it": Effects of emotional disengagement on children's memory for educational material. *Emotion, 7*(4), 812–823.

Rinne, L., Gregory, E., Yarmolinskaya, J., & Hardiman, M. (2011). Why arts integration improves long-term retention of content. *Mind, Brain, and Education* (in press).

Robertson, P. (2002). The critical age hypothesis. *The Asian EFL Journal (Online),* Retrieved from http://www.asian-efl-journal.com/marcharticles_pr.html.

Robinson, K. (2001). *Out of our minds: Learning to be creative.* Oxford, UK: Capstone Ltd.

Rohrer, D., & Pashler, H. (2010). Recent research on human learning challenges conventional instructional strategies. *Educational Researcher, 39*(5), 406–412.

Rohrer, D., & Taylor, K. (2007). The shuffling of mathematics problems improves learning. *Instructional Science, 35*(6), 481–498.

Rose, D. H., & Meyer, A. (2002). *Teaching every student in the digital age: Universal design for learning.* Alexandria, VA: Association for Supervision and Curriculum Development.

Rotherham, A. J., & Willingham, D. (2009). 21st century skills: The challenges ahead. *Educational Leadership, 67*(1), 16.

Runco, M. A. (2004). Creativity. *Annual Review of Psychology, 55,* 657–687.

Runco, M. A., & Albert, R. S. (1986). The threshold theory regarding creativity and intelligence: An empirical test with gifted and nongifted children. *Creative Child & Adult Quarterly, 11*(4), 212–218.

Rundus, D. (1971). Analysis of rehearsal processes in free recall. *Journal of Experimental Psychology, 89*(1), 63–77.

Ruttle, P. L., Shirtcliff, E. A., Serbin, L. A., Ben-Dat Fisher, D., Stack, D. M., & Schwartzman, A. E. (2011). Disentangling psychobiological mechanisms underlying internalizing and externalizing behaviors in youth: Longitudinal and concurrent associations with cortisol. *Hormones and Behavior, 59*(1), 123–132.

Sapolsky, R. M. (2004). *Why zebras don't get ulcers.* New York, NY: Henry Holt and Co.

Sawyer, R. K. (2006). Educating for innovation. *Thinking Skills and Creativity, 1*(1), 41–48.

Schlaug, G., Jäncke, L., Huang, Y., Staiger, J. F., & Steinmetz, H. (1995). Increased corpus callosum size in musicians. *Neuropsychologia, 33*(8), 1047–1055.

Schmahmann, J. D. (1997). *The cerebellum and cognition.* New York, NY: Academic Press.

Schmidt, S. R. (1994). Effects of humor on sentence memory. *Journal of Experimental Psychology. Learning, Memory & Cognition, 20*(4), 953.

Schwabe, L., & Wolf, O. T. (2010). Learning under stress impairs memory formation. *Neurobiology of Learning and Memory, 93*(2), 183–188.

Schwartz, D. L., Bransford, J. D., & Sears, D. (2005). *Efficiency and innovation in transfer.* In J. Mestre (Ed.), *Transfer of learning from a modern multidisciplinary perspective* (pp. 1–51). Greenwich, CT: Information Age Publishing.

Scruggs, T., & Mastropieri, M. (2000). The effectiveness of mnemonic instruction for students with learning and behavior problems: An update and research synthesis. *Journal of Behavioral Education, 10*(2/3), 163–173.

Shepard, R. N. (1967). Recognition memory for words, sentences, and pictures. *Journal of Verbal Learning and Verbal Behavior, 6*(1), 156–163.

Shiffrin, R., & Nosofsky, M. (1994). Seven plus or minus two: A commentary on capacity limitations. *Psychological Review, 101*(2), 357–361.

Shonkoff, J. P., & Phillips, D. (2000). *From neurons to neighborhoods: The science of early childhood development.* Washington, DC: National Academy Press.

Singleton, D., & Lengyel, Z. (Eds.). (1995). *The age factor in second language acquisition: A critical look at the critical period hypothesis.* Clevedon, UK: Multilingual Matters.

Slamecka, N. J., & Graf, P. (1978). The generation effect: Delineation of a phenomenon. *Journal of Experimental Psychology: Human Learning and Memory, 4*(6), 592–604.

Smith, S. M., Glenberg, A., & Bjork, R. A. (1978). Environmental context and human memory. *Memory & Cognition, 6*(4), 342–353.

Smithrim, K., & Upitis, R. (2005). Learning through the arts: Lessons of engagement. *Canadian Journal of Education / Revue Canadienne De l'Éducation, 28*(1/2), 109–127.

Smyth, V. (1979). Speech reception in the presence of classroom noise. *Language, Speech, and Hearing Services in Schools, 10*(4), 221–230.

Sperling, G. (1960). The information available in brief visual presentations. *Psychological Monographs, 74,* 1–29.

Squire, L.R., & Kandel, E.R. (1999) *Memory: From Mind to Molecules.* New York, NY: W.H. Freeman & Co.

Steinberg, L. (2008). A social neuroscience perspective on adolescent risk-taking. *Developmental Review, 28*(1), 78–106.

Steinberg, L., Dahl, R., Keating, D., Kupfer, D. J., Masten, A. S., & Pine, D. S. (2006). The study of developmental psychopathology in adolescence: Integrating affective neuroscience with the study of context. *Developmental psychopathology, vol. 2: Developmental neuroscience* (2nd ed.) (pp. 710–741). Hoboken, NJ: John Wiley & Sons.

Stevens, C., Lauinger, B., & Neville, H. (2009). Differences in the neural mechanisms of selective attention in children from different socioeconomic backgrounds: An event-related brain potential study. *Developmental Science, 12*(4), 634–646.

Strick, M., Holland, R. W., van Baaren, R., & van Knippenberg, A. (2009). Finding comfort in a joke: Consolatory effects of humor through cognitive distraction. *Emotion, 9*(4), 574–578.

Swanson, C. (2008). *Cities in crisis: A special analytic report on high school graduation.* Bethesda, MD: Educational Projects Research Center.

Sylvan, L. J., & Christodoulou, J. A. (2010). Understanding the role of neuroscience in brain based products: A guide for educators and consumers. *Mind, Brain, and Education, 4*(1), 1–7.

Tallal, P. (2004). Improving language and literacy is a matter of time. *Nature Reviews Neuroscience, 5*(9), 721–728.

Talmi, D., Anderson, A. K., Riggs, L., Caplan, J. B., & Moscovitch, M. (2008). Immediate memory consequences of the effect of emotion on attention to pictures. *Learning & Memory, 15*(3), 172–182.

Tanner, C. K. (2008). Explaining relationships among student outcomes and the school's physical environment. *Journal of Advanced Academics, 19*(3), 444–471.

Taylor, J.B. (2008). *My stroke of insight: A brain scientist's personal journey.* New York, NY: Viking Penguin.

Thompson, W. F., Schellenberg, E. G., & Husain, G. (2001). Arousal, mood, and the Mozart effect. *Psychological Science, 12*(3), 248–251.

Toch, T. (2011). Beyond basic skills. *Phi Delta Kappan, 92*(6), 72–73.

Tomlinson, C., & McTighe, J. (2006). *Integrating differentiated instruction & understanding by design: Connecting content and kids.* Alexandria, VA: Association for Supervision and Curriculum Development.

Toppo, G. (2011, March). The search for a new way to test school kids.*USA Today.*Retrieved from http://www.usatoday.com/news/education/2011-03-18-schooltesting18_ST_N.htm.

Tyler, S. W., Hertel, P. T., McCallum, M. C., & Ellis, H. C. (1979). Cognitive effort and memory. *Journal of Experimental Psychology: Human Learning and Memory, 5*(6), 607–617.

Unsworth, N., & Engle, R. W. (2007). On the division of short-term and working memory: An examination of simple and complex span and their relation to higher order abilities. *Psychological Bulletin, 133*(6), 1038–1066.

Valeski, T. N., & Stipek, D. J. (2001). Young children's feelings about school. *Child Development, 72*(4), 1198.

Varma, S., McCandliss, B. D., & Schwartz, D. L. (2008). Scientific and pragmatic challenges for bridging education and neuroscience. *Educational Researcher, 37*(3), 140–152.

Warm, J. S., Dember, W. N., & Parasuraman, R. (1991). Effects of olfactory stimulation on performance and stress in a visual sustained attention task. *Journal of Social Cosmetic Chemistry, 42,* 199–210.

Webb, N. (2002). *Alignment study in language arts, mathematics, science and social studies of state standards and assessments for four states.* Washington, DC: Council of Chief State School Officers.

Wentzel, K. R., & Wigfield, A. (1998). Academic and social motivational influences on student's academic performance. *Educational Psychology Review, 10*(2), 155–175.

Willingham, D. T. (2009). *Why don't students like school? A cognitive scientist answers questions about how the mind works and what it means for your classroom.* San Francisco, CA: John Wiley & Sons.

Wilson, D. (2004). The interface of school climate and school connectedness and relationships with aggression and victimization. *Journal of School Health, 74*(7), 293–299.

Zaromb, F. M., & Roediger, H. L. (2009). The effects of effort after meaning on recall: Differences in within- and between-subjects designs. *Memory & Cognition, 37*(4), 447–463.

Zentall, S. (1983). Learning environments: A review of physical and temporal factors. *Exception Education Quarterly, 4*(2), 10–15.

Zentall, S. S., & Zentall, T. R. (1983). Optimal stimulation: A model of disordered activity and performance in normal and deviant children. *Psychological Bulletin, 94*(3), 446–471.

Zhao, Y. (2009). *Catching up or leading the way: American education in the age of globalization.* Alexandria, VA: Association for Supervision and Curriculum Development.

Zins, J. W., Weissberg, R.P., Wang, M.C., & Walberg, H.J. (2004). *Building school success on social emotional learning: What does the research say?* New York, NY: Teachers College Press.

Ziv, A. (1988). Teaching and learning with humor: Experiment and replication. *The Journal of Experimental Education, 57*(1), 5–15.

Zylowska, L., Ackerman, D. L., Yang, M. H., Futrell, J. L., Horton, N. L., Hale, T. S., ... Smalley, S.L. (2007). Mindfulness meditation training in adults and adolescents with ADHD. *Journal of Attention Disorders, 11*(6), 737–746.

Index

CORWIN

A SAGE Company

The Corwin logo—a raven striding across an open book—represents the union of courage and learning. Corwin is committed to improving education for all learners by publishing books and other professional development resources for those serving the field of PreK–12 education. By providing practical, hands-on materials, Corwin continues to carry out the promise of its motto: **"Helping Educators Do Their Work Better."**